HOMICIDE:
LIFE ON
THE SCREEN

D0556418

HOMICIDE:
LIFE ON
THE SCREEN

Tod Hoffman

ECW PRESS

The publication of *Homicide: Life on the Screen* has been generously supported by The Canada Council, the Ontario Arts Council, and the Government of Canada through the Book Publishing Industry Development Program.

CANADIAN CATALOGUING IN PUBLICATION DATA

Hoffman, Tod
Homicide: life on the screen
ISBN 1-55022-358-5
1. Homicide – life on the street (Television program).   I. Title.
PN1992.77.H62H63 1998   791.45'72   C98-931382-4

All photos courtesy NBC Entertainment.

Cover design by Guylaine Régimbald.
Imaging by ECW Type & Art, Oakville, Ontario.
Printed and bound by Imprimerie Gagné, Louiseville, Québec.

Distributed in Canada by General Distribution Services,
325 Humber College Blvd., Etobicoke, Ontario M9W 7C3.

Distributed in the United States by Login Publishers Consortium,
1436 West Randolph Street, Chicago, Illinois, U.S.A. 60607.

Distributed in the United Kingdom by Turnaround Publisher Services,
Unit 3 Olympia Trading Estate, Coburg Road, Wood Green, London N2Z 6TZ

Published by ECW PRESS,
2120 Queen Street East, Suite 200,
Toronto, Ontario M4E 1E2.

www.ecw.ca/press

PRINTED AND BOUND IN CANADA

CONTENTS

One   Realism and Reality   11

Two   Baltimore   30

Three   The Murder Police   42

Four   On the Screen   83

Five   Issues 159

Six   An American Epic 180

Appendix: Episode Guide 189

ACKNOWLEDGMENTS

A number of people were kind enough to assist with this project in a variety of ways. Foremost, Tom Fontana was gracious in allowing me complete access to the *Homicide* set and to anyone with whom I wished to speak. Without this level of cooperation, this book would not have been possible. He showed great courage in supporting an author who would be analyzing and critiquing his work, and for that I owe him thanks. His assistant, Sunil Nayar, was most helpful. As well, I thank Barry Levinson for his interest.

I visited Baltimore twice — from May 27 to June 1, 1997 and September 15 to 24, 1997 — for research purposes. I want to thank David Simon for writing an infinitely inspiring book and for seeing me when it wasn't always convenient. His honesty and forthrightness gave me insights into his work and the Baltimore City Police I would not otherwise have enjoyed. On the *Homicide* set, Miles Perman and Holly Unterberger were saddled with guiding me around and facilitating interviews. Baltimore Police Captain Gary D'Addario was tremendously cooperative and indispensable in helping me make contact with others in the department.

For their time and consideration, I want to thank every member of the *Homicide* cast who spoke with me: Richard Belzer, Andre Braugher, Reed Diamond, Michelle Forbes, Clark Johnson, Yaphet Kotto, Kyle Secor, and Jon Seda. Also, James Yoshimura, Eric Overmyer, and Darryl LaMont Wharton, who were equally forthcoming.

Baltimore police officers, past and present, were exceptionally gracious and helpful. Sergeants Terry McLarney and Tom Pellegrini showed me things in Baltimore I wouldn't otherwise have seen. Harry Edgerton, Donald Worden, and Ed Burns shared their stories.

Joseph Wambaugh and Warren Littlefield also submitted to interviews, for which I thank them. Ed Kane was an invaluable fount of knowledge concerning Baltimore past and present. I thank Gil Stotler for all his help during my first visit to Baltimore.

My thanks to Nancy Caudill and the entire staff at the Admiral Fell Inn in Fell's Point for providing me a place worthy of being called home in Baltimore.

Joanna Giddon of NBC in New York was invaluable.

Boris Castel, editor of *Queen's Quarterly*, gave me my first opportunity to write about *Homicide*. The first chapter of this book owes much to an essay I published in the summer 1997 issue. Robert Lecker, Jack David, and Holly Potter make it a pleasure to work with ECW. Stuart Ross's thoughtful and attentive editing is much appreciated.

Finally, to my parents, Bernard and Florence, who are always supportive. And, most of all, to my wife, Sally, who once said to me, "Be a writer."

All quotations in this book are drawn from exclusive interviews granted to the author, unless otherwise attributed. For analytic purposes I have relied on *Homicide: A Year on the Killing Streets* by David Simon (Boston: Houghton Mifflin, 1991) and *The Corner: A Year in the Life of an Inner-city Neighborhood* by David Simon and Edward Burns (New York: Broadway Books, 1997).

It goes without saying that I, alone, bear responsibility for the contents of this book.

Tod Hoffman
Montreal, Quebec
August 1998

As the strong man exults in his physical ability, delighting in such exercises as call his muscles into action, so glories the analyst in that moral activity which *disentangles*. He derives pleasure from even the most trivial occupations bringing his talent into play. He is fond of enigmas, of conundrums, hieroglyphics; exhibiting in his solutions of each a degree of *acumen* which appears to the ordinary apprehension praeternatural. His results, brought about by the very soul and essence of method, have, in truth, the whole air of intuition.

— Edgar Allan Poe, *The Murders in the Rue Morgue*

O N E

REALISM AND REALITY

Were it merely another run-of-the-mill cop opera — the sort that clutters prime-time television, not to mention cinema screens and bookshelves — *Homicide: Life on the Street* would hardly warrant the attention of a book. But it is more than that. Even apart from the consistent quality of its writing, the unprecedented cinematic feel it brought to network TV, and the excellence of its ensemble cast, *Homicide* is exceptional. Its themes reach out beyond the confines of its characters or their role as police officers. In telling its stories of murder, it is actually telling a tale of urban America in the 1990s. And doing so in a fashion rarely before seen. As Joseph Wambaugh, the former policeman whose books established a new benchmark in realism and who was the creative force behind the groundbreaking *Police Story* in the 1970s, says, "*Homicide* violates the rules of serial TV. It does things no other cop show has done." Consequently, it gives viewers the most realistic glimpse at big city policing they're ever likely to get from a safe distance.

The basis upon which we judge the believability of a story is most often spurious at best. Usually it's a pure act of faith, earned by a writer, director, or actor through the skill and honest commitment with which they exercise their craft. If we can't believe in them, our interest quickly wanes. If we can, they come to personify whoever and whatever they portray. Fairly or otherwise — without any actual knowledge, and often having only superficial contact with real members of a particular profession — we feel an intimacy, based solely on what we've read or seen on television and movie screens. Thus we expect our doctors will be caring perfectionists, our lawyers eloquent and passionate, our cops courageous and dedicated. We come to look for real practitioners to resemble our entertainers, rather than vice versa.

It is the nuances that distinguish realistic police characters from their more familiar cardboard cutouts. Those who've never ridden a radio car or confronted a killer need to be brought into the world of those who have. Face it, the average producer or writer has precious little experience of the world inhabited by police. They make it up. They imagine how police feel, create characters to express outrage, righteous indignation, sympathy, and compassion, and research procedure well enough that these characters' actions hold up to superficial scrutiny. Then they rig up a back lot to resemble some generic figment of a ghetto and populate it with some shabby-looking extras who seem like nothing so much as shabby-looking extras (out in the real world even marginally successful dope dealers are decked out in the latest Nike, Fila, and Tommy Hilfiger sports logo gear, and whatever else is cutting-edge in urban fashion). Finally, they set about conceiving crimes that, regardless of their complexity or implausibility, can be neatly wrapped up in the forty-seven minutes allotted between commercials.

Don't knock it. This formula has been wildly successful for nearly fifty years. Police are an entertainment industry archetype, a mainstay of prime time since Los Angeles Police Chief William Parker teamed with Jack Webb to bring us *Dragnet.* The blandly stoic, ever dependable Webb gave a generation their sound bite for police work: "The facts, ma'am, just the facts." Justice is blind and impartial. Opinions, emotions, prejudices have no place in an investigation. Just the facts, ma'am.

Dragnet created "a crime-and-severe punishment myth that ordained the LAPD with a chaste image and god-like powers," writes James Ellroy in *My Dark Places.* His novels about corrupt and brutal Los Angeles cops from the same era have so incinerated the myth that its ashes will never rise. He adds, "The LAPD took their myth to heart. They stuck their heads up their asses and isolated themselves from the public."

Dragnet never bothered with such a troublesome quality as subtlety. Today it is laughable, a blatant public relations piece on behalf of the department. But the ingredients of its formula can still be detected in most crime drama. In the 1950s that formula was simple: police equalled right, criminals equalled wrong; right supersedes wrong. Right wins the day. Indeed, right was never seen to lose a battle; hence, it couldn't but win the war.

Then came the 1960s and suddenly the formula was being tested against new values, unprecedented rules. Even before things started to go haywire, a — perhaps unintentionally — subversive show hit the air in September 1963. *The Fugitive*, starring David Janssen, presented us with the pursuit of a man wrongly accused of murdering his wife by a single-minded bloodhound cop who deafly ignores his fantastic tale about a one-armed killer. Of course, Janssen's character — based on the sensational Sam Sheppard case in Cleveland — was telling the truth and viewers were made abundantly aware of this from the outset. There was no ambiguity, no place for doubt as to who was in the right.

The theme of *The Fugitive* was really nothing new. It was lifted from Victor Hugo's classic of pursuit and obsession, *Les Misérables*. What was new was that TV was conspiring to debunk the legend of the infallible cop, which it had been largely responsible for creating. While the show still presented a childishly simplistic morality play (recall that it never challenged viewers to question the fugitive's innocence), suddenly the formula for right and wrong was reversed.

The '60s and early '70s was a tumultuous period when such inversions seemed to be the rule, rather than the exception. Civil rights, Vietnam, new moral standards, drug use all exerted unprecedented pressures on a justice system few people had realized was on the verge of a breakdown. Cynicism would no longer be an affected pose of the hip few; it would be the national norm. President Kennedy's head had been blown off and the conspiracy theorists were converging on the scene of the crime. African Americans had to protest in the streets to achieve nothing more than the dignity and respect promised by the Bill of Rights. The United States was losing a war they didn't quite understand. A culture that had once been safely relegated to the margins as *counter* was embraced by a generation. Libidinous youth gave vent to their passions, experimenting openly with sex, narcotics, and politics. Confused and overwhelmed, the police were somehow to keep order. A job that had once been about arresting criminals was now about quelling demonstrations. Young cops, who were reined in by 1950s codes of behavior, were increasingly segregated from civilians. And civilians, whose recreational drug use was criminal and whose sexual practices were felonies in some jurisdictions, wanted no part of police.

Rifts within American society — between races, classes, generations — were becoming more visible and vocal. They had always been there, but now they were making the nightly news. Police, shown whaling away on anti-war activists who were asserting their own concept of patriotism and blacks who had the effrontery to demand equality, were seen defending a political status quo that was fading fast.

And then there were a series of police corruption scandals, the most spectacular of which was that precipitated by a New York City officer named Frank Serpico. Immortalized in Peter Maas's book and the film adaptation starring Al Pacino, Serpico exposed a department that seemed more preoccupied with breaking the law than with enforcing it. Just as we accuse police of generalizing and stereotyping on the basis of color or class, we allowed revelations of wrongdoing by several police to taint the reputation of all police. Once their moral authority was called into question, all their authority became suspect. But, hey, this was the era of secret, unauthorized bombing blitzes in Cambodia, and of Watergate. Authority and legitimacy were up for grabs. We can't trust the president; maybe we can trust the press. The cops are dirty; maybe the criminals are a bit clean. Addicts are felons, but recreational users are living next door. These matters had always been unclear, but we had never before had this fact shoved in our faces.

By the time we reach the crime-sick, law-and-order-craving 1990s, we want to see absolutely *real* police TV. Along comes the Fox network with *Cops*, in which camera crews accompany police on actual patrols or prearranged raids. With its fellow travelers, *LAPD: Life on the Beat* and *Real Stories of the Highway Patrol* (with its endlessly fascinating reenactments of state troopers issuing traffic tickets), *Cops* dishes up such a disconcertingly *real* representation of police work as to achieve hyperreality. The officers being tailed are so conscious of the cameras that they end up doing a parody of reality. These cops invariably act with superhuman restraint. No abuse or resistance is enough to push them to lose their cool. The sorriest excuse for an addict, pervert, or thief is invariably addressed as "sir." Even while squirming on the ground against three cops trying to apply handcuffs, they're being told, "Please, put your hands behind your back, sir." In one memorable scene, an officer is being cursed out viciously by a motorist after a traffic stop. "Why do you use profanity so much?" the officer inquires without the least trace of irony in his voice.

It isn't so much that *Cops* has no plot or dramatic quality; it isn't meant to have either. It is intended to be a sequence of adrenaline rushes. What is shameless about the show is its wanton misrepresentation of who police are, while pretending it's the real thing. Consider this story told me by a Baltimore cop. A female officer was struck while attempting to make an arrest. The suspect fled into a row house. The officer had failed to call for assistance, which in fact arrived only because a citizen had dialed 911 to report that a cop was being beaten.

"Did somebody hit you?" the first sergeant on the scene demanded of the cop.

"When I tried to cuff him, he swung his arm around and hit the side of my head and I lost my hold on him," she ruefully admitted.

"So he hit you."

"Yes."

"Did you see where he ran?"

"Yeah," she indicated the house into which he'd disappeared.

By now several radio cars had converged.

"OK, here's how things are done," the sergeant explained calmly. "Anybody hits you, you send out a 13 (emergency code for officer needing assistance), we come, and we beat him up.''

Real police doing real police work beyond the camera's glare.

As David Simon explained it in *Homicide: A Year on the Killing Streets*, the book upon which the series is based: ''Honor to a cop means that you don't hit a man who's wearing cuffs or is unable to fight back, you don't hit a man to obtain a statement, and you don't hit a man who doesn't deserve it. Police brutality? To hell with that. Police work has always been brutal; good police work, discreetly so.''

What has this to do with *Homicide*, the show?

Homicide is the best incarnation of realism in police drama. It shows cops for who they are and what they are. If there is a single spine of concern that supports the entire body of work it is the question of what it means to live life in contact with death every single day. It continues a tradition that can best be traced to Wambaugh's 1970 debut novel, *The New Centurions*, in which he follows a group of rookies from the virginity of the training academy to the fire and brimstone of the Watts riots five years later. Along the way, their shining armor gets chipped and bent. Each had joined for the opportunity at a career with decent pay and good benefits. Some saw it as a stepping stone to better things. None was fearless in the face of danger, one ended up boozing on the job, another indulged in soft drugs.

''*The New Centurions* was the first real psychological police story,'' Wambaugh says. ''I tried to tell the story of how the job acts on cops, rather than how cops act on the job.''

Homicide actually seeks to illustrate both sides of that coin. To examine cops on the job and the job on cops without relying on clichés is a tall order. For one thing, there is no direct cause and effect, one to the other. Each cop works and copes in his or her own way. Someone with no police experience is going to be hard-pressed to respect the complexities of the subject if they've nothing to rely on but their imagination. But executive producers Barry Levinson and Tom Fontana, who had also been behind the acclaimed hospital drama *St. Elsewhere*, did not dream *Homicide* up from thin air. They had David Simon's descriptions and observations of the Baltimore police.

Levinson received a copy of Simon's book, as he receives just about anything with a Baltimore angle. That's the reward — and occasionally the price — of being Baltimore's most famous native chronicler. He made his initial mark as a writer-director with *Diner* (1982), a pre-Gen X coming-of-age drama that launched the careers of Kevin Bacon, Ellen Barkin, and Mickey Rourke. He'd write and direct two more Baltimore-based films: *Tin Men* (1987), a funny and poignant story of unscrupulous siding salesmen in the 1950s, and *Avalon* (1990), based on his own family's immigrant experience (as an aside, Baltimore's Fell's Point was second only to Ellis Island as a landing ground for Eastern Europeans in the 19th century). Between, and since, these films he's been responsible for a highly acclaimed body of work as writer (. . . *And Justice for All* in 1979, *Jimmy Hollywood* in 1994, and *Sleepers* in 1996) and director (*Rain Man*, for which he won the Oscar in 1988, *Bugsy*, for which he was nominated in 1991, *Disclosure* in 1994, *Sleepers*, and, most recently, 1997's *Wag the Dog*).

A practitioner of what he terms ''stand around and watch'' journalism, Simon spent all of 1988 in the company of the Baltimore City Police homicide unit contemplating the frightening, absurd, surprising, and banal qualities of violent death in a city within a country where murder is so commonplace that it doesn't ensure headlines. His book is the most insightful and honest ever written about the daily grind of policing.

Levinson felt the book was particularly suited for adaptation to television. He explains, ''For a feature, you extract one major story line and end up throwing out four-fifths of the book. A TV series would allow for continuous coverage of the characters.'' And that element of continuum — the overlapping of stories, the progress of the characters' lives — is the central feature of the book.

Fontana was fascinated by Simon's book, but nonetheless hesitant to turn it into a series.

''I thought there couldn't be any better cop show than *Hill Street Blues*,'' he confesses, referring to Steven Bochco's innovative production of the 1980s that introduced viewers to the large ensemble cast, multiple independent plotlines, and stories that went unresolved over several episodes. Furthermore, he feared that the book was too much from the detective's perspective.

"I felt better about it when Barry said we could toss the book aside," Fontana relates. "I wanted to draw on the events from the book, but to tell a dramatic story we'd have to let the facts go. Let's be clear about it: we're telling stories, not recounting news events."

Given Fontana's comments, it is of greater credit to Simon that so much of the series has been drawn directly — sometimes word for word — from his pages. Much like a good detective, Simon is an exceptional observer and listener. His brand of journalism requires that he be at the forefront of the action, yet all the while go unnoticed. He records without interfering, is present without becoming involved.

That Simon succeeded in insinuating himself so completely within the homicide unit is nothing short of amazing. Police are notoriously guarded around outsiders, whom they expect to be hostile at worst, incapable of understanding them at best. Either way, to their way of thinking, nobody — least of all a reporter — is going to portray them as they believe themselves to be. Of course, this was never Simon's purpose. His objective was to portray them as they are. Ask cops about their job and they'll smoothly launch into a greatest-hits package of their best cases, as if they had been waiting all their lives for the question. But, that's not the cop's grind. What about the things that went wrong? The unanticipated twists that threw everything for a loop? The hunches that splattered against a wall? What of the plain routine that numbs the brain? All this stuff seems irrelevant to the participants. They don't have the perspective to recognize those fleeting moments that expose who they are. In this regard, Simon was like a therapist, picking up on the telling details that account for the behavior.

Though the routine of people whose job demands that they carry guns and hunt down those who most decidedly don't want to be found is bound to have its extraordinary quirks, it is routine. If it is to be described fairly, the extraordinary elements must be set up in the context of those routines that dominate and define the occupation. Police work is not a succession of car chases and gun battles, but time marked while crammed into a compact car undertaking surveillance on people who never appear, watching doors that don't open, following up clues that fail to materialize, interviewing individuals who willfully and without imagination lie, and — as much as anything else — slamming headlong into an unyielding and backlogged bureaucracy that has become immune to outrage. Through it all, Simon was there absorbing and committing to paper the lives of police and the deaths of the city. Like the detectives, readers have to pause to remind themselves exactly which suspect belongs to which corpse. It is chilling how casual it all becomes.

The idea of doing a book on a year in the life of the murder police took shape after Simon, then the *Baltimore Sun*'s crime-beat reporter, spent a Christmas shift in the squad room for a feature story. Although that particular shift had been uneventful, he knew that the tone and texture of what went on there would make a great book. Fortuitously, as it would turn out, a reporter's strike in 1987 left him bitter about the newspaper business (without dampening his passion for journalism) and looking for something to fill the time. So he set about seeking permission for unfettered access to the inner workings of the homicide unit.

Not surprisingly, a straw poll within the thirty-six-man unit found thirty-three opposed to his presence. And Sgt. Terry McLarney, who would serve as the model for Steve Crosetti, dismissed the three in favor as mental cases. Lt. Roger Stanton, one of two shift commanders, resolutely insisted that Simon not be attached to his squad. The other lieutenant, Gary D'Addario, to whom the character of Al Giardello would owe much, was more open-minded about the project.

"Initially I was opposed," he admits, "but it wasn't absolute. I wasn't worried, I didn't feel like I had to watch my back or anything. I had confidence in the job my guys did."

Once then-commissioner Edward Tilghman approved of Simon's project, the unit had no option but to suffer his presence. But they didn't have to hide their hostility. Nothing as insignificant as a commissioner's order could dissuade veteran detective Donald Worden, upon whom Stanley Bolander would be based, for example, from greeting Simon with a contemptuous "Simon, you piece of shit."

How did he overcome the opposition?

"You keep telling people what you're doing until they believe it. Then you hang around until you become as close to invisible as you can."

He allows that for the first few weeks there was some hesitation in the behavior of the detectives — their actions would momentarily stutter as it flashed on them that they were being scrutinized. Within a month, however, everyone was acclimatized to having him around. "Everybody's got to revert to form eventually; you really can't play false with your life for any length of time.

"Besides," he adds, "I think their attitude was, if the department agreed to this over their objections, it would be the department that would have to live with the consequences."

Even Worden's hostility disappeared with time. In retrospect he says, "I had known Dave from when he was with the *Sun* and I didn't mind his being around. But why did we need him? I couldn't see any harm coming from it, but I didn't see any good, either. You just never knew what he was putting down."

Initially, Worden ignored Simon, allowing him to tag along because he couldn't refuse, but never inviting him. Finally, Simon sat him down over a drink and told him frankly that when he asked around about which detective could teach him the most about working murders, the answer was invariably Worden. Maybe it was that revelation, or maybe it was the beer, but The Big Man did cooperate and, for his trouble, is depicted as an intelligent and intuitive investigator.

D'Addario agrees that once the commissioner assented, it was a done deal. The detectives took solace in the expectation that Simon would hang around for a while and eventually give up.

"None of us thought anything would come of it," D'Addario admits. "But he worked hard and was around morning, noon, and night. It's not too much to say that he almost became one of us.''

''I was surprised to find Dave there *all* the time,'' concurs McLarney, joking. ''That's how he wore us down.''

Clearly, over time, Simon won the police's respect for his work ethic. He would keep it for having written a book which they, to a man, concede got it right. Worden gave him 95 percent, D'Addario a whopping 99.9 percent.

That's not to say there were no complaints. Simon agreed to have each detective look at the portions of the manuscript that concerned them and consider their feedback. He was, however, under no obligation to revise in accordance with their wishes.

''Everyone saw things they didn't like,'' Simon allows. ''But I told them to read it to the end and reflect on whether it captured their year.'' Once they'd considered the book as a whole, most detectives withdrew their complaints.

It's no easy chore to confront your own life as interpreted through someone else's eyes. The pages glare up at you angrily. The moments of struggle or failure, the petty embarrassments, the bad moods, the insensitivities seem to tower above the rest of the text, bleeding over passages that serve to explain or qualify. The positive things are all written in a smaller script, grotesquely understated beside the negative. But that's only in the eye of the beholder. To a stranger, the police of Simon's *Homicide* are drawn in complex hues that defy immediate identification. Simon writes with the sensitivity of one who has experienced the world through his subjects. He took their perspective and made it his voice.

''Narrative demands that your subjects are given their voice; journalism demands that you tell the whole truth. Journalists have ceased to believe in writing this way,'' he scoffs. ''They resort to a pretext of objectivity, as if objectivity should prevail over the view of the people involved. You have to get emotionally involved to succeed in writing from another person's point of view. That doesn't mean that you have to be anything less than honest. My intent was to get readers to *feel* what it is to be a Baltimore homicide cop.''

Simon's researches call for a controlled schizophrenia: he

has to become emotionally involved with his subjects in order to tell the story as they breathe it; he has to remain detached in order not to get caught up in the casual lies people tell for self-justification.

"The price of my mission is that I've got to put everything down on paper and show it to the people I write about," he admits. "I do my best to write their bad moments with as much sympathy as I can. In the end, I need to be able to look people in the eye and tell them that what I've written is the truth. Usually they can see it."

Notwithstanding all that *Homicide: Life on the Street* owes to Simon's book, it has had to forge a personality suited for a totally different medium and audience. For one thing, its cast is not strictly derivative of the real Baltimore police. Some of the characters owe particular features to real people, others are compendiums of several people, and some — most notably the recent additions — are entirely fictional. Though they draw on reality in recreating specific cases taken from actual events, the actors are not tied to imitating one specific individual, and this has become clear as their characters have evolved. Controversy and hard feelings have arisen between the producers and some of the police as a result of the latter's belief that their lives have been exploited. The producers, however, argue that they have imagined their characters and then put them in true-life situations as recounted in the book *Homicide*, often giving them the words to say that Simon wrote.

"We did everything we could to convince them that our characters were not them," asserts Fontana. "We went out of our way to treat them fairly, but some of them felt this was the one time they were going to see themselves on TV and they couldn't get beyond the idea that we were making a show about them."

Where television is most at odds with books (and why, I would imagine, so few TV series have ever drawn inspiration from them) is in how time passes. In this regard, books are far better able to reflect reality. Life doesn't accommodate short attention spans; television does. Breaking each episode into 12-minute segments, it must solve every problem within the hour. Tedium, the prevailing atmosphere on most police shifts, doesn't hold out much promise for captivating viewing — unless the script and acting are so superlative, the characters drawn with such nuance, and the plot so intriguing that the normally impatient TV watcher adapts to the tempo of the scene, allowing it to unfold at a pace that evokes the same boredom and irritation felt by the character who can't elicit a confession, or has to spend hours at a computer screen checking telephone records or vehicle registrations, or can't find his assigned car in the parking garage, or has to wade through mounds of senseless forms (all situations that *Homicide* has presented).

The secret, according to Clark Johnson (who plays Det. Meldrick Lewis), is as follows: "You take banal conversation and let it drip with irony."

Homicide exhibited the fearlessness that has marked much of its existence in just its third episode, "Night of the Dead Living." During a steamy graveyard shift, the detectives sit around the squad room sweating and bitching about the lack of air-conditioning, while an appropriately smoldering blues track plays. Nary a murder is committed. No calls come in. No one leaves the building. Partners John Munch (Richard Belzer) and Stanley Bolander (Ned Beatty) bicker about their respective relationships, the former lamenting his girlfriend's having left him, the latter agonizing over whether to call the medical examiner for a date. Steve Crosetti (Jon Polito) tries to come to terms with his teenage daughter's sexual awakening. Meanwhile, a suicidal Santa Claus is arrested, only to escape somewhere in the building. Detectives Beau Felton (Daniel Baldwin) and Lewis busy themselves with the mystery of who places a lit candle by the case board every night. The most urgent dramatic tension occurs when an abandoned baby is found in the basement, but he turns out to belong to the cleaner, a lovely girl who arouses the interest of Tim Bayliss (Kyle Secor). The episode is *Barney Miller* done as film noir.

What was so risky about this was the timing. Barely had we been introduced to the eight regulars who populate the unit, much less get to know or care about them, when we were asked to watch them in an inane circumstance. But the timing is also appropriate, coming as it does in the midst of the investigation into Adena Watson's murder, which was the pivotal case of *Homicide*'s premier season. At the very end of episode one, the body of eleven-year-old Adena was found in an alley. By the bad luck of the draw, rookie Bayliss was the primary investigator. The first steps in this investigation are among three cases handled in episode two. Proper television procedure would have seen such a heinous crime quickly, decisively, and — most importantly — successfully closed within one or two episodes. Actual police procedure is nothing like television. Many inquiries stumble down false trails before they get on track. Some never get on track. Bayliss's only advance on the case during episode three was to identify a fingerprint off a schoolbook found beside the dead girl's body. He sent uniforms to pick up the person he now felt was his prime suspect. It turned out that the bearer of the print was a twelve-year-old boy who had borrowed the book from the library two years earlier.

Only in the final moments of the episode does a promising new lead present itself. Frank Pembleton (Andre Braugher), the rookie's reluctant partner, realizes the body might have been dumped where it was found because it was disposed of from the roof of an adjacent row house, rather than via the alley, as they had assumed. This causes the detectives to conclude that she may have been murdered by residents of one of the adjoining homes. They resolve to conduct a raid at the appropriate address, but the shift comes to an end and the action will have to await another episode. Inserting this episode at this point in the series was an effective device to give a sense of the time lags suffered during actual case work.

"Stakeout," an episode written by Noel Behn in the fourth season, carries forward this tradition of not relying on sensationalism to rush along the plot. Instead, dialogue and characterization maneuver the story. The crime becomes almost a distraction from the banal conversation. Real stakeouts or surveillance operations are about as dull as life can get.

Rarely are you blessed with a situation where the target does what you are waiting for him to do quickly and in plain sight. It's Murphy's Law adapted for police: Whatever pattern has been established for the target will be broken as soon as he is placed under surveillance. As a result, most of these operations occupy hour upon uneventful hour. Since you must remain watchful and alert, there's no alternative but to gorge on coffee and try somehow to make conversation with your partner.

The stakeout begins on a tip from Daryl Nettles, who is facing charges for solicitation and possession. He claims to have seen one Robert Bakasik torture and murder several young men. The suspect is learned to be visiting Pittsburgh. Giardello (Yaphet Kotto) orders a stakeout be set up on Bakasik's house so he can be arrested as soon as he returns. They establish an around-the-clock vantage point from inside a neighbor's home. And they wait.

And shifts change.

And they wait.

Bayliss contemplates resigning from the force. Giardello is tormented by his daughter's impending wedding in San Francisco to a man he's never met. Megan Russert (Isabella Hofmann) muses about how strangers will bare their souls to each other; Lewis complains, in response, that no one ever confides in him. The Buxtons, whose home they're in, are experiencing obvious marital tensions, the husband being out of work. Mike Kellerman (Reed Diamond) frets over a curse a Gypsy he arrested placed on his entire family. Munch moons that his efforts to get closer to Stan are constantly rebuffed. Giardello and Frank discuss smoking and their mutual testiness. When Bakasik returns in the final scene and is cuffed, it's an afterthought. The grisliest of serial murderers and it barely takes a minute to bring him in, after all the waiting.

Books have an easier time with such time-sensitive pacing. Gaps in the course of events and periods of reflection can be far more elegantly recounted in print than on the screen. Simon's *Homicide*, which runs to over 600 pages, would have failed as a 250-page quickie. The reader is not taken from crime to conviction in the breathless, uninterrupted rush typical of much crime writing; instead, there are obstructions, intrusions, and the circularity of genuine police routine.

Television, however, is generally in a rush. It doesn't graciously suffer ambiguity. It's a medium that feels most confident when it bombards with action or overwhelms with melodrama. As Wambaugh put it in *TV Guide*, successful cop shows "fill the screen with suds and fury." Television is particularly ill at ease with opaque mysteries. They can baffle for an hour, so long as they come clear in the end. Killers are supposed to wind up in jail, put there by the show's star. On the personal side, if a relationship is in flux, limbo won't be tolerated indefinitely; some denouement is required. That life doesn't always work like this seldom stands in the way of a satisfying ending.

Simon wrote a straightforward procedural. He made a conscious decision not to follow the detectives home. That's not to say he didn't see them off-duty. He accompanied them on their frequent bar hops across Baltimore at the end of shift, but the talk and the mood on these beer-soaked occasions were decidedly job-related. Conventional wisdom, however, is that a television series — an American television series, at any rate — couldn't last without a good dose of personal drama.

During the early years, the series stayed relatively true to Simon's decision. Except for some post-shift winding-down at the Wharf Rat, a Fell's Point tavern, there was little development of the characters' personal lives. Like most overworked people, these cops didn't make much effort to socialize with their colleagues after work. The traditional cop show depicts the police partnership as the most intimate of friendships. It's a tired cliché and one that owes more to convenience than truth. In *Homicide*, as in the department, members of the squad frequently dislike each other and are critical of each other's work habits. Egos clash. Collaboration can be reluctant.

Bayliss complains to Frank — four years into the series — that he gets no sense of family among the homicide detectives, that he's never been to anyone's house for dinner, that he isn't even sure where Kay Howard (Melissa Leo) lives, that the unit doesn't have a softball team. Impatient with the whole notion, Pembleton replies, "We're like a real family. Opinionated, argumentative, holding grudges, challenging each other. We challenge each other to be better than we are. Kinda thing doesn't happen at barbecues and ball games. It happens on the job, where it's supposed to. Putting down a murder.''

Gradually, however, the show has clawed deeper into the private aspects of its characters.

''Television viewers seem to need personal drama to accompany the professional,'' shrugs Simon. ''*Homicide* never wanted to be strictly procedural. Hell, *Cops* does that. We couldn't keep explaining the same things every week.''

Herein lies the seldom acknowledged truth about police work: it is repetitious. While each investigation is unique, the process followed is familiar. In an open-ended endeavor like serial television you have to unveil new stories. Some of the personal plots have been daring and successful: Frank's stroke, Tim's abuse as a child, Crosetti's suicide, Mike's delinquent brothers, Giardello's relationship with his kids; others less so: Mike's contemplation of suicide, Meldrick's marital difficulties, Howard's vacation in her hometown being marred by a murder.

One of the homilies of the television industry is that, in choosing to watch a show, viewers are inviting the cast into their home. Thus, the creative pressure to make characters likeable, endearing. Books, on the other hand, are not bound by this constraint.

Some of the officers depicted in Simon's work are exceptional investigators: diligent, thorough, creative; others are less so. Some are sensitive to issues of gender equality in the department and race on the street; others are not. These matters are addressed frankly in the book, but not so directly on TV, where a more egalitarian blend of race and gender has become the norm.

Hence, though all the detectives in the squad Simon joined were men, a female was put on the show. Indeed, Warren Littlefield, president of NBC's Entertainment Division, was blunt with Levinson and Fontana: ''If you don't have a woman, you don't have a show.''

Fortunately, they settled on Melissa Leo in the role of Kay.

She eschewed glamor, abstaining from makeup or sexy apparel. She was allowed to be as tough and cynical as any of the guys. It was given to her to refer contemptuously to uniformed policewomen as "secretaries with guns." It's common enough to hear cops utter such comments. A male cop once told me he was so exasperated with a female who had resolutely refused to jump into a fight to help out her fellow officers that he asked her why she had bothered to join the force. She defiantly stuck out her chin and said, "Because my typing days are done." But on TV it's more acceptable for a woman to express exasperation over such a situation than for a man.

Race is another delicate issue that is handled, well, delicately. Pembleton and Felton have a minor conflict when Felton refers to Martin Luther King Boulevard by its previous name, and Pembleton infers a racial slight. The black Lewis good-naturedly makes fun of Crosetti's Italian ancestry, but never with malice. It is certainly not a constantly simmering issue.

"Television is stark," says Simon. "You can draw characters more subtly in a book. On TV, you can't have a character express offensive racist remarks or bitterness toward women police and still have viewers relate to them. If you tried, you'd destroy him. People are not prepared for that."

The exception to this is when it's plain that within the offending character beats the clichéd "heart of gold." Thus, you can have an Archie Bunker type so long as there is nothing vicious about him. You can have a brutal cop, but only if it's abundantly clear that the brutality is directed against someone deserving. Unwilling to succumb to easy characterizations, Homicide sometimes leaves the issue on the periphery, or finds a way to bring in a dispensable individual who will take a regular off the hook. But this has usually been done with the integrity that has been the series' strong suit.

To my mind, Homicide is the best police series ever produced. Two small but defining scenes illustrate this. The first came in its debut episode ("Gone for Goode"). Detectives Munch, Lewis, and Crosetti are out on a dreary, deserted Baltimore street in the dead of night discussing ways and means of getting out of police work. After much debate, Lewis settles on the burgeoning mail-order adult-diaper market as the most promising financial alternative to a civil-service paycheck and pension. While all this is going on, a young black man skulks in and out of sight. Munch, spotting him, pulls his badge and caustically yells, ''We're cops — go rob somebody else.'' No demands about what he's doing, no frisk for weapons or drugs, no arrest to ensure the safety of the good citizens of Baltimore. Just a plea not to be troubled.

The second scene was played out in season two (''Happy To Be Here''). Lieutenant Giardello confronts the half-witted kid who has been jailed for assassinating his friend, investigative reporter Sam Thorne, for the paltry fee of $500. Unable to comprehend the enormity of what he's done, the kid tells Giardello that he did it because he wanted to purchase a fully equipped, top-of-the-line mountain bike. With smoldering grief and the weariness of the spirit-crushed, Giardello quietly replies, ''There are no mountains in Baltimore.''

These vignettes illustrate the audacity to delve into those sides of police life that television has traditionally ignored. Cops are not on a mission. Whatever zeal they possessed at the start of their careers is quickly strangled in the red tape of administration and compromises of the justice system. Cops have a job to do and most do it with workmanlike pride. But they still put in for every minute of overtime earned, and a favorite pastime is calculating service time and pension benefits. Portraying this doesn't diminish the characters, it humanizes them. What heroism most of us see is in the struggle to endure the pounding that life inflicts, to adapt to our essential powerlessness. Each of *Homicide*'s characters and the real detectives upon whom they are based personify this restrained valor.

T W O

BALTIMORE

In many respects, Baltimore personifies urban America circa the 1990s, with its sheen of glossy, geometrically elegant towers to dazzle and divert attention from the swarms of ragged people in their shadow. Walking the streets, you can't help but watch out for the types who populate *Homicide*: from the slouching, furtive-looking West-side street-corner dealers to the extravagantly tattooed, snaggle-toothed South Baltimore hillbillies. You see these types, sure enough, and you see everything in between. There is nothing about Baltimore you'd confuse with Los Angeles glamour or New York sophistication. Both of these cities are excessively familiar — even to those who have never been there — for being overused as sets. Indeed, Baltimore is a city refreshingly without pretension, a city whose local flavor overwhelms chain-brand conformity. A city with its own particular cadence, a sort of Southern drawl revved up to a Northern tempo.

"It's an ordinary workaday city," says Barry Levinson, which alone makes it unique for television. "Baltimore is representative of urban struggle."

The city — with its distinctive neighborhoods, its better- and lesser-known landmarks, its mean ghettoes — is a pivotal character in *Homicide*: this is very self-consciously a Baltimore show. It captures the city's charm and misery to establish a distinctive sense of place.

"Shooting out in real life in Baltimore is what sets us apart," according to Reed Diamond. "We have real people, real smells. I can tell immediately if a show is made on a Hollywood back lot. No matter where they pretend the piece is set, it's got this blinding, sunny glare characteristic of California, and you just know it's fake."

Being surrounded by reality roots the actors in Baltimore, and Baltimore's personality — not some designer's conception — is all over this show.

"Our screen lives overlap with our real lives in Baltimore in a way they wouldn't in other towns," Clark Johnson says, referring specifically to the more celebrity-keen Hollywood and Big Apple.

Larger cities don't spark the community feeling that marks the smaller town (Baltimore city is home to only 800,000). My first day in Baltimore I was having my morning coffee at the Daily Grind (the only place to have coffee; Diamond is adamant that it is absolutely the best thing about Baltimore), when Andre Braugher casually ambles in with the *Sun* under his arm. He stands in line like all the other bleary-eyed working stiffs, gets his coffee and muffin without fanfare, and sits down to his breakfast on a rickety chair at one of the mismatched tables. He doesn't slink off and hide in a corner. He doesn't hide himself with shades. He just sits there and drinks his coffee and reads his paper. And nobody bothers him or stares.

I walk into Kooper's Tavern, across from the *Homicide* set on Thames Street, with Johnson. It's around 5:00 PM and there's only a handful of regulars at the bar. He's welcomed almost like Norm coming into Cheers. He responds with waves and a warm smile. We then sit down, are served, and are left in peace. It's no big deal to have Johnson in their midst because it happens so frequently in the neighborhood. Most of the cast members rent in Fell's Point, so they're not only at the bars and restaurants, but also at the grocery store and the laundromat. They've immersed themselves in the community.

And Baltimore has embraced them as their own. With a few exceptions, of course. There are the snide bumper stickers that complain "*Homicide: Life Without Parking,*" protesting all the spaces procured by production vehicles, particularly in Fell's Point, where parking is already at a premium. And, naturally, there are the alternative subversives at the weekly

City Paper, who voted *Homicide* "Best Psychic Vampire Draining the Soul-Essence of the Community" in 1997's annual Best of Baltimore issue. "We're fed up to the gills with hearing some skin-puppet deliver lines in a Baltimore restaurant or beloved local institution," they rant. "We've had it with jackbooted thugs annexing primo parking spaces just because they want to shoot a scene in our neighborhood. We're done with the thrill of seeing on the idiot tube streets we see every fucking day." And everybody bitches when they stop in at a particular watering hole only to find it closed because *Homicide* is filming. There are also those occasions on which a citizen has been left exasperated when seeking the assistance of police only to find that the uniforms so mercifully congregated right where they're needed are extras and that the real thing is — what else is new? — nowhere to be found. But these are the exceptions.

In its October 1997 cover story, *Baltimore* magazine bemoaned the thought of losing *Homicide* once and for all now that the city and show have become so entwined. Most Baltimoreans I spoke with are still enthusiastic about the instant familiarity they have with the show. Do any New Yorkers really care that *NYPD Blue* purports to be about them (even though it's filmed on a lot in LA)? Or *Law and Order*? *Homicide* attracts a larger proportion of its audience in the greater Baltimore region than elsewhere. There's even a walking tour, called Hollywood on the Harbor, that guides fans to the Fell's Point locations used by the show. And everybody is pleased about the estimated $27 million per year the production pumps into the local economy.

Baltimore is a noir kind of town. Its predominant residential architecture — the squat, compacted row house — casts a peculiar angular shadow along the street. Most often there's no green space, just concrete hard up against brick. Where there is a lawn, it's usually a meager, fallow patch scratching vainly for some fertile purchase. The rows are separated by narrow side alleys that bisect with narrow back alleys, offering plenty of badly lit corridors through which to flee and become lost.

Natives include two of the classic pulp writers of the 1930s and '40s. Dashiell Hammett, born in St. Mary's County, gained invaluable experience that would inspire his fiction while working for Pinkerton's Detective Agency in Baltimore. He went on to write a number of classic potboilers featuring steely detectives, the Continental Op, Sam Spade, and the Thin Man. James M. Cain wrote novels of lust and greed featuring tough men and tougher, scheming women, including *The Postman Always Rings Twice* (1934), *Double Indemnity* (1936), and *Mildred Pierce* (1941). Both men ended up in California and set much of their work there. Back then, Baltimore was less a place to be than a place to be from.

Baltimore is among several cities to stake a claim to Edgar Allan Poe. Born in Virginia, he had family, and spent several years of his youth, in Baltimore before moving on to Philadelphia and New York. That he happened to die while visiting Baltimore and is buried in the city's oldest cemetery — at Fayette and Greene — bequeathed it perhaps the best known monument to Poe. The row house where he resided for three years at North Amity Street has been preserved as a museum. Would it appeal to Poe's sense of darkness that his home stands in an especially dreary, dilapidated part of town?

Among Poe's literary accomplishments is to be credited with inventing the detective genre. Biographer Kenneth Silverman writes of "The Murders in the Rue Morgue" (1841) that "few other works can claim its authority in giving rise to a new popular genre and setting its conventions. At the time Poe wrote, the word *detective* did not exist in English, and for many readers his story had the delight of profound novelty." Notwithstanding the significance of this contribution, thanks in large measure to film and the uniquely eerie voice of Vincent Price, Poe will always be best known for his macabre and grisly stories and poems.

How Baltimore would *Homicide* really be if it failed to pay homage to Poe? Season four's "Heartbeat" is the tale of a ten-year-old murder of which the police had never even been aware. Thanks to a tip, a skeleton is unearthed from behind a brick wall where it had been sealed. In his last agonizing hours, the victim, in darkness, fading fast in the thickening air, with drying veins and unnourished body, scratched the letters C-A-R-D-E-R in one of the bricks of his tomb. That and other evidence pointed to Joseph Cardero (Kevin Conway), a would-be Poe-esque poet and drug dealer whose corner was Fayette and Greene, the very corner where Poe's remains lie. He is even shown pondering his muse in the cemetery itself.

Munch dogs Cardero like the telltale heart of Poe's imagination. Wherever Cardero turns, around every bend, behind every wall, at the end of every hallway, there is Munch, reminding him of the endless agony of his victim, who waited for death with no other sound to distract him save the ever-weakening beat of his own heart. When Munch brings Cardero into the interrogation room — the box — he fills it with a maddeningly rhythmic heartbeat. All he can elicit from his suspect is that the victim had stolen his copy of Poe's collected works. Munch assures him, "You killed him but you can't escape him."

Returning to his apartment, Cardero is haunted by the sound of a beating heart. He truly cannot escape the cruelty he has inflicted. His only recourse is to consign himself to the fate of his victim. With only a feeble candle and memories of the poems of Poe for comfort — what comfort could these darkly twisted visions offer? — he seals himself behind bricks from which not even his screams would escape.

One of America's oldest cities — it celebrated its bicentennial in 1997 — Baltimore was among the first of the great northeastern centers to slide toward disintegration. By the late 1960s the inner city was as economically depressed as it had been during the Great Depression. The downward swing hit bottom in 1968 when riots laid further waste to the city following the assassination of Martin Luther King, Jr. But determined local efforts were already under way to erect breakwaters against the lapping waves of urban decay. In 1967 a plan to demolish the dilapidated warehouses and rotting piers that pocked the Inner Harbor cleared the way for the development of the hotels and cultural, entertainment, and shopping facilities that today make it Baltimore's centerpiece and unrivaled tourist mecca.

The other major reclamation project of the period focused on Fell's Point, the original seaport community from which Baltimore grew in 1726. The current incarnation of the Point is an eclectic co-mingling of gentry and grunge, one of the last remaining residential downtown waterfront communities in the eastern United States, and Baltimore's liveliest concentration of nightlife. But it wasn't always quite so upmarket.

"When I was a kid in the late 1930s, my parents allowed me the run of the city," reminisces Ed Kane, proprietor of the city's Water Taxi service and one of the great repositories of Baltimorean lore. "With one exception: Fell's Point. I wasn't permitted to go down Broadway below Eastern Avenue because it was just too rough, even for a kid. Then in the 1950s, when I was in the Navy, the out-of-bounds list for Baltimore was five pages, and three and a half of them dealt with the Point."

As recently as 1965, when it was still a haven for sailors and brothels (Kane swears the term "hooker" stems from a little hook of marshy land at the base of Fell Street where the ladies kept their establishments back in the 1800s), a large tract of the area was condemned to make way for an expressway. Only a concerted community effort saved this great historic treasure, the largest concentration of Revolutionary-era buildings in the United States — nearly 350 structures dating from 1785 to 1810.

The 1985 restoration of the Admiral Fell Inn — at the crossroads of the Point, Broadway and Thames — was the linchpin for Fell's Point's renaissance, establishing a hub for neighborhood tourism. Originally a seaman's hostel in the 1780s, it has also served as a ship chandlery, YMCA, distilling plant, and theater, but was an abandoned hulk when refurbishment began. *Homicide* acquired the empty city recreation building — a brick behemoth in the middle of Thomas Street at Brown's Wharf — and turned it into a studio back in 1992, which injected even more life into the district. Later, the walking tour was added, bestowing celebrity on a number of local establishments.

I've already praised the Daily Grind, the on- and off-screen café of choice for *Homicide*rs. In what ranks among the best soliloquies ever delivered on the show, Pembleton sings a suitable ode to caffeine as life's blood. The episode is "Every Mother's Son" (written by Eugene Lee), and Frank has just processed a fourteen-year-old murder suspect. Kay Howard approaches him in front of the squad room coffeepot to seek his counsel on a case about which she has doubts. Frank replies:

"Every day I get out of bed and I drag myself to the next cup of coffee. I take a sip and the caffeine kicks in, I can focus my eyes again, my brain starts to order the day. I'm up, I'm alive, I'm ready to rock." He pauses. "The time is coming when I wake up and decide that I'm not getting out of bed. I'm not getting up for coffee or food or sex. If it comes to me, fine; if it won't, fine. No more expectations.

"The longer I live the less I know. I should know more. I should know that coffee's killing me. You're suspicious of your suspicions? I'm jealous, I'm so jealous, Kay. You still have the heart to have doubts? Me, I'm going to lock up a fourteen-year-old kid for what could be the rest of his natural life. I gotta do this; this is my job. This is the deal, this is the law, this is my day. I have no doubts or suspicions about it. Heart has nothing to do with it anymore. It's all in the caffeine."

Munch, Bayliss, and Lewis pooled their funds in season three and purchased the Waterfront Hotel, facing headquarters on Thames. All dark wood and weathered comfort, it's the perfect retreat for cops craving haven from the battering they take out in the world. The Waterfront really is a popular local tavern, catering to *Homicide* fans as well as regulars who have become accustomed to its periodic unavailability during taping. Before adopting the Waterfront, the detectives would repair to Ann Street's Wharf Rat for their drinking. Across Ann is another series landmark: St. Stanislaus Church, behind which was found the first in a series of bodies dumped behind churches in season three. It also served as the setting for Steve Crosetti's funeral and the baptism of Pembleton's daughter.

Real-life justice is meted out some distance from Fell's Point, within six square blocks downtown, immediately north of the Inner Harbor, between North Calvert and President streets. Starting west, at the corner of Calvert and East Fayette, stands the Clarence Mitchell Courthouse, a stolid *beaux arts* building that Simon described in his book as being "as fine and glorious as any structure ever built in the city of Baltimore." Several scenes depicting the detectives on their way to or from court have been shot in front of the building. Directly facing the courthouse is the Battle Monument, erected in 1814–15 to commemorate those who died in the defense of Baltimore during the War of 1812. The Battle Monument is the official insignia of the city, superimposed over the Great Seal of Maryland on the police uniform shoulder patch. Police head-quarters, home of the real homicide unit, is a couple of blocks over at Frederick Street. It's an unremarkable modern office block. The show's squad room is an excellent replication of the real squad rooms inside.

Homicide has paid tribute to so many major Baltimore landmarks.

- Poe's grave site was used in "Heartbeat," as discussed earlier.
- The birth home of Babe Ruth, another native Baltimorean who went on to claim fame elsewhere, has been converted into a museum on his life and other glories of Baltimore baseball. During season five ("Wu's on First"), Kellerman was visited by his delinquent brothers, Drew (Eric Stoltz) and Greg (Tate Donovan), who were on the run from some Cleveland hoods. They had in their possession one of the Babe's original uniforms, which they stole from a guy who had stolen it from the museum. At Mike's insistence, they break into the museum to return it to its rightful place. There, they engage in a standoff with the hoods, broken only when the police arrive and take everyone into custody.
- Pimlico Race Course is the site of the Preakness Stakes, one of the jewels in horse racing's triple crown. In a fifth-season episode, Detective Munch followed a tip from a small-time mobster and dug up an entire section of the parking lot in search of a body.
- Druid Hill Park is the largest green space in the city, and home to the Baltimore Zoo. The accomplice of a serial killer led the detectives to the bodies of several young boys who

had been hastily buried in an isolated section of the park (in "Stakeout"). It was here, also, that the pivotal confrontation between police and drug lord Luther Mahoney began.

- The Block is the city's notorious tenderloin. Far less extensive than it once was, the Block now is, literally, one city block: on East Baltimore Street, between Holliday and Gay. Here is an intensely concentrated selection of strip bars, peep shows, and porn shops. Ironically, it ends abruptly across Gay from the Central District station. The establishments along the Block are not of the stylish, well-kept variety, but are down-and-dirty, raincoat-wear smutty. The Block figured most prominently in season two's "A Many Splendored Thing," an investigation that carried Bayliss into the demimonde of sadomasochistic sex. After the case was closed, his curiosity peaked, Bayliss was last seen strolling the Block and scanning the action. Gordon Pratt (Steve Buscemi), the prime suspect in the shooting of three of the detectives, was taken into custody at a massage parlor on the Block ("End Game," season three).

- Memorial Stadium is Baltimore's sports shrine, where memories of Orioles past and the still-lamented Colts echo. Before the Cleveland Browns restyled themselves the Ravens and put up shop in Baltimore, the city briefly embraced the Canadian Football League Stallions. In an opening sequence that provided Bolander the chance to bemoan the Colts's midnight run to Indianapolis, the Stallions trotted out the homicide unit for a pre-game introduction.

- Camden Yards, a model of baseball stadium architecture and one of the focal points of downtown rejuvenation, was used as the backdrop for two murders. The first involved a tourist who was gunned down in a mugging outside the Yards ("Bop Gun"). The second, in the opener of season six ("Blood Ties"), took place right inside the stadium during an Orioles game. An obnoxious Yankee fan killed his companion for inducing him to go to Baltimore for a game on the pretext that the Yanks would be playing, when it turned out to be the A's. In that first instance, a run-down residential neighborhood that isn't, in fact, near the Yards was juxtaposed through the magic of editing. "That was the one episode that caused us some concern," admitted Gil Stotler, then director of communications for the Baltimore Area Convention and Visitors Association. "We got several phone calls from people wondering if Camden Yards was safe."

- The National Aquarium in Baltimore, regarded as one of the world's important marine exhibitions, was opened in 1981 at the Inner Harbor. It is credited for much of the vitality enjoyed by the entire harbor development. It provided an appropriate soothingly lit environment in which Bayliss and Pembleton met clandestinely with a shadowy National Security Agency cartographer involved in a convoluted plot to murder the man who may have been his biological father ("Map of the Heart," season four). Perhaps the most unrealistic thing ever depicted on *Homicide* was an aquarium that wasn't teeming with tourists and kids. On another occasion, the same detectives met in front of the exterior seal tank with a man who was preserving his wife's quickly ripening corpse in their home weeks after her death.

- The B&O Railroad Museum is home to the most extensive collection of railway memorabilia in America. The display of vintage locomotives provided the backdrop as Felton and Russert put an end to their affair ("Extreme Unction," season three).

- The Orchard Street Church in West Baltimore is supposed to have served as one of the stops on the Underground Railroad. Lauded today for being "the northernmost southern city," a compliment to the relaxed hospitality the South is supposed to embody, it bore a whole other meaning back when slavery was a major Southern institution. Baltimore had a large free black population and the Railroad ferrying runaway slaves to the North ran right through it. Slavery's ugly legacy proved the motive for the murder of Martin Ridenour, great-great-great-grandson of Patty Ridenour, a female bounty hunter who dragged escaped slaves and free blacks alike back into bondage in the South ("Sins of the Father," season six). He is found, whipped and lynched, in a vacant row house just around the corner from Orchard

Street. How this white executive ended up on the predominantly black west side, not to mention the method by which he was dispatched, are mysteries. The case breaks when Frank hears the victim's name and recalls Patty as the boogieman in the nursery rhyme his grandmother had used to scare him into obedience. With that, Meldrick realizes the motive hinges on long-suffered memories and is drawn to a suspect whose interest in African-American culture is fuel for rage. With an imaginative blend of past and present, Daryl LaMont Wharton's screenplay ties Ridenour's heritage to that of his killer, Dennis Rigby, whose great-great-great-grandfather had been kidnapped by Patty and sold into servitude. Rigby is an expression of the pain and anger that such indignity continues to incite. Slavery is not left as an historical anachronism, but is living history from which America has yet to recover.

- Fort McHenry was instrumental in the defense of Baltimore from the British during the War of 1812. It was the pivotal battle that inspired Francis Scott Key to pen "The Star-Spangled Banner." Bolander, his date Linda (Julianna Margulies, before ER propelled her to fame), and a lovesick Munch saw fireworks here one evening after Munch crashed their date ("A Many Splendored Thing").
- The Bromo-Seltzer Tower, rising 308 feet, is one of the more distinctive features of Baltimore's skyline. It is a constant reminder that the remarkable elixir Bromo-Seltzer was invented right in Charm City. This was one of the vantage points from which a sniper terrorized the city ("Sniper," a two-part episode from the fourth season).
- The Washington Monument at Mount Vernon Place, significantly smaller than the Bromo-Seltzer Tower at 178 feet, is nonetheless significant for having been the first monument erected to honor George Washington. As from the tower, the sniper fired indiscriminately, including toward the nearby Baltimore Museum of Art.

Furthermore, the Homicide cameras have found their way through every compass point: the corner drug markets of

West Baltimore, the projects of the East, the Pigtown section of South Baltimore, the affluent North side. Of course, the distinctive character of Fell's Point has been particularly prominent, but we've also seen Federal Hill and Little Italy. The show has even taken a day trip out to Annapolis, where Bayliss and Pembleton interviewed the ex-husband of a murder victim on the pristine grounds of the Naval Academy ("Control," in the fifth season). Lewis and Crosetti made a pilgrimage of sorts to Washington, DC, following up on the possibility that the murder of a Chinese student in Baltimore may have been tied to China's embassy. They went on to take the opportunity to visit Ford's Theatre, an indulgence to Crosetti's fascination with the Lincoln assassination ("And the Rockets' Dead Glare," in season one).

What all of this illustrates is how *Homicide* has never packaged itself in the plain paper of a generic catchall. Obviously, this is the key to using place as a crucial element within stories. Writer/consulting producer Eric Overmyer, who had no previous experience of Baltimore, says, "It's very liberating not to be writing about a place you've seen a thousand times before." Similarly, looking at a place we haven't seen a thousand times before is very appealing.

T H R E E

THE MURDER POLICE

"Even if you don't believe in anything else the cops do, if someone's been killed and they're out to find who did it, wherever you come from, you can't help but feel some allegiance with their task," argues David Simon.

And about what else can you say that? Everyone with a driver's permit has had a reason to hate traffic cops. Vice touches upon too many things that tempt the otherwise law-abiding citizen. For all the just-say-no bullshit, drugs are bought and consumed in all those nice suburban enclaves where taxpayers sit around lamenting the deterioration of the city. You gotta believe in what the robbery division does, but they never seem to accomplish anything more than taking down good reports for the insurance company when it's your stuff that's been pinched. But homicide finds demonstrably dangerous people and gets them off the street. They may not be the worst criminals, but they've committed the worst crime.

To any cop who has ever worked homicide investigations, there is no question: It is the most important thing they ever have done or ever will do. They may be formally employed by a city, a state, or a province, but in practice they are God's own police. It's not *crime* they deal in; it's *commandments*, His word: "Thou shalt not kill." Priests and rabbis may spread the message, but it's the murder police who exact His just retribution. If for no other reason than that, they constitute an elite.

"Because in a police department of about three thousand sworn souls," wrote Simon with reverence, "you are one of thirty-six investigators entrusted with the pursuit of that most extraordinary of crimes: the theft of human life. You speak for the dead. You avenge those lost to the world.''

In the city of Baltimore there is an excess of vengeance to be sought. In 1988, the year about which Simon wrote, 234 human beings were murdered. This represents a fairly tame tally by local standards. Over the past decade, only 1987 saw fewer killings (226). Since 1990, more than 300 homicides have been committed each year, topping out at 353 in 1993.

''Being in homicide is like mowing the lawn,'' Simon shrugs. ''There's 250 murders this year, there'll be another 250 next year.'' Something to count on in contemporary America.

On the surface, a homicide investigation is an overwhelming task. The victim — often the only person with a heartfelt interest in seeing justice served — can no longer help investigators identify or locate suspects. Witnesses are difficult to find, dedicated as they are to forgetting whatever they know. Co-operating with the police can be a dangerous act in the drug-soaked inner-city neighborhoods where so much of the violence occurs. Unless you want to get buried very deeply beneath something of which you — quite sensibly — want no part, you can only have two responses when a detective asks what you know: lie and deny.

The thing Simon found most surprising when he began observing police work from the inside was the sheer volume of lies detectives must filter. Hence, the first truism he learned: everyone lies.

''Police expect everyone to lie to them because that's their experience,'' he says. ''When they realize that someone is actually telling the truth, you can see them perk up, they'd be genuinely shocked. In this sense, police earn their cynicism.''

Life is fleeting, expendable in the ghettoes. Kids grow up without expectations of a future, so they seldom agonize over consequences. Minor beefs that could be shrugged off in more genteel society become issues of pride and status where both are in short supply.

According to Edward Burns, a former homicide detective, now a teacher at a Baltimore high school and co-author with

Simon of *The Corner: A Year in the Life of an Inner City Neighborhood*, "When you expect to be dead at 21, but you're not, you find yourself grown up with a natural indifference."

Baltimore was hard-hit by the decline of traditional heavy industry and the resulting disappearance of steady and decent-paying jobs for workers with minimal skills and low education. The result has been the routine triple play of urban poverty: frustration to rage to drugs. Before the 1980s, most of the drugs that were abused either mellowed users or left them in a stupor — in either event, drugs were of little concern to anyone outside the affected community. Then came crack cocaine and everything changed. An intensely addictive and volatile drug, crack was the spark that ignited random violence and casual murder on an unprecedented scale. An addict needs $10 to score a rock, so he pops someone who moves a bit too slow in handing over a wallet. Stick-up crews know that there's easy money to be had by holding up the corner dealers flush from the fruits of ghetto retail. If you've got them out-gunned, this is low-risk crime; the victims can't exactly flag down a passing radio car and make a complaint. And if they decide to complain at source, somebody gets hurt. Then there are the truly entrepreneurial spirits, about whom the phrase *caveat emptor* — let the buyer beware — was coined. Rather than getting dirty slinging drugs, they sell bags of pure, uncut baking soda to the unwary. Consumers disappointed with their purchase often let their displeasure be known with the blade of a knife or the barrel of a gun.

Fortunately, Baltimore hasn't been divvied up by well-structured gangs, as have Los Angeles and Chicago. It's still pretty much a free-enterprise city. Dealers take to the corners to market their wares and users can shop the strip in the hope of scoring the best available blast. Free samples get distributed at the start of business so that word-of-mouth will create a demand. What this means is that there are few sustained turf wars or disputes over territorial infringement. There are invisible boundaries between neighborhoods, and East-end slingers are ill-advised to hone in on the West side, and the Fayette Street crews don't stray too far south. But the strict borders and drive-by enforcement are largely absent from the mix. On the other hand, there is no supreme warlord to intervene in minor disputes and minimize the violence.

The drug killings are undoubtedly the most frustrating to investigate. They are the least likely to produce credible, cooperative witnesses. They are the least likely to involve a victim who *matters*. Among the ideas the book *Homicide* got across so effectively was that some victims inspire greater fervor from a detective than others. How can it be otherwise? Divide nearly 300 murders into 36 police and you get about eight killings per cop. Does anybody really expect the police to shed tears over every corpse?

Well, yes, some people apparently do. And they all seem to have gold braid on their caps. The very brass who had turned Simon loose in homicide disapproved of some of the things he revealed. They were bothered by the suggestion that investigating officers don't take every case personally and that something like the rape-murder of a child is given greater importance than the stabbing of a street hustler. On the other hand, they are the ones who give impetus to the so-called "red ball," a case into which all available — and some unavailable — resources are poured. In doing so, they openly acknowledge that some calls for vengeance are more compelling than others.

It's no sin to admit that cops recognize those killings where "the dead man is indistinguishable from his killer," and their level of emotional expenditure will be adjusted accordingly. Simon eloquently posed the "American detective's philosophical cul-de-sac: If a drug dealer falls in West Baltimore and no one is there to hear him, does he make a sound?" The rate of burnout among police is high enough as it is; if they invested their souls in every victim, they'd implode. Police commanders, who long ago sacrificed themselves to appearances, apparently felt otherwise. Or, at the very least, they didn't want to see it expressed in print.

It is important to distinguish between detachment and disinterest. The primary investigator has an interest in solving every murder to which their name is attached. His reputation and, ultimately, his tenure in homicide depend on it. There was never a suggestion that detectives neglected to follow viable leads in any case. No sergeant or lieutenant is going to accept failure on the argument that the victim was a knucklehead lowlife.

"Red-ball pressures were real," admits Gary D'Addario to me. But he quickly adds, "In my 10 years in homicide, rich or poor, black or white, every victim got an honest investigation. Every case was a job for the detective and he was obliged to bring the killer to justice.

"Something each of us learned about in homicide was grief. And the grief is just as painful for the mother of a drug dealer as the mother of a little girl. And they get the same benefit of closure when the person who killed their child is convicted."

Nevertheless, there is such a thing as a *genuine* victim, that person who deserved the simple reward from life of a peaceful death, whose body should be spared the indignity of an autopsy, whose secrets should never be intruded upon by police. The domestics, the burglaries, the molestations, and, above all else, the children.

Homicide pushed the envelope in choosing to illustrate emotional detachment in a second-season episode involving a very genuine victim. David Simon co-wrote the teleplay for "Bop Gun." In an Emmy-nominated performance, Robin Williams guest-starred as Robert Ellison, a man vacationing in Baltimore with his wife and two children. In the vicinity of Camden Yards they are confronted by three armed young blacks who shoot the mother. Beau Felton is the primary investigator of the red ball that ensues.

Sitting in the squad room, unknowingly within earshot of Ellison, Munch jokes, "The husband was standing there for the whole thing. He doesn't think he can ID anybody. I asked him to describe the gun, you know what he says? 'It's big and metal.'"

"With a hole in it like this," Felton adds amid general laughter, holding his fingers in a huge circle. "Why is it every civilian says the same thing about a robbery? Three nondescript yos, with a hole in the end of the barrel the size of the Fort McHenry tunnel." Throughout this episode, the taboo ghetto slang "yo" is used in reference to black males.

As Ellison approaches the detectives from behind, Felton goes on gleefully, "I am telling you, I am going to rack up the overtime on this one."

Understandably incensed at Felton's coldness, Ellison insists on filing a complaint with his superior. Giardello takes him into his office. "He's not going to feel what you feel," he explains. "None of us are. . . . You need him to solve your murder, not to grieve."

A decade has passed since Simon's year in homicide, seven years since his book was released, and six since it debuted as a television series. The murder rate is still astronomical. Baltimore is one of the ten most violent, murderous cities in the United States. The number of officers assigned to homicide has more than doubled, to over seventy investigators. Furthermore, a Violent Crimes Unit has been established to investigate all the shootings, cuttings, kidnappings, and other major crimes that used to be juggled by homicide in between the murders. The solution rate, however, has plummeted. Few of the men Simon wrote about survived the decade in the unit. As effusive as they are in their praise for the book, some are less enthusiastic regarding the series. There are mutterings that the attention heaped upon them has had a detrimental impact on their careers. Command's response has ranged from the petty to the profound.

On the extreme petty end of the scale, consideration was reportedly given to bringing some of the officers up on charges of conduct unbecoming for all the profanity lacing their talk. That anyone who is supposed to be a cop could be surprised to hear them swearing is astounding. Police use obscenities. It's an obscene profession practiced in an obscene environment. You're looking down on an eviscerated body and, somehow, courteous manners are not what come to mind. An old cop joke has it that a police could recite the entire Gettysburg Address using only "fuck" and "motherfucker" and other police would understand every word.

Of greater profundity was the 1994 decision by Commissioner Thomas Frazier to implement a program whereby officers are regularly rotated between coveted units and more routine duties on a four-year cycle. Some homicide veterans believe the public exposure of the unit provided an excuse for such a radical movement of senior personnel. There had been grumblings within the ranks that homicide had become a closed shop, to which openings only came up when someone retired or died. Certainly if Frazier, an outsider recruited from the San Jose Police, was looking to score points with younger officers, promising easier access to elite units was one way to do it. As more than one homicide veteran put it, the new commissioner had a hard-on to push out the fat, old, white guys. One went so far as to entertain suspicions that Frazier is either a frustrated homicide wannabe, or was badly screwed over on some occasion by a murder police.

Those with a less suspicious inclination would point out that not everyone in the unit was fat or white. As for old, well, they were all seasoned investigators. But, then, that used to be a given for homicide. You couldn't get in unless you had served in patrol *and* distinguished yourself in an investigative assignment, whether in the district or a centralized squad. Under Frazier's plan, the road to homicide would be faster and less obstructed.

Without a comprehensive appreciation for the political machinations and maneuverings of the police bureaucracy, it is impossible to say whether anything like retribution was exacted against the homicide officers. One senior officer commented to one of the men that, ''Homicide has been cracked.'' Exactly what he meant is a bit obtuse. If he was implying that something had been revealed which should have remained hidden, he didn't read the book. Perception, however, can always be counted on to survive fact. Taken as a whole, within its proper context, there is nothing negative — save a few specific incidents — to be construed from the book or show. If anything, both depict complex and humane people coping with horrific situations.

Police administrators are an interesting species. Once upon a time they surely had it in their minds to be real police. They were moved by a sense of duty to patrol the streets with a mind toward keeping people safe. They desired to conduct investigations and apprehend criminals. But both tasks speak to a certain vocation. As with any profession, you can fake it for a while, but eventually talent and aptitude — or lack thereof — will be revealed. Those with the slipperiness to stay out of trouble, the political savvy, the ability to file a good report, and the temperament for mind-deadening paperwork can fast-track the admin route. This is a perfectly legitimate career. And if those who selected this path only realized it, they'd cause far less trouble than they do. Ironically, they seem unable to overcome the notion that they are something other than *real police*. Not that there's anything wrong with that. An administrator doesn't have to have been a good cop, nor is a good cop necessarily good administration material. The trick in a police department, as in life, is to know yourself and do what you do best.

The admin police are damned by the delusion that they think like other police. They don't. As a result, they're shocked to be faced with the fact that those doing police work feel obstructed by bureaucrats whose paperweighted idea of the street is filtered through the morass of the General Orders Manual, the bible of policy and procedure for the Baltimore police. Real police think of a way to deal with a problem and then check to see if they're covered by the GOM. Admin put decisions on indefinite hold to see what the GOM tells them to do.

Make no mistake, the police environment is a tough one. Until you're taken in as one of the boys (and this applies equally to women), you're made to dance through a minefield to prove yourself. You've got to be able to swagger wearily up to the bar with a good night's worth of reckless war stories. You've got to earn the right to curse and swill, to laugh at and tell tasteless jokes. You've got to ooze the attitude. At the end of the day, you may hightail it out to the county refuge where you stow your family, but the streets of Baltimore are your turf. Citizens may rent property on your post, but you own the space. And don't bother some veteran of the wild Western District with tales of woe if you have the nerve to work across the street in the Central. Better put on a cup when you come down here, bunk, 'cause this is the side where your balls drop off. And don't even bother ordering a drink if you got your stripes out of policy division.

This shouldn't be a problem. If you want to make colonel at a preposterously young age, admin is the route. All the patrolling in the world through the Western won't earn you that. Just understand that you won't have earned your rank in the eyes of the men you'll command. Oh, they'll obey you all right, call you sir, snap off a regulation salute, but you'll never be police in their eyes. If you could recognize that, seek camaraderie with the other gold braids, and leave the men to their job, all would be well. Why insist on the rank *and* pretend to be a police officer? There's the problem.

The superior officers on *Homicide* have been a slithery coven of blatant careerists, incompetents, and equal-opportunity tokens. Their narcissism is frightening because they have the authority to harm. Deputy Commissioner James Harris (Al Freeman, Jr.) is most devious and blunt about it, as befits his holding the highest of ranks. Vindictive and venal, he wears his self-interest on his sleeve. Harris showed himself capable of blatant falsehood when he denied to Pembleton's face that he had agreed not to pursue misdemeanor charges of making a false police report in the bizarre case of Congressman Jeremy Wade, who concocted a ridiculous story about an attempted kidnapping to cover up a fight with his homosexual lover ("Cradle to Grave").

Colonel Granger (Gerald F. Gough), the first of Giardello's commanders to appear, wasn't an especially assertive ruler. Giardello was instrumental in his demise, exposing how he handed city plumbing contracts to his brothers-in-law, who always left things worse than they found them so as to parlay each job into ever more lucrative work. He was replaced by Colonel Barnfather, played with conscience-free relish by Clayton LeBeouf. He has guile and backroom smarts, but none of the street smarts or decisiveness a subordinate would value in a leader. He shows up at crime scenes when the appearance of someone of rank is mandatory, but is not one to take the tough decision on his own authority. The successful bureaucrat always has a paper trail protecting him from above and a vulnerable subordinate protecting him from below.

Then there was the ill-fated Megan Russert, whose roller-coaster career soared from lieutenant to captain, only to plummet again to detective. She was promoted over Giardello expressly because she was female. At the time there were enough black senior officers (including Barnfather and Harris) that Giardello could only hope to advance on merit, inevitably the last quality to be considered. Finally, there is the thoroughly detestable Capt. Roger Gaffney (Walt MacPherson) — bigoted, incompetent, and revealed to have been that squad-room larcenist, the Lunch Bandit. Yet again, Giardello had every reason to believe he deserved the captaincy when Russert was demoted. But Harris had a score to settle and the best thing about being deputy commissioner is you always find an occasion to settle scores. Commanders act essentially as the men expect of them. Their motives seem far removed from those that propel working police. This incongruity is one of the greatest sources of frustration for police everywhere: the department for which they work seems to have some elusive agenda that is never spelled out.

A less ephemeral issue than the mindset of the brass was the passing of Commissioner Tilghman, who died before Simon's book was completed. Having authorized the project, he would have had little recourse had he not been satisfied with the outcome. His successors, however, were not constrained by any stake in the matter. And the fact is that the careers of some of those in the book have not flourished, even those of some highly competent policemen. Several have left the city police rather than risk a return to uniformed patrol. Sgt. Jay Landsman, to whom Munch owes some of his personality, is a homicide investigator with the Baltimore County Police. Rich Garvey, some of whose cases were assigned to Kay Howard, is an investigator with the Harrisburg, Pennsylvania, public defender's office. Donald Waltemeyer, from whom some of Lewis's early dialogue was drawn, is with the Aberdeen, Maryland, Police. Others have retired from police work altogether, while many soldier on in other capacities on behalf of Baltimore.

HIS EMINENCE

It's ironic how the higher one rises in a bureaucratic structure, the lower one's self-confidence sinks. Perhaps it's the pressures of having to satisfy insecure superiors and the fears of being blamed for the actions of incompetent subordinates. In the "stab 'em in the back and step over their corpse" atmosphere of any politically charged power structure, an every-man-for-himself panic afflicts every decision.

That's precisely why it is so refreshing to encounter a leader like Gary D'Addario. To a man, anyone I spoke with who has served under him would jump at the opportunity to do so again. They admired his grace when low clearance — or solution — rates threatened his command and his willingness to stand up for his people. This is what defines leadership. Unfortunately, a lieutenant commanding a homicide unit is only a leader of sergeants and detectives. All the while, he is being second-guessed by captains, majors, colonels, and deputy commissioners. Homicides sometimes make headlines, and when an investigation is an unqualified success, seeing your name in the paper becomes a good thing. But when it's not, the stampede to find cover can leave more bodies strewn in the hot sun than the bull run at Pamplona.

In an era when so many command positions in a police force are doled out to functionaries, D'Addario stands out as a real police officer. Having been promoted to lieutenant in homicide from uniform patrol sergeant in the Northern, he had spent his time riding a radio car, not a desk, and it shows. You can tell he doesn't just look out over the street; he reads it. Big without being imposing, D'Addario is a man of presence. He is comfortable draped in the authority of his uniform, having earned it by deed, not appointment. He transferred out of homicide in October 1989. He has since been promoted to captain, and is currently acting commander of the property division.

He considers himself less authoritarian than his TV counterpart, Al Giardello. "I always maintained the perspective that my detectives were the experts. I ran the unit along a two-way street of loyalty and respect." This style exposed him to criticism when detectives' performances slipped. He also proved himself too willing to stand up for his men in the face of his own superiors' arbitrariness. That his loyalties often ran down before up, has cost him. By his count, he has been passed over for promotion on four occasions.

D'Addario brought a rare level of refinement to homicide. His dignified disposition was honored in the exaggerated politesse with which he was addressed. He was often referred to as "your eminence," not mockingly, but as a means of distinguishing genuine deference and regard from the required use of rank titles in address and perfunctory salutes.

D'Addario serves as *Homicide*'s regular technical advisor, ensuring accuracy on procedure, such as the serving of warrants, conducting searches, securing crime scenes, making arrests, etc. He is an indispensable source on how Baltimore police talk. He says he's never heard a cop talk about making a "bust" except on TV. In Baltimore, they make an arrest, or they lock someone up. He also ensures the authenticity of uniforms and some of the cosmetic details of the set.

Homicide viewers will recognize him for his recurring role as Lieutenant Jasper, the fast-draw commander of the Quick Response Team. Not surprisingly, his favorite episode was the second of three parts dealing with the shooting of detectives Bolander, Howard, and Felton ("Dead End"), wherein he has a confrontation with Pembleton about how to go about arresting a suspect. It was a thrill to be challenged with going face-to-face opposite Andre Braugher.

He praises *Homicide* for its realism, conceding, "Television skims over a lot of the nitty-gritty and background work of an investigation. Where *Homicide* has been most instructive regarding real police work is in Andre's scenes in the box. He has been near perfect in portraying a detective conducting an interview."

So, do outsiders come away from *Homicide* with a better understanding of police?

"I don't really think so," he answers upon consideration.

"People tend to see things in stereotypes. They can't know because they're not participants."

Police are existentialists at heart.

LATONYA'S GHOST

Latonya Wallace was eleven years old in 1988. Tom Pellegrini had been in homicide for only two years, a policeman for ten. Their lives would converge and Pellegrini would never get over the encounter. No one who worries about a cop's capacity for callousness has ever sat down over a beer and discussed Latonya Wallace with Pellegrini. As he speaks, his eyes fade away to the distance and you get the impression he is seeing the beautiful twenty-one-year-old woman she would be today had she not gone the few blocks from her Reservoir Hill home to the local library and encountered the wrong man at the wrong time that fateful February day.

In all, Pellegrini spent eight years in homicide. He left in August 1994, returning to uniformed patrol in the Southern District. Promoted to sergeant a little more than a year later, he transferred to the Western to supervise a patrol shift over three and a half of the most crime-infested square miles within the jurisdiction of the Baltimore City Police. Indeed, to call it patrol is a misnomer. On a typical night shift, there's not enough down time to just cruise a post, showing the colors and letting the locals know the constabulary is on the lookout. Eight hours on the street is spent careening from call to call. Almost every one involves potential violence. Because there are only nineteen one-man cars out per shift, if there's no indication of violence, there's little possibility of response. The residents know this, so when they call 911 they almost always toss in the presence of a weapon.

"I wanna report kids sellin' dope outside my house." Pause. "Oh, yeah, and I seen one of 'em has a gun."

Dealers are so plentiful, it would have to be an awfully slow night for a radio car to make it to a corner to break up the action. *But* if someone's out there with a gun, that's another matter.

"We'll be right there, ma'am."

And, hey, the report probably isn't much of a lie, even if the complainant didn't actually see a gun. Chances are there is one in the mix. The 17-shot Glock 9 mm carried by the patrolmen is no advantage; it's just an equalizer, if that.

Pellegrini left the Western in March 1997 and went back downtown to drug enforcement, where he works today.

Where you see the most resemblance between any of *Homicide*'s fictitious police and their real alter egos is in the earliest episodes. Tim Bayliss, like Pellegrini, was burdened with the expectation among the other squad members that he would swiftly expose himself as a hump, unworthy of working murders. Truth of the matter was, the very background that led his colleagues to underestimate his value was the thing that had gotten him into homicide. Pellegrini accepted an assignment to the mayor's security detail because the traditional reward for eating the shit served up by a politician for a couple of years is a transfer into the unit of your choice. Pellegrini wanted homicide and he didn't want to wait fifteen years to get there. Sure enough, when Mayor Donald Shaeffer headed off for the governor's mansion, Pellegrini seized his chance and claimed his reward.

Latonya wasn't Pellegrini's first case, as Adena Watson was for Bayliss. Pellegrini knew he could solve killings. But this was the one that mattered. This was the one where true evil had been committed. This was a crime without mitigating circumstances, without doubts to be absolved. This was sin, pure and simple. Latonya had left her home in broad daylight and walked to the library, where she checked out some books. She never returned home. She was found early the next morning, raped, stabbed, and strangled in the backyard of a Newington Avenue row house. Because the actual killing had been done elsewhere, there was little physical evidence and no witnesses at the scene. When a killer succeeds in concealing the site of the crime, they most effectively destroy the physical linkages between themselves and the victim. Without something tangible to tie killer to victim, there is little leverage for eliciting a confession. And without either, there is no charge.

Talk to the detectives today and there is consensus on one point: Tom Pellegrini worked the Wallace murder as aggressively and thoroughly as was humanly possible. Sometimes, they admit, there is simply not enough evidence to solve a crime. When all was said and done, did he mark the right man as his suspect? This question leads to debate, though none of it heated. The detectives, however, exhibit the kind of doubts that lose jury trials. And if these men, predisposed as they are to project guilt, have reasonable doubts, no jury that could be assembled in Baltimore would ever have convicted.

Pellegrini, however, *knows* he made the culprit. He's had ten years to ponder the case and he's resolved it in his mind. The proprietor of a Whitelock Avenue fish shop, where Latonya had occasionally done odd jobs, murdered her. She would most likely have trusted him enough that he could lure her from the street to a place where he could rape and kill her. There was enough ambiguity in the Fish Man's sex life to suggest a potential for deviance. His alibi for the presumed time of the murder was weak enough to be questionable. Enough, but not quite. That he failed to break down and confess during the most intense interrogation permitted by a justice system that prevents its police from employing physical or psychological torture did nothing to shake Pellegrini's certainty. It merely convinced him that the Fish Man is a stone sociopath.

''The last interrogation we conducted lasted nearly 12 hours. He had conditioned himself to say 'no' to any question we put. At one point I was so frustrated I asked him, 'Is your birthday March 6?' Without a thought he answers, 'No.' He just wasn't capable of saying yes to anything by then.''

''Want to see where the Fish Man lives?'' Pellegrini asks as we tour his old stomping grounds on a warm fall night.

It's around midnight and the Western is humming. The corner drug markets are in full swing, as they are twenty-four hours a day, seven days a week. Anytime you have the cash in hand and need to score a blast, this is where to get it. You don't need to search for the touts, they'll find you. Just cruise by nice and slow with the window down and let your poison be known.

Hell, you can get drive-through service. Unless you're two white guys with short hair who look older and better-fed than the average doper. In that case, you'll get a real close eye-fuck. Give it back, keep your pace to a crawl, and you're made for cops. Otherwise, maybe you're insurance adjusters or some other citizens who shouldn't be in this part of town at this time of night. In which case, you're moved down the food chain to prime stickup bait.

We cruise around the backstreets, watching the drug action. Business as usual for Pellegrini. "Yup, this here's the ghetto," he says with proprietary pride. His eyes narrow as he observes the action. His hair is still thick and combed back, as it was in 1988. He still has the groomed moustache that was once de rigueur for police, but both show more gray. He has put on weight after another decade of bad food from carryouts anxious to get a reputation for feeding cops — a deterrent against those who would use them as a substitute ATM, hitting them for the register on any night of the week.

Turning onto Gilmore Street, we come to a stop outside a beaten-up row house set a few feet off the street by a weed and garbage patch that might once have passed for a lawn. "That's the Fish Man's place."

He stares at the door. Maybe he's reliving that pivotal inter-rogation. Maybe he's wondering if another opportunity will come for one more attempt to shake loose the truth.

"You know" — he's speaking even lower than usual — "I knew I was being transferred out of the Western at the end of last March. So, on March 6 I knocked on his door. I wanted to see him again and wish him a happy birthday. 'Happy birthday, W.,' I said and smiled. He looked at me, said, 'Yeah, happy birthday and fuck you,' and slammed the door."

We pull away from the curb and drive north toward New-ington Avenue in Reservoir Hill. Latonya's body had been discovered behind the mean 700 block. Look this place over and you *expect* to see tragedy skulking in the shadows. This is a place where fear accompanies every little girl's trip to the library. A place where trust and innocence are fatal qualities. The worst of the dwellings, 702, was raided because a check of the residents had turned up several criminal records. It's now boarded up, 10 years less habitable than at the time. All the while Pellegrini is providing a running commentary of what befell Latonya as best they could reconstruct it.

Finally, we drive to Whitelock Street, where the Fish Man's store had stood until burning down the week of the murder. The ruins have all been cleared away, and what had been a commercial strip is now another vacant patch in a neighborhood with an infinite genius for finding a way to get worse. Based on traces of tar found on Latonya's clothing, Pellegrini is sure she spent her last hours there.

"Somehow, the broad was lured up here —" He suddenly shuts down. Time hitched its breath. *The broad.* Involuntarily, he had assumed the protective membrane that keeps Latonya out of his heart. Broads aren't fragile, delicate little girls. The break lasted only a second, maybe just a fraction. He takes a deep breath and continues, "*Latonya* was lured up here . . ."

He says her name softly, tenderly. He'd love to forget that she was just a child.

What makes this moment all the more poignant is that it precisely mimics one from Simon's book. Discussing the case with Det. Eddie Brown in the squad room, he catches himself saying, "I think this broad . . ." before he corrects himself with "this girl."

Pellegrini needs this distance. He is paid to investigate, not to agonize. On this case, he failed to heed that distinction. Notwithstanding the occasional mercy of forgetting who Latonya was, he has never ceased the agonizing. Nothing has succeeded in hardening him to this one murder. He travels back the 10 years without effort, recalling minute details easily. This case may not have been closed with a suspect charged, but it has never been filed away.

Simon wrote, "His obsession is not with the victim but the victimizer . . . if the case stays open, if somewhere in this world the killer lives to know that he has beaten the detective, then Pellegrini will never be quite the same." Detectives get beaten all the time. The clearance rate proves it. Closing a case means only that a charge had been laid. It doesn't even begin to account for all the cases diminished by plea bargains, lost on technicalities, witness recantations, and other eventualities. By the time all the statistics are in, a lot of murderers have evaded capture, justice, or both. This case was special because of its victim. And somewhere a killer has beaten the detective.

"That case nearly killed me," he confesses. "It took an incredible mental and physical toll. I just couldn't get interested in another drug murder after this. You can't protect yourself from what you see in homicide. You carry it with you for the rest of your life. Still, I felt obliged to stay in homicide because I knew I was good and was getting better."

He left only when it became clear the commissioner was determined to dismantle the unit.

Pellegrini has nothing but praise for Simon's book. He is rather less complimentary toward the TV series. While he wasn't thrilled to see some of his own negative thoughts about senior officials spelled out on the page, he can't deny that he entertained them. This was part of the danger of having a reporter around day in and day out to which the squad was exposed by these very same senior people. At least he can't argue with the veracity of the reporting. Simon wrote it as it was and, therefore, can't be blamed.

The TV show, he feels, lurches in a reckless zigzag over the boundary between fact and fiction. Bayliss is clearly identifiable with him. They share the same career path — the Quick Response Team to mayor's security to homicide — and Bayliss was the overwhelmed, inexperienced, and very earnest primary on Adena's murder, which followed Simon's reporting of the Wallace case. He even developed the same stress-related afflictions, like the hacking cough, that dogged Pellegrini. So far so good. He served as technical advisor for these episodes, ensuring as much accuracy as possible.

"Then, they had Bayliss go off and do things I'd never done. Now, the producers argue that he's not me, but fact is that for everyone who knows me, the association has been established. So, you base a guy on me, then you have him losing it and holding up a liquor store, having sex in a coffin. I had lieutenants in my department stopping me in the halls to ask about these things. It was my credibility at stake.'' Pellegrini — and others — felt it unfair to start from reality, then blend it with a fictitious character. They would have felt far more comfortable had a choice been made: use the detectives as portrayed in the book, or create wholly original characters.

Another matter that raised the ire of several of the detectives was the episode in which Detective Felton's close friend Chuckie Prentice reluctantly shoots his cancer-riddled father when the old man is unable to take his own life (''See No Evil,'' in season two). Felton advises Chuckie to stand firm by his story that his father shot himself, informing him that there isn't enough physical evidence against him to justify a murder charge. Lewis, the primary, is convinced that Chuckie did the shooting and intends to have him tested for gunpowder residue. He sees Beau talking to Chuckie before he has a chance to interrogate him and figures something is wrong. After a heated exchange, Lewis consents to turn his back while Felton takes Chuckie to wash off the residue so the test will come back negative and the shooting can be written off as suicide. The real detectives objected to the implication that they would conspire to cover up a murder under any circumstances. They felt the episode cast doubt on their collective integrity.

Again, the issue came down to the fact that the characters can reasonably be mistaken for representatives of the Baltimore police. Having been the subjects of the book upon which the series is based, the detectives were sensitive to the prospect that even fictional cases would attach to them. A letter signed by the squad was sent to Barry Levinson on the matter, but Pellegrini never received an answer.

He and his fellows weren't interested in the moral issues the episode was taking pains to address — the distinction between homicide and assisted suicide. Nor were they appeased by the fact that the offending detective was not as clearly identifiable with any one of them as Bayliss was with him. At that point in time, they extrapolated every incident on the screen directly to themselves. It is probably fair to say that, short of disowning their debt to the book or making a strictly factual documentary about the Baltimore police, the producers were not going to appease the detectives. The bitterness that ensued — on both sides — was almost inevitable.

Those were the major points of contention. There was another concern, about which Pellegrini speaks openly.

"I asked Dave once what might be in his book for us. You know, 'cause without us, there's no book. He said, well, if anyone makes a movie, that's when we'd see some money. Well, he sells the rights to Levinson, and still we see nothing. But then they come to us to sign releases and I refused. I figured that if they needed my release to make the show, there should be something from that."

For the first season's episodes, a variety of detectives were utilized as technical advisors. Pellegrini said that paid $25 per hour — hardly serious cash. Eventually even that dried up as D'Addario was taken on exclusively to provide such advice. Because he had never signed the release, Pellegrini sued and a settlement was reached.

There's really no need to take sides. A case can be made for either party. On the one hand, the show is, without a doubt, a dramatic fiction. What it takes from real life, on the other hand, is undeniable, nor is the strength that reality has given it. However, the depth buoying up the characters is a function of the life they have taken on, unbound by the constraints of factual biography. For all that you may recognize some Tom Pellegrini in Tim Bayliss, there is, at this point, more distinguishing the two than linking them. As the series has probed different angles of his personality, Bayliss has emerged more as a fully rounded individual than a derivation. But it is understandable that these differences might be more apparent to someone viewing it from a distance.

THE BIG MAN

"The series sucks."

These were the first words spoken by Donald Worden after I introduced myself and explained why I wanted to meet.

The remark made me all the more anxious to talk to him, since no one else whose opinion I'd solicited had been so succinctly negative (he later qualified this comment, saying he was referring to specific elements about which he went on to elaborate).

Worden provided a base for Bolander, the cantankerous character played by Ned Beatty, whose seeming greatest delight came from tormenting and belittling his long-suffering partner, John Munch. Worden is by far the bigger of the two, towering a bulky six feet four inches. His blue eyes hover somewhere between piercing intensity and watery kindness, a pretty good combination for a detective.

Worden is especially unhappy at how real details from his personal life were appropriated and twisted for Bolander. In particular, he felt that marital problems he was experiencing back in 1988 were unfairly represented.

"I'm very upset about how they portrayed my ex-wife. She didn't deserve how our relationship was used," he says.

Bolander had been married for twenty-three years, when his wife decided they had problems. She up and left him on little more than a whim and the advice of a marriage counselor. Stanley was understandably embittered and spent no small amount of time bemoaning women's penchant for fickleness, not to mention their greed for alimony. He also experienced all the insecurities of a middle-aged, overweight man's efforts to assert himself in the singles game.

At first, he was enamored of the medical examiner, Dr. Carol Blythe (Wendy Hughes). They went through a rather tender and humorous courtship. Then he had a crush on Linda, the violin-playing waitress. In all, it was a touching account of male menopause: too old for overt sexuality, too young for abstinence. Beatty was occasionally too cuddly for his own good and too vocal about his desires in the context of the squad room, but was generally able to pull off his character's awkward search for love.

Worden dismisses the suggestion that all of this was pure fiction. "There were elements of my real life in there." He would have appreciated being consulted on these matters.

A further critique: "I don't think they showed Bolander much respect in the squad room."

D'Addario echoes this sentiment. Worden was known as the Big Man, only partly for his physical size, but also for the esteem in which he is held by his colleagues. Less senior detectives would frequently bounce cases off him, both to hear a fresh view on possible investigative avenues and because he has a virtually photographic memory for past cases and old suspects. D'Addario says a true representation of Worden would have had Bolander serving as more of a mentor to younger colleagues. In *Homicide*, Bolander is recognized as no more or less of an authority than anyone else.

Edward Burns, the homicide veteran who escaped notice in the book because he was seconded to a joint operation with the Drug Enforcement Agency in 1988, calls Worden "the greatest natural police detective in America. He has this amazing instinctive feel for whether someone's lying. He's probably the last person on earth who could explain it, but that's the mark of the natural."

Part of being a natural is the ability to sift through clutter and penetrate to the heart of the matter. And the heart of all police work is talk. When Worden worked the Northwest he was, wrote Simon, "on a first-name basis with anyone in the district who was worth arresting." That's the type of familiarity that breeds respect for a cop.

"There was a time when we knew everyone on our post and everyone knew us," Worden says, recalling fonder days when crime was at a reasonable level. "People would feed us stuff they'd hear. Even when they didn't witness something themselves, they'd hear talk and let us know. That doesn't happen anymore."

When you're investigating a crime, you've got to induce someone to talk to you. According to Simon in *Homicide*, "Worden carried a credibility that somehow transcended the excesses of his profession. On the street, people who had contempt for every other law officer often made a separate peace with Donald Worden." In other words, people talked with Worden.

The alchemy of police work is to read the person across from you quickly and accurately enough to know what you need to say to get them talking. You're not going to put the fear into the fearless. Don't even try. No way are you going to out-tough the street tough. Bluster is just going to get you silence. Never play to their strength. Find the weakness. Jab it like an infected sore. Death by a thousand cuts. Probe and move, go back, plunge ahead, circle to someplace off the map, then drive right down Main Street. Act lost, then look like you're found. Pretend to know nothing, then show them you know all. Let them see you as world-weary, then look surprised. Make them feel smart in the face of your stupidity. Pull out the rug, give them a glimpse at your intelligence. Let them be whoever they want, then turn them into who they really are. Find their defenses, then batter them down. Listen to the lies, then dismember them until you extract the nugget of truth.

Donald Worden has been a Baltimore police officer since he was twenty-two years old. He tried his hand at retirement in 1995 after thirty-three years on the force, ten of them in homicide. The lure of his garden, however, wore off after barely a year. In October 1996 he returned as a civilian analyst in homicide's cold cases unit, where he lends an untainted eye to unsolved murders and reviews new leads to see if they constitute evidence that might mean a break in the deadlock.

To this day he loves being a police. You can tell by the way he pronounces the word: POH-lice, drawing it out as if he relishes saying it every time.

There are a lot of myths about the isolating nature of the profession. True, it does tend to shape your worldview in a peculiar way. Seeing human nature at its most dishonest and violent on a regular basis does cause you to think the worst of people. It creates a longing to associate with those you don't feel you have to test before you can trust. Fellow members of the fraternity get an automatic buy. But it's untrue that police necessarily want this isolation.

"Police do have a certain mindset. You might spend your entire working life without having a single non-police as a friend,'' admits Worden. ''A lot of that's because other people don't want to be around you. Everyone's got some larceny in their hearts, so they're uncomfortable with police.''

Civilians are undeniably guarded around police. They figure every conversation is a potential open inquiry. As if police don't have enough crime thrust at them on the job, maybe they're moonlighting for some extra work during a social encounter. Better not mention that shoplifting when you were eight, or out'll come the cuffs. That hilarious story about how you drove home after guzzling half a bottle of whiskey gets cut off midsentence as you picture the cop breaking out the pocket breathalyzer to check for alcohol residue years after the fact.

That police protect each other behind a so-called blue wall of silence is somewhat exaggerated; it's less conspiratorial than commonly imagined. A good part of it is undoubtedly simple apathy. If it doesn't jump up and bite me on the ass, it's not my problem. Let someone else handle it. Sure, cops shouldn't be apathetic about wrongdoing, but they aren't likely to be blowing the whistle at every suggestion of impropriety, regardless of the seriousness. If they witness a fellow officer administering an excessive thumping out on the street, there's no question that benefit-of-the-doubt discretion kicks in. If a cop were to be seen indulging in some sort of corruption, the easy way out is to turn your back.

Occasionally a policeman is implicated in a crime where there's no turning away and benefit of the doubt is lost in absolute denial. Worden ranks a suspected police-involved shooting in an alley off Monroe Street as the most frustrating case of his career. The incident was carefully documented in the book, and dramatized in the series, where the affair was given to Pembleton to handle and some extraneous personal details were added.

Several things must be kept in mind when considering Monroe Street. First, as Simon so succinctly wrote it, ''In the United States, only a cop has the right to kill as an act of personal deliberation and action.'' Put that way, it's an awesome power to be able to legally decide to discharge your weapon at another human being with the intent of killing him. Second, having taken such a decision, a cop *always* stands by the body and calls it in. Third, the only time this decision is proper and just is when it is taken in the interest of protecting lives, whether the cop's own, that of fellow officers, or of civilians. Finally, the second and third points are what allow the rest of us to sleep easy with the first.

Worden believes in all facets of the police code. The discretion you get from membership in the fraternity is earned by your adherence to the responsibilities of being an honorable cop.

"I still feel disillusioned at having been lied to by other police," he reflects sadly on this ostensibly unsolved killing.

John Randolph Scott was on the wrong end of a police chase in a stolen car that began in the Central District. Scott and his companion ditched the car in the Western and hoofed it through the ghetto alleys. Some minutes later, he was a lifeless heap with a .38 round through his back. Buttons that had been ripped from his shirt were found beside him, as if he had been involved in an altercation before being shot. Police from three districts — Central, Western, and Southern — were swarming the area in response to the stolen-vehicle pursuit call. Nobody saw Scott take the bullet. Who killed him? Was it a cop who, firing on an adrenaline burst, quickly realized there was no way to write his way out of having shot an unarmed suspect in the back? Did he conclude that it was better to deny involvement and hope nothing could be proven than to try to explain how an out-of-control situation had spiraled into chaos? Worden could relate to out-of-control and could sympathize with chaotic, but he couldn't accept anarchy, and that's what he had if police were not going to stand up and report when they had shot someone.

As with most murders, you start with who discovered the body and work from there. Sgt. John Wylie called it in. If he didn't shoot the suspect, didn't he at least see anyone else in the alley? No, he just heard the gunshot. While he showed deception on a polygraph test, ballistic tests couldn't tie him to the fatal bullet. There was a possibility that a civilian had shot Scott, but no viable suspect was presented. If you're looking for a shooter, you concentrate on the people with the guns, especially when they were in the process of chasing the victim.

Charges were never laid in the killing. Wylie ended up leaving the department about a year after the incident with a stress-related disability. Worden goes back and forth in his own mind about what happened that night. He tested over 60 guns, belonging to all the police in the vicinity of the scene and never came up with a match. He's still in the market for that elusive witness, anyone who might have seen anything that would tie someone to Scott in the seconds before he died. Whenever he hears that someone from the 700 or 800 blocks of Monroe has been brought in on anything, he makes sure they're questioned about this shooting.

"Maybe we'll get a hold of someone who's jammed up on a charge who'll be willing to talk." Only an optimist at heart can work cold cases.

The Monroe Street scene was tackled faithfully by *Homicide* over two episodes in its second season, "See No Evil" and "Black and Blue." Many of the details were changed; for instance, the shooting followed on a crack-house raid and fictitious tension was tossed in, in that Lt. Jimmy Tyron (Michael S. Kennedy), who parallels Wylie, had had an affair with Kay. Like Worden, Pembleton was indignant at the thought of a cop failing to stand by his shooting. Good or bad, you do not abandon a body in an alley. However, he was not overly troubled by the prospect of revealing a cop as the shooter. Every case is the same challenge for Pembleton, a personal affront. A killer has had the temerity to take a life on his watch and expects to get away with it. Pembleton's pledge is that this not happen. Whoever or whatever you may be, his mission is to absolve you of the delusion that you can evade the consequences of your brutality. The whys are of peripheral importance, little more than a curiosity. All he need really concern himself with is the who.

This precept flies in the face of mystery convention. The real point, after all, of the whodunit is actually whydunit. Sherlock Holmes, Hercule Poirot, Adam Dalgleish don't just get their man, lay a charge, and move on to the next body. It's not enough to match the suspect to a latent print at the scene, or have an eyewitness who ID's the killer. They explain — usually in meticulous detail — *why* the murder was committed. In real life, as well, we're more interested in why than who. We all sleep a little easier when we know that an unsolved killing can be written off as a mob settling of accounts, or that a kid gunned down on a corner was the victim of a drug deal gone sour. Even if their killers are never arrested, the rest of us know we're not prospective victims.

A police department cannot function on reassuring the citizenry that, while no arrests are imminent, at least they can tell us why the victim was killed. What they need is to lock someone up. If that person never gives up why they did it, but there's still enough evidence to prove his guilt, that's a keeper. One of Simon's more prescient insights was on the issue of motive: "[A] known motive can be interesting, even helpful, yet it is often beside the point. Fuck the why, a detective will tell you; find out the how, and nine times out of ten it'll give you the who." Detective Felton paraphrased these sentiments in an early episode.

To Pembleton's mind, whatever special treatment a police officer may have been entitled to had been abdicated when he elected not to stand by the body. With a little creativity, poor judgment, or a mistake in the heat of battle could be written up to look better than it had been. But once responsibility had been denied and all the police on the scene claimed not to have seen anything, it became a straight-up murder investigation like any other.

Giardello opposed a zealous pursuit of the police angle. Since the victim was out of sight for some unspecified period of time in the alley, he hypothesized that a civilian may have been responsible. Although this was a long shot, he wanted that possibility exhausted before seeing cops treated as suspects. He forcefully warned Pembleton of the consequences of turning "brother against brother." He pointedly refused Pembleton's request that the gun of every cop on the scene be submitted for ballistic testing. In a frighteningly intense moment between two unnervingly intense actors (Braugher and Kotto), Pembleton tells his superior he's been left with no choice but to go over his head. The sequence ends with Frank leaving his lieutenant's office and Giardello muttering, with chilling menace, "You son of a bitch, Pembleton."

Giardello feared that a policeman would be sacrificed for political expediency. Indeed, Captain (soon-to-be Colonel) Barnfather conceded as much when he said that any public outcry would necessitate that someone be handed up. He was casually prepared to serve up whatever the public might order, as if he were running a fast-food joint and cops were cheese steaks. Later on, Giardello would chastize Pembleton and the brass for failing to pursue any scenario other than that the shooting was police-involved.

This element of the plot had some basis in fact. Normal chain of command would have had Worden reporting to his squad supervisor, Sergeant Terry McLarney, who would, in turn, report to D'Addario. However, McLarney was an old Western man and the captain, *evidently*, feared his closeness to several of the potential suspects. Therefore he had Worden report directly to the administrative lieutenant, which also shut D'Addario out of the case. This was an extraordinary move, and one that reflects the public volatility around a botched police shooting.

The thought that a policeman of McLarney's stature and professionalism would compromise an investigation under any circumstances could only occur to a jittery political creature with the self-preservation instincts of a gazelle, ever twitching to the scent of danger. McLarney feared that the currents were moving so swiftly in the direction of police involvement that an innocent person might get swept away. In fact, he believes this is what happened. At the time, he wanted to pursue the case parallel to Worden's investigation, on the supposition that someone other than a cop may have shot Scott. The result would be one of two things: either it would uncover a potential suspect, or it would reinforce the theory that police were involved. McLarney wasn't suggesting that the investigation of police be interrupted, merely that a complementary investigation be undertaken. He was refused.

Like Worden, McLarney carries his own frustrations about Monroe Street. Principally, he doesn't believe Wylie is responsible. He doesn't dismiss the possibility, but he hasn't seen enough to condemn the man. Furthermore, he is still troubled by untested theories.

"Isn't this appropriate," he laughs, kicking at a spent syringe that marks the exact spot where Scott fell 10 years earlier as we stroll down the alley. Not much has changed on Monroe Street. "I think too many minds were made up before the case was investigated. I'm not saying Wylie couldn't have done it, just that cops became the exclusive focus too quickly. And remember, the bullet was never matched to a cop's gun. The way it was supposed to have played out, I don't think a cop would have had time to go to a secondary weapon. And if there had been a struggle and Scott had been disarmed and shot with his own gun, there would have been no reason to panic and not own up, plus the gun should have been at the scene. That leaves a possible third party, a civilian that Scott encountered before Wylie gets there."

In the *Homicide* on-screen version of the story, Lane Staily (Isaiah Washington), a witness seen dashing out of the crack house with the victim, is brought in for questioning. Giardello suggests that Staily might even be the killer. As a peace offering of sorts, an appeasement to his lieutenant's sensibilities, Pembleton coerces a confession out of him. He accomplishes this with a masterful manipulation of Staily's guilt over his friend's death, compounded by his fear about having witnessed what really happened. In a gut-wrenching scene, Pembleton gives Staily race, rage, indignance, sorrow, and, finally, blame. Braugher plays the scene through an astonishing range of emotions. He switches from friendly to intimidating to consoling in a heartbeat. He twists Staily's guilty mind into the guilty act. A sweat-soaked Pembleton shamefacedly hands the confession to Giardello.

Knowing the confession is bogus, Giardello urges Staily to come clean about what he saw and he gives up Lieutenant Tyron. The victim had surrendered, but then turned to run. Tyron had time to pull out a second weapon, and shot him in the back. In a far cleaner conclusion than life would afford Worden or McLarney, Tyron is arrested.

IN THE BROTHERHOOD
OF COPS

Of Sgt. Terry McLarney, David Simon writes, "one of the most intelligent, self-aware men in homicide. . . . Generations from now, homicide detectives in Baltimore will still be telling T.P. McLarney stories." When he refers to someone as self-aware, Simon has paid them the highest compliment he knows. Self-awareness is the great equalizer, causing one to acknowledge one's shortcomings as much as one's strengths. It's a quality that can only enhance one's respect for others.

At the end of a shift spent cruising downtown as sector supervisor in the Central, McLarney was peeling off the Sam Browne belt — laden with gun, reloader, mace, cuffs, keys — uniform shirt, and Kevlar vest. He paused, looking at the accoutrements of his trade, and shook his head. "Is this any way for a grown man to go to work?"

For McLarney, it's been the way for twenty-one years. Out of choice. After joining the force, he studied for his law degree and could have pursued the six-figure salary the bar would have brought him, were it not for the instinctive disdain all cops feel toward lawyers. It's almost more honorable — certainly less deceitful — to just go criminal and be done with it than to don the trappings of the court. More to the point, policing is something he believes in. It calls for fewer of the stomach-burning compromises that lawyers pride themselves on brokering. Somebody hurts somebody else, you hook 'em up and lock 'em up. That the courts may turn them out within hours is something to keep someone else up at night. The cops did their decent day's work.

Good old-fashioned police work is what McLarney likes to do best. And he personifies the good old-fashioned cop in so many ways. He knows his beat intimately. Each block of Sector Two has its own criminal history. He knows where the bodies have fallen and where the troublemakers congregate. When things are slow he likes to parade the radio car through St. Mary's Park, the only green space in the sector. If the dealers and derelicts expect regular passes, they won't gain a foothold. With every pass, McLarney reaffirms the citizens' claim to this peaceful haven for their own. He's at home in his car, doing what police do. What he resents are the shifts when he's so bogged down in the paperwork that goes with his stripes that he can't leave the office. Worse still is when he's stuck inside because there aren't enough cars to go around.

Advancement in the department comes with administrative chores. Given his choice, he'd ride all the time, backing up his guys, making sure they have support on tough calls. Some shifts are so busy and responding officers so scarce that they can only spare the time to lock up the worst of the worst. Hours wasted processing lesser offenders are hours off the street. As well, there are the routine hassles that every supervisor has to address. Of his men, McLarney says, "None of them is a fuckup, but every one of them fucks up 10 percent of the time. With twelve guys, that's 120 percent of fucking up."

In the best tradition of who police used to be, he repairs to the bars to unwind after a shift. In his path, beer doesn't stand a chance, and he topples one soldier after another. He's laid-back, almost serene, soft-spoken and thoughtful. He's done a lot of policing over the past two decades.

Ten years ago, Kavanaugh's on West Madison was the preferred watering hole of the murder police. It was dark and a little ragged at the edges, just disreputable enough to appeal to cops. Here, they could find fellowship or solitude, as the mood struck. Everything changes, however. Hughie Kavanaugh sold the bar and his name came off the shingle. Today, it's a lesbian club, called Coconuts. In the spirit of reminiscence, it was fitting that we should quaff a couple there on our swing through Baltimore. McLarney walks in comfortably, ambling up to the bar. He greets the owner. If we are conspicuous amid the women swaying to the throbbing disco beat, he pays no heed. This is a bar, it serves beer, we're home. The only thing he seems to lament is the tacky pastel color scheme and the pink felt on the pool table.

Simon praises McLarney for being the first member of the squad to realize what he was up to. While others dismissed Simon, figuring nothing would come of his efforts, or that he would tire of the chore and abandon it, Terry really *got* it. He knew there was going to be an actual book. Despite that, he never ceased to be himself.

"It could have been a disaster, but I think we came off pretty well. We were seen to do our job and to do it effectively," McLarney concludes.

He didn't follow the series beyond the first year. He never made any effort to become involved with the production. After Simon's research was completed, his only participation was at the various launch parties where the beer flowed. He ventures to say that he thinks it's childish how some of his colleagues became so upset with the fictions worked in to the characters they took to be themselves. Great liberties were taken with Steve Crosetti, who is loosely based on McLarney. Physically there is little resemblance. Actor Jon Polito is a bald, dark butterball of a man, while McLarney is sandy-haired, Irish, and still retains memories of the build of the football lineman he was. Crosetti was divorced; McLarney lives in the suburbs with his wife and sons. Polito's departure after the second season was dealt with by having Crosetti commit suicide. This was an opportune means of exploring the usually overlooked issue of police suicide. McLarney didn't strike me as the suicidal type.

It was for Crosetti to bear the scars that make a jagged topography across McLarney's gut. McLarney took a bullet for the city while responding to a call for an armed robbery in progress at a gas station. It took him eight months to recover from his wounds. Far from being reluctant to get back on the job, he couldn't wait. He says he's never thought back on that day while en route to other potentially dangerous encounters. He also denies ever stripping down to unveil his scars before a superior so as to get his way. Crosetti, on the other hand, did just that as a way of illustrating why Giardello owed him the investigation into the shooting of his friend, Officer Chris Thormann (Lee Tergesen), in season one's "A Shot in the Dark."

You don't shoot cops. Whereas any other murderous assault may be looked upon with indulgence — this is Baltimore, after all — this rule is non-negotiable. A police officer may be resisted, to a degree. You might even get in a swing or two. Oh, make no mistake, you'll get beat down, but nothing out of line. It's understood. A street cop can't be shown up. He, and he alone, owns his post. Challenge that and he's got no choice but to reclaim his turf. If he can't do it on his own, backup is just a signal 13 away.

Once upon a time, if you did make the mistake of shooting a police, your best bet was to leave town or turn yourself in. As Simon writes it, if you compounded the error by letting yourself be found within Baltimore, you were pretty much done for. Times have changed. Cops aren't going to open themselves up to criminal charges or civil liability for the sake of a fallen comrade. Today, simple arrest has to suffice for vengeance.

When Officer Gene Cassidy was shot twice in the head while on patrol in the Western, McLarney went on a crusade. No shooting of a Baltimore police officer had ever gone unsolved, and that of McLarney's old bunkie wasn't going to be the first.

Nothing can shake witnesses loose like an entire police department on the rampage. Cassidy's survival was in grave doubt on the night of the shooting. Even as he began his miraculous recovery, he was left blind and with no memory of the hours preceding the incident. It was McLarney's mission to find the shooter and ensure that there was enough evidence for successful prosecution. There would be no plea bargains, no compromises, no way out, no alternative to trial by jury. The shooter would down the entire load, the maximum penalty.

After an initial misstep, in which the wrong man was arrested, Butchie Frazier was apprehended. Knowing his post as he did, Cassidy had recognized Frazier for being wanted on an outstanding warrant. While trying to effect an arrest, a tussle ensued, and Cassidy was shot. Frazier was tried and convicted, in large measure due to the tireless hustle of McLarney.

On *Homicide*, Cassidy was personified by Thormann. His relationship with Crosetti was developed over the first several episodes, before the shooting took place. Originally, Giardello insisted that Crosetti was too emotionally involved to lead the investigation, but he relented after a viewing of his battle scars. If each character has had a defining case at one time or another, this was Crosetti's. What Simon wrote about McLarney could apply equally to Crosetti: "a man defined by the badge as few men are anymore, a true believer in the brotherhood of cops, as pagan a religion as an honest Irishman may find." That Thormann was a friend lent a personal dimension to the case, but you can't help but believe he would have found the same urgency in any cop shooting.

Crosetti's relationship with Thormann was followed beyond his quest for the culprit. In a particularly poignant scene, Crosetti is visiting him soon after his return home. Sightless, confined to his bed, Thormann is unable to withstand the need to relieve himself in his sheets. Humiliated, he begs Crosetti to leave. Genuine brotherhood wouldn't tolerate his giving in to the reflex of disgust. With an immense compassion that was merely human, Crosetti gently goes about changing his bedding, insisting he is only doing what he would expect of Thormann were their positions reversed. A less gifted actor than Polito could have ruined the scene by overacting and turning it into something maudlin. But Polito lets quiet mercy rule his performance.

McLarney expressed satisfaction with how the Cassidy incident was dramatized. He also said that Cassidy himself had been pleased. Closure is a popular concept, thrown around a lot by radio talk-show shrinks, as if some simple ending can be tacked on to life-altering traumas. When Butchie Frazier was convicted of attempted murder in the first degree, it could be argued, Cassidy and his loved ones had closure. But did they? Cassidy still lives the effects of his wounds every day. That's not to say he hasn't adjusted exceptionally. Today he is an instructor at the Baltimore City Police Academy, helping to train new recruits. But in 2005, Frazier will be eligible for his first parole hearing. From that date on, Cassidy will have to relive his nightmare through victim-impact statements if he is to help keep Frazier locked up. Life sentences rarely mean life.

Homicide took up this facet of the story during the fifth season

("Double Blind"). A riot broke out in the prison and Thormann's shooter, Charlie Flavin, saved a guard's life during the melee. His reward was to be granted an early parole hearing, at which Thormann is compelled to give a statement to prevent his release. It was a powerful sequence, abnormal for TV, which rarely expects its viewers to possess an attention span encompassing several years. In reprising the Thormann situation four years after the fact, *Homicide* was, in effect, saying that tragedy is not conveniently closed, repaired like a bad muffler. Wounds can heal and still be very much open. It helps to be reminded of that every once in a while.

THE HARRY EDGERTON STORY

The first time I met David Simon I asked him whether, in retrospect, there was anything in his book that he had gotten wrong. One thing, he replied without hesitation.

"I gave Harry Edgerton too much credit for being antisocial. I presented it as being healthier than it actually was, when, in fact, being a lone wolf is very dangerous and potentially self-destructive. I didn't foreshadow that at all. In the end, Harry suffered because of who he was and because he'd burned lot of bridges. I learned that if you're going to be the way he was, you'd better produce every time; if you slip up, there'll be a dozen guys waiting to get you."

Simon balked at recounting the story of what had happened to Edgerton, saying that it was only fair that if Harry wanted it to be told, he should be the one to tell it. Thus began my odyssey to track down the elusive Harry Edge. I had been led to believe that the man was difficult to pin down. Much to my surprise, after a few phone calls, followed by a couple of missed appointments, he warmly accepted my invitation to meet at the Hyatt Inner Harbor, where he is on the security staff. A charming man, outgoing and friendly, he happily rattled off old war stories over several hours.

Edgerton's fate is important, since he served as the model for Frank Pembleton, who has emerged as *Homicide*'s pivotal figure. Pembleton shares his alter ego's preference for working alone. Only with great reluctance did he agree to a regular pairing with Bayliss, and only after Giardello in effect ordered him to do so. In the opening episode he was goaded when sent out with Felton on a routine call. The great Pembleton, Felton chided, didn't trouble himself with anything but important murders. Edgerton's reluctance to handle his share of the drudge work and to perform supporting duties for other detectives was a source of resentment within his squad. His saving grace was being, by all accounts, a great detective. That can earn you some slack, but only so much. In the case of Pembleton, it's always been enough and, by all appearances, it should have been enough for Edgerton.

Harry wanted to do police work on a grand scale. He and his partner, Ed Burns, cultivated major investigations into violent drug gangs in conjunction with the FBI and DEA. For four years (1984–88) he was, in effect, separated from the Baltimore police, working on such an operation.

"You don't have a doctor doing brain surgery one day and sweeping floors the next, know what I mean?" he asks rhetorically. "Rookie detectives could answer phones and type up questionable death reports."

Harry Edge is an enigma. While most policemen pride themselves on being insiders, he took perverse pleasure in being an outsider. It is with pride and a smile that he refers to himself as an "outcast." A native New Yorker — that fact alone made him suspect to Baltimoreans — with an ear for jazz, Harry Edge has a rhythm all his own. Every other cop gulps down beer; he sips Manhattans. The consensus was that he was a certified weirdo. That he openly admits to being one of the three detectives who were in favor of Simon's presence confirms him as certifiable.

A homicide detective since 1980, he had his own particular approach to the job. "To Edgerton, the consummate loner, homicide investigation is an isolated, individual pursuit," wrote Simon. "It is, in his mind, a singular contest between one detective and his killer, a contest in which the other detectives, the sergeants, the lieutenants, and every other organism in the police department have no appropriate role beyond getting out of the primary detective's path. This was, in essence, Edgerton's strength and at the same time his weakness.'' It was a strength because of his talents as an investigator, a weakness for its alienating effect on those he felt were in the way. He lacked the patience to sidestep what he perceived as obstructions; he just barreled right over them.

To deliver his best, he had to be indulged. D'Addario knew he could count on Edgerton to work a whodunit until it could be worked no more. He also knew he couldn't count on him to jump at the chance to do the paperwork on a suicide. He was an enlightened enough manager that he was prepared to play to his men's strengths and steer away from their weaknesses. But bureaucracy is about nothing so much as grinding every peg into the same hole.

The cause of his demise seemed rooted in a volatile mix of political jealousies emanating from others and poor judgment on his part. Among people for whom cover-your-ass is as natural a precaution as brushing their teeth, Edgerton exhibited bad instincts. Doing effective police work has never been enough. Being seen to do it according to established procedure was of equal importance. Harry either never understood that or, being Harry, was unwilling to concede the point.

Take the example from Simon's *Homicide*, where he's on the receiving end of a miracle: a witness to a drug murder who's willing to talk. Judging that a chat at the scene is less likely to spook the witness than a trip to headquarters, Edgerton takes him aside and gets what he needs then and there. Soon after, he closes the case. Not good enough. He catches flak for failing to bring the witness in for a formal statement. Minor breaches by others could be overlooked, but were occasions for payback against Harry for the irritations he caused.

By his own account, Edgerton was a rising star in the department in the mid to late 1980s as a result of the successful operations he and Burns were running with federal agencies. Seeing how the FBI and DEA were able to pour resources into deep investigations of known repeat offenders convinced him that this was the way to do police work. Intelligence, he felt, was the long-term solution to crime. Instead of reacting to individual criminal acts, violent gangs should be studied, targeted, infiltrated, and shut down as soon as major crimes could be proven. Running such cases are resource-intensive and time-consuming, two elements city police forces can rarely accommodate.

In 1993, Edgerton drew up a proposal to establish a Violent Crimes Task Force, which would serve as an intelligence-coordinating and reactive unit for all violent offences, except homicide. The concept was to use computer analysis to chart patterns of violent crime, determine which gang leaders posed the greatest threats, and then launch precision strikes against them. Edgerton was to be the coordinating detective, leading a hand-picked squad of ten detectives and twenty patrolmen. They were to engage in the most sophisticated intelligence techniques, including wiretapping, source recruitment, and undercover activities. According to Edgerton, the department was prepared to implement such an innovative program because the mayor was in trouble over soaring crime rates. Though Edgerton hadn't devised the plan in response to a political situation, it was conveniently appropriated by those with grander visions.

Edgerton was soon embroiled in bureaucratic complexities for which he had neither feel, nor aptitude. Or, as he puts it, "I never honed the bullshit ability." A mere detective — a rank no greater than that of patrolman — he was reporting to the deputy commissioner level. As the task force attracted media attention, senior officers began jockeying for credit and control of the unit. Not having nurtured a network of political allies, Edgerton had no influential friends to protect his status as effective head of the force. In December 1993 he was offered a return to homicide. Never enamored with the chore of run-of-the-mill murder, he wanted something more.

"This was a defeat. I had already created a legend in homicide," he now says, still disappointed by the vagaries over which he rose and fell. "I wanted to go to the Career Criminals

Unit and turn it into a substantial operative intelligence unit.''

At the time, Career Criminals was a desultory posting. He intended to restore its vitality and make it a repository of information on recidivist dangerous offenders to which other squads would turn for support when they needed hard intelligence about suspects already known to the police.

Here's where the Edge file gets positively paranormal. Not only had he failed to cultivate friends in the right places, he had sowed enemies in high places. To listen to him, they were looking for a reason to cap his career. How they found it was most strange. Of his routine, Simon had written that Edgerton revolved to ''a time clock all his own. Perennially late for roll calls and shift relief on night work, Edgerton might just as easily be discovered putting together a case file at 3:00 AM when his shift had ended at midnight.'' This was how Harry worked. While insightful commanders had seen the benefits in leaving him to his own devices, in Career Criminals he worked for a captain who liked to see his men behind their desks during regular business hours.

One night, Edgerton had been in the office until 2:30 AM working on a warrant. The next day his captain fumed when he didn't show up at the office until 5:00 PM. He immediately suspended him for being AWOL, demanding that Edgerton turn in his badge and gun. Flabbergasted, Harry had no recourse but to comply.

''It was suggested to me that I might be under stress and I should see the department psychiatrist.'' He complied and was reassigned to the strictly nine-to-five, office-bound duties of cheque fraud. ''Everybody knew that the way to punish Harry Edgerton was to chain him to a desk.''

One circumstance under which police work can never be reduced to the clock is where informants are concerned. A productive relationship with a source depends on the personal relationship the investigator establishes. From an emotional standpoint, the source does not work for an organization, he makes a connection with an individual cop. When he gets in trouble, he doesn't expect the department to be there for him, he relies on his handler to help him out.

Edgerton's work in homicide, Violent Crimes, and Career Criminals had caused him to recruit several sources. It was one of the things he did best. One night after he had been reinstated to fraud, he got a call from one who needed to see him.

He says, "I couldn't tell him, 'Hey, thanks for helping me out, but I don't do that any more, so you deal with it.' And I wasn't going to go out into the mix without a weapon." Since his return from suspension, he hadn't been reissued his service revolver. So he loaded up his personal .38 and went to attend to his source.

On his way home he got pulled over in the Western for having expired tags on his car. The uniforms advised him that it'd have to be towed. Nothing further would have come of this, except that they turned up his unauthorized handgun. As a result, he was resuspended. When he returned to work he was shucked off to the pawnshop unit, where his assignment consisted of checking the hawk shops for possible stolen goods.

"Man, I was a murder police. I don't sit at my desk with that bullshit. I'd come in to work and just sit there with a book. I said, 'When you got someplace for me to do real work, you give me a call.' Finally, I just stopped showing up. I just needed six months to get in my twenty, so I'd basically just show up for my check. As soon as I hit twenty, I agreed to take my pension," he recounts sorrowfully.

It was a sad and inglorious ending to a career. Edgerton undoubtedly brought some of his troubles upon himself by willfully ignoring the political currents that eventually won the day. Maybe he was so naive that he never caught wind of them. Or maybe it really was a case where he needed some friends to alert him to the brewing storms. In any event, bureaucracies don't give much leeway to individualists. They only celebrate creativity after it has proven beyond any possible doubt to be risk-free. And sometimes, the lower echelons have to defer when credit is doled out. Dutiful team players are more highly valued than charismatic free spirits. Loners live and die on the fluctuating measures of merit, rather than the more stable support of patronage. When Edgerton could have used someone to step forward on his behalf, there were no takers.

Unlike Pellegrini and Worden, Edgerton basks in the notion that he is Pembleton. And who wouldn't? In Pembleton, one sees the consummate investigator. Charming, poised, inventive, brilliant, instinctual, Pembleton has all the faculties to assimilate and assemble minute details until they lead him in the most logical direction to solve the crime. For the most part, however, as with the other characters, Pembleton has owed less and less to any particular person over time.

"I hung out with Harry for a long time when we first started," recalls Andre Braugher. "I tried to incorporate some of what he told me about techniques, but I never impersonated him. Besides, there are so many different people who have had a hand in writing the character over the years that it flies off in so many directions. The character ends up doing things you never would have expected."

Pembleton was cured of his lone-wolf instincts early when he was assigned to partner with Bayliss. He has tread some choppy political waters and been burned. He even turned in his resignation when Deputy Commissioner Harris lied and saddled him with the blame in the case of Congressman Wade's false police report. He has walked the precipice between pursuing higher rank and the case work that is his passion. He has sometimes attracted the sort of media attention that causes lingering resentments. His is not a personality that blends harmlessly into the blue screen, and that poses certain risks in a paramilitary structure that values malleability. At the same time, he's the type to get the call when there's a job that needs doing. This is a paradox with which every police force struggles, and along with it struggle those who don't quite fit.

ON THE SCREEN

NBC's Warren Littlefield makes no bones about it. He's in the eyeball business. His job is to make sure that as many eyeballs as possible are glued to NBC at all times. That's how he pays his rent, how his bosses measure his success. I'm not sure he'd admit it in so many words, but the overall standards of network TV speak loudly to the fact that quality is the first casualty in the ratings battle. That's not the fault of Littlefield or his counterparts at the other networks. If it really was *Masterpiece Theatre* we were all watching, prime time would be filled with nothing but. Network programmers spend their time trying to replicate those shows proven to attract viewers. The crux of their job is to give us ever closer approximations of what we've been watching all along. Cloning, as opposed to innovating, is the standard of commercial entertainment.

But true greatness is found in originality. From the outset, *Homicide* has gone out of its way to innovate. And innovation in the visual arts, it goes without saying, means giving the audience something new to look at. Past experience shows, however, that television audiences are stubbornly resistant to anything new. It unsettles them, makes them uncomfortable — exactly the responses *Homicide* purposely elicits. The show's look is uniquely its own. It uses only two fabricated sets: the squad room in the old city recreation facility and the medical examiner's office, set up in a warehouse just around the corner off Fell Street. For the rest, Baltimore provides the set. If a scene calls for a home, the locations manager finds one to film in, whether it be a tenement or a luxury condo. If an arrest is to be staged on a Federal Hill street corner in the middle of the night in the dead of winter, that's exactly where and when the shot is filmed. If the squad needs some relaxation in a Fell's Point tavern, that's where they go.

To better reflect real life, *Homicide* is shot with a single handheld camera on 16mm film. The resultant look is rough and jittery. The camera weaves and bobs, in and out, circling warily like a boxer searching for an opening. Cuts are fast and uneven, as if the perfect angle was nailed for a split instant with a fleeting blow, and then was gone. Early on, there were complaints from viewers who found the movement too dizzying. They failed to register how the camera work was a mirror to the action it was recording.

Exterior shots were easy to capture with a roaming camera. The squad and interrogation rooms presented a greater challenge. Levinson told the *New York Times*, "We set it up for 360 degrees so that the camera operator can come around completely in here. When we're shooting the squad room, the actors will always be at work. They will be in many more shots. They'll never know if they are definitely in or out of a given shot. It will look ragged. All I care about is that the audience notices something is different, something is not the way we have seen things before on television."

The actors, too, would have to adjust. Most TV shows are shot from several angles at once with stationary cameras. Scenes are done in many very short takes, sometimes requiring that actors perform almost line by line. When sequences need to be re-shot, it is important, for the sake of continuity in editing, that they hit their marks precisely and try to mimic their exact body position from earlier takes.

In contrast, *Homicide*'s scenes are done in long takes, run through in their entirety several times until the single camera has captured it from every conceivable vantage point.

"It's a jaggedly edited show. I'm sure if you checked it closely you'd find lots of continuity errors," allows Kyle Secor, who has directed two episodes ("Diener" and "Shaggy Dog, City Goat"). "But you get a lot of energy doing long takes. It's a technical challenge to capture the proper tone when you have to repeat line by line.''

Even with the aggressive editing and the double- and triple-take stutters that *Homicide* has patented to drive home telling phrases, glances, or action, the acting has a seamless feel to it. The actors are clearly playing to each other, rather than to the camera. Because of the editing, they are free to approach each take freshly, unconcerned about whether they have delivered a precise duplication of the previous one.

This approach came about partly by chance. ''Before it became our signature, we used jump cuts because you simply couldn't play out the scene exactly the same way each time,'' affirms Levinson, who directed the premier episode, ''Gone for Goode,'' as well as ''The Gas Man.''

Clark Johnson — who has also directed several episodes (''Map of the Heart,'' ''Betrayal,'' ''Valentine's Day,'' and ''Full Court Press'') and has previous directorial credits — says he had an epiphany during the making of the debut episode. It came while he and Polito were walking through a cemetery with the caretaker discussing the exhumation of a body. They had already dug up one corpse from the plot where he was supposed to have been interred, but it turned out to be the wrong body. The cops finally get the caretaker to admit he was burying people willy-nilly and had no idea where to find the body they needed.

''I'm used to knowing exactly where the camera is at, but here we are, walking along, the dialogue is so funny, and this camera is just everywhere,'' Johnson recalls. ''It came to me that the camera was to us what Simon had been to the detectives. I just stopped worrying about where it was. My job was to go about my business and the camera would do what had to be done to capture it properly.''

If you want quality commercial entertainment, you've got to consume it. Money follows the audience, not vice versa. Advertisers line up behind the screen that's being watched by all the eyeballs. And for six seasons, huge numbers of eyeballs have not been focused on *Homicide*. Some of the blame for this surely rests with the network schedulers, who have tucked it into the execrable 10:00 PM Friday slot. Industry wisdom has it that this is when hip urbanites between the ages of twenty-five and forty (the ideal demographic) are out and about, not shut in watching TV, as they would be on weeknights. Even though *Homicide* stands up reasonably well to its head-to-head competition (ABC's *20/20* routinely wins the slot, but *Homicide* frequently scores as the number-one drama, over CBS's atrocious *Nash Bridges*), it can't compete in the overall ratings with shows presented at more coveted times. Ratings as of mid-April 1998 gave *Homicide* 80th place out of 168 network programs. What has secured its survival is a consistent, loyal following within that important demographic.

But *Homicide* has not always been consigned to the Friday-night wasteland. Indeed, it premiered in one of the most sought-after positions of the entire year: on January 31, 1993, following the Super Bowl, which delivers one of the great lead-in audiences of the television season. With Barry Levinson's name figuring prominently in the heavy promotion that preceded its airing, and recognizable actors like Beatty and Kotto, a good springboard seemed to be in place.

The *Homicide* debut, "Gone for Goode," was a remarkable hour of television. To this day, with 100 episodes in the can, it stands as Richard Belzer's favorite.

"I thought it was amazing," he says. "In one hour we introduced eight different characters and succeeded in defining each one."

Was Jenny Goode killed in an accidental hit-and-run, or was she willfully murdered? Munch is stymied by vague witness descriptions of a man with blond hair in whose company she was last seen leaving a bar and contradictory identifications of the car he was driving. More than anything, he wants the medical examiner to declare her death an accident so it can be turned over to the traffic squad, sparing him the agony of a murder investigation with no obvious leads, one likely to remain forever unsolved, a statistical blotch against his name. There's just one detail that gnaws at him: one of Jenny's shoes was missing. If she was walking along a dark road and struck by a passing car, where was her other shoe? The most likely explanation is that it had been left behind in the car in which she had been riding. This suggests she had exited in a hurry, meaning the driver of that car could have been responsible for her death, indicating homicide. Bolander berates his partner for trying to ditch a murder by having it ruled an accident, thus denying Jenny Goode her fair justice. He questions the mettle of any detective who would wriggle out from under a tough investigation on a technicality.

Munch is as resentful of Bolander's insinuation as he is desperate to win the older man's approval. He works the case as much out of spite as anything else. And it pays off. In matching photos of those with criminal records to the registrations of vehicles similar to the one in which Jenny was last seen, he notices an individual with dark hair and blond eyebrows. Why does a man suddenly dye his hair? Munch inspects the suspect's car and confronts him, coming away with a closed case. Bolander grudgingly concedes his good work, allowing that he has earned the title Detective.

In the same episode, Howard and Felton are blessed with a most cooperative killer, who not only leaves the body of a bill collector in his own basement, but calls home while the detectives are examining the scene and makes an appointment to meet with them at headquarters. The scenario might seem inconceivable, except that it is drawn directly from a real case in Simon's book.

The affectionate, insult-riddled relationship between Lewis and Crosetti emerges as they trace the murder-for-hire spree of Calpernia Church, an elderly lady who has systematically dispatched of successive husbands for the insurance money. Crosetti's obsession with the Lincoln assassination is introduced.

The boyish Bayliss joins the squad with eagerness and a how-to textbook on solving homicides. He is the viewer's point of entry to the show, the outsider seeking a way in. Naturally, he is teamed with Pembleton, the outsider intent on staying out. Their partnership gets off to a rough start when Pembleton's methods stray far from anything the textbook ever envisioned.

And overseeing it all is their discerning yet benevolent leader, Lieutenant Giardello.

Homicide has won recognition for its outstanding achievements, though it has been largely ignored by the Emmys. It took home two of the coveted statues in season one, for outstanding direction (Levinson, "Gone for Goode") and outstanding writing (Fontana, "Three Men and Adena"). It received two additional nominations (Gwen Virdon in "A Ghost of a Chance" for outstanding guest role, and Mark Pellington for outstanding graphic design and title sequence). In season two, Robin Williams was nominated for his guest appearance in "Bop Gun." *Homicide* was then shut out from Emmy consideration until 1996 when it garnered three nominations, but no wins (Andre Braugher for outstanding lead actor, Lily Tomlin for outstanding guest actress in "The Hat," and Lou DiGiaimo and Pat Moran for outstanding casting). Braugher was again nominated in 1998

It has won awards for outstanding drama series of the year in 1996 and 1998 from the Television Critics Association, best quality drama of 1994 and 1996 from the Viewers for Quality Television, and best dramatic series (for "Hate Crimes") of 1996 from the Media Access Awards. In 1995, it was honored with the Quill and Badge Award for outstanding police drama. The Peabody Awards named it outstanding series in 1993 and 1996. An unprecedented third Peabody was won in 1998 for the searing episode "The Subway." The Writers Guild of America has bestowed two episodic-drama writing awards on *Homicide*, for "The Night of the Dead Living" (Fontana and Frank Pugliese story, Pugliese teleplay) in 1993 and "Bop Gun" (Fontana story, Simon and David Mills teleplay) in 1994. Surprisingly, only one award has been presented to a cast member, a 1994 Viewers for Quality Television best-actor nod to Braugher.

Homicide very nearly didn't make it to air in anything like the form it's taken. Upon purchasing the rights to Simon's book, Levinson sought an experienced television producer-writer with whom to partner on the project. Knowing this, his agent,

Creative Artists Agency — the largest talent agency in Hollywood — sent him several scripts. Among them was *Polish Hill*, written by John Wells, another of their clients, who had made his mark with the 1988 series *China Beach* and would go on to be executive producer of *ER*. It was an ill-considered move. The script lifted entire passages of dialogue from the book, along with several essential concepts. Warner Brothers had already signed on to produce Wells's pilot for CBS. The matter was brought to Simon's attention.

Appalled though he was at the blatant plagiarism of his material, there is only so much that can be done, unless one is prepared to engage in years of litigation. Matching lawyer fees against Warner was not a happy prospect. And, at that point, it would have been left to Simon to carry any lawsuit. True, Levinson would be out the rights fee, but that represented a small loss. So far, he had only invested the $10,000 he paid Simon for the option on six episodes. Simon stood to be the big loser if *Homicide* were to be shelved.

"I spent three years on this book," he would tell the *New York Times*. "Some guy comes along, reads it, goes to his processor and steals it."

Warner, on the other hand, had invested serious money to produce *Polish Hill*. When it comes to civil suits, if the party with the greatest resources is the party with the most at stake, they're the odds-on favorite to ride the legal magic carpet to exhaustion, if not victory. Besides, even if Simon was eventually to win, the Warner show would have gone to air, thus ensuring *Homicide*'s consignment to mothballs. The irony of the situation was that the first show to air would appear to be the source of original material, regardless of the real sequence of creation.

After reading the first draft of *Polish Hill*, Simon — who is also represented by CAA — contacted Wells. This was a tactical risk, in that it gave Wells an opportunity to revise the script enough to disguise what had been lifted from *Homicide*, but not necessarily enough so that Levinson would still be convinced to go on with his project. Wells responded to Simon with a new script that omitted the most egregious appropriations.

"This showed that the plagiarism had been conscious. But, even having tried to revise it, he had forgotten everything he'd stolen, so there were still a lot of elements directly out of my book."

Levinson stepped in and had his lawyer send a letter to Warner advising them that the show they were producing contained material of which he was the rightful owner and told them to remove the offending portions. Warner exhibited no intention of forcing changes.

Simon makes it clear that he and Levinson were not concerned about the quality of *Polish Hill*. Which product might be the better show was not the issue. They simply knew they would be left in the wings if it was broadcast with details crucial to their story. The thing that worried them most, once the revised script eliminated much of the dialogue taken out of the book, was that Wells's script called for "the board." Now familiar to all *Homicide* fans, the board is a genuine article in the Baltimore police homicide unit. Inscribed upon it in red grease pen is the name of each murder victim under the heading of the primary detective. Red indicates an open case. With an arrest, the name is dramatically rewritten in black. The board is more than a mere prop; it lurks as a witness to murder, a silent monument to the victims, tribute to the detective's successes, reminder of their failures.

"Isn't it pretty?" Giardello asks Mike Kellerman sarcastically when too much red is under his name. "The way the board just stands here, a silent sentry to the dead and gone. I love the way the red and black meld together in harmony, a haiku of color and vengeance."

The board has become a signature for the series. It's the sort of device that cannot be repeated without being derided as derivative. Indeed, Levinson is convinced that the network would not have gone ahead with *Homicide* had *Polish Hill* proceeded with all of the elements it procured from Simon's book.

Shockingly, Wells and Warner exhibited no embarrassment over the plagiarism so long as it was confined to a private exchange of letters between the parties involved. However, in June 1992 Levinson took the matter public through the *New*

York Times. Now it was a source of embarrassment. By this time, Warner was afraid that to concede to any changes would be an admission of wrongdoing and would expose them to lawsuits. Furthermore, the pilot (now called *Angel Street*) had been completed and contained elements that Levinson was insisting be eliminated. However, both parties were amenable to a settlement that wouldn't scuttle either of their projects. Levinson wanted to bring *Homicide* to air and Simon wasn't interested in a legal wrangle. In the end, Warner agreed that the board, which was used in the pilot, would be excluded from future episodes, as would other factors that could be traced directly back to the book.

Simon was incensed when Warner followed the settlement by publicly announcing, "Warner Brothers is willing to make minor changes in a good will effort to stop these endless, scurrilous and unfounded accusations." He responded, "I don't believe so-called scurrilous accusations and minor problems could make a major studio reshoot portions of a pilot and reedit a major pilot. They're doing it because John Wells plagiarized from *Homicide* and got caught." He still bristles at the thought that Wells made money off selling the pilot in the first place.

As it turned out, *Angel Street* would air on CBS in the fall of 1992, starring Robin Givens. It was cancelled after only three episodes.

That *Homicide* has survived so long is something of a miracle. Levinson admits that it is too challenging a program to ever have held the promise of breakout commercial success. On the other hand, he asserts, it is making money for the network. Could the network make even more money in the slot *Homicide* occupies? Conceivably.

But as Warren Littlefield explained, "If we were the number-three network and struggling, we might be under pressure to give up on shows, but that's not the case. Being NBC, and being highly successful at the moment, we can afford to have patience with shows and to make choices. We think *Homicide* is excellent TV, it's as simple as that."

Choices have to be made. The components for commercial success are no deep secret. You can decide to pander and repeat whatever has worked for others in the past, or you can create a body of work that will stand apart.

Says Johnson, "Originally I expected we'd have *NYPD Blue* numbers. But I now know that what we do won't appeal to everyone. We won't reach that huge audience. Still, I prefer that to compromising. I don't want to be doing *Dukes of Hazzard* or *Nash Bridges*."

Michelle Forbes (Chief Medical Examiner Dr. Julianna Cox) professes confusion as to why escapism is equated with mind-lessness, rather than stimulation. "It's a release to think and to be affected," she argues. Staring listlessly at a screen and not being compelled to think is a mind-deadening experience. And yet, apparently, the preferred experience of millions.

Yaphet Kotto is expansive on the subject: "Packaging is what determines your audience. It all depends upon what you want to do as a producer. Bells and whistles will attract people's attention. Imitators have come along and been more successful than us. But we didn't bend to sex and violence; this has been our undoing. The man who chose to show nudity realistically read the arena he was in and put out what was wanted. The same people who demand good TV are watching this and not a man delivering a soliloquy.

"We have no choice but to say that that which we have created is what we wanted. We bring a sense of self to our art, and the self is our vehicle for acceptance. Once the vehicle has been accepted, we feel exonerated.

"There is no outlet for art anymore. I'm not going to do art in a cesspool. To church I will bring holy water, but not to a cesspool. Unless we distinguish between the two, we aren't being fair to ourselves. When you deal with the public you deal with commercialism. Art is something you deal with after a society is done. Picasso and Rembrandt were treated as mad-men in their time; only afterward were they revered as artists."

So, *Homicide* has managed with a dedicated cult following and the notoriety that comes from critical praise. This has been enough for 100 episodes, renewal for a seventh season in

1998–99, and syndication runs in the United States, Canada, and Europe. And a body of work that will stand apart as insightful and innovative.

Homicide's original ensemble — for the most part — defied the stereotyping that is the science of most casting exercises. Yes, there was the requisite woman. Aside from that concession, the cast bore a striking resemblance to reality. Credit the inspiration drawn from the real police.

What few people seem to understand is that the "police type" is largely a creation of pop culture. There is something within the fraternity known — whether positively or negatively depends on where you sit — as PMS, or Police Mentality Syndrome. It refers to an attitude that most police adopt. Cynicism, weariness, an affinity for gallows humor, a capacity to react with cold one-liners to any situation, a steel-cased what-the-fuck shrug always at the ready. Any cop can affect PMS, and most do. So long as you're careful to recognize it as an affectation, you can drop it when outside the company of other police, if ever you get outside. Once you take it on as part of your personality, you'll soon find yourself unfit for any other company. These are tenuous slivers of character for an actor to convey or for a writer to capture. As a result, it has been more difficult for each character to carve out his or her own presence within the collective. *Homicide* has pursued the difficult process of establishing characters without resorting to the crutch of artificial eccentricities. (Crosetti's strange obsession with the Lincoln assassination was a rare exception.)

Once a chemistry has been established on set and a rapport cemented with viewers, a regular's departure can prove very disruptive. Neither Levinson nor Fontana would agree with this premise.

"It's part of the growth process of a series," says Levinson. "Just as it happens with the real squad, you make adjustments and try to bring in a new dynamic."

"Cast changes can be healthy for writers, as well as actors," Fontana asserts. While he is reluctant to discuss the specifics behind individual changes, he does say, "In some cases we felt the character had been written out, that we had run him or her into a brick wall and there was nowhere to take them that other characters couldn't go. In other cases, an actor was so unhappy that I felt it best for the spirit of the show that they shouldn't have to be there." (I asked Kyle Secor about the reasons for specific cast changes and he laughed, "Creative differences, it's always creative differences.")

Warren Littlefield echoes Fontana's explanation, adding with regards to the Crosetti character, "He was stepping into territory already being mined by others in the ensemble. There comes a point where a character no longer opens new doors."

"I thought we had the most realistic cast at the beginning," opines Johnson. He is, however, quick to compliment the two cast additions who have served as his on-screen partners, Diamond's Kellerman, and the newest member, Jon Seda as Paul Falsone.

Given the evolution of the cast, there appears to have been a prevailing sentiment that members of the original troupe bore too close a resemblance to one another. Fact is, they also bore the closest resemblance to what one would see in any homicide squad in America. Later additions tended — with varying degrees of success — to plug into perceived demographic gaps.

FRANK PEMBLETON
AND TIM BAYLISS

The Pembleton and Bayliss partnership is an exceptional pairing of characters, as it is of actors. Played by Andre Braugher and Kyle Secor, respectively, they have evolved with, and largely because of, each other. At the same time, both actors have grown, enabling them to take their characters to unexpected places.

As executive producer Tom Fontana explains it, "Bayliss, the ultimate innocent, would become corrupted; Pembleton, the ultimate cynic, would become human."

Though each stands out in his own right, it is hard not to think of them together. Therein lies the genius of their chemistry: each is such a strong individual, yet dependent on the relationship.

"Bayliss and Pembleton are the greatest love story in the history of television," Fontana asserts.

Braugher laughs at the characterization. "Yeah, I'm Kathy Baker and he's Tom Skerritt," he says, referring to *Picket Fences*, the CBS show that for so long beat out *Homicide* in the ratings and at the Emmys.

"Andre and I decided we'd do their relationship as intimately as possible," offers Secor. "We've gone through as many shades of a relationship as a marriage."

In a fourth-season episode ("Stakeout"), Pembleton rather curtly tells Bayliss to match dental records of missing teens with John Does at the morgue. Tim balks, complaining that Frank never so much as says "please" or "thank you." Exasperated, Frank says, "*Please* don't be an idiot. *Thank you.*" That sets Bayliss off about how he doesn't have to be in this job, that he could go off and pursue other options. Even more exasperated, Frank invites him to do so, complaining, "All you ever do is keep repeating yourself over and over again." Quick cut to the home at which Howard and Lewis are on stakeout and the angry voice of the husband to his wife, "You keep repeating yourself over and over again. . . ."

It's been a frequently reluctant love, fraught with tension. Pembleton is a loner by nature who has gradually come to appreciate his partner's qualities. Bayliss was an eager tag-along, ready to defer to his more experienced partner to gain his acceptance — at the outset. As he came of age as a detective, and as a man, he became less willing to suffer Pembleton's arrogance, seeking — and finding — opportunities to assert himself. Together they've ridden a pendulum, always looking for equilibrium through its turbulent arc. If love can be equated to respect, trust, and dependence, then these men have come to love each other. But in many respects it is love without friendship. They don't hang around together or attend each other's barbecues. Bayliss once complained about never having been to Frank's house, to which Pembleton responded that he didn't particularly want to have him over. After Frank and Mary had their first child, Bayliss had to invite himself to see her. This is no sensitive, huggy, new-age partnership. These are real police. They work in a real squad room where you don't show too much vulnerability to your colleagues. If your dog died during the night, you don't want to come to work the next day in mourning. That's a sure way of encountering a rash of cruel dead-dog gags. Whatever you hold dear is best held close to the vest.

Charisma is the most mysterious of human qualities. What is the source of that magnetism some people exude? They manage to pull you into their orbit and grip your attention. Their presence is nearly hypnotic. You watch them intently, as if there's something weighty to their every gesture. Andre Braugher is the most purely charismatic actor on network television. Each pause, each heavy sigh, each pass of his hand across his gleaming pate, each smile, each marginally controlled rage.

Julliard-trained, he spent his last hiatus from *Homicide* performing the title role of *Henry V* at New York's Shakespeare Festival, for which he won an Obie Award.

"In a perfect world I'd do Shakespeare all the time," Braugher asserts. He's already done *Much Ado About Nothing*, *Richard II*, *Othello*, and *Macbeth*, among others. "For me, there's no greater challenge in the theater."

Challenge is the theme of Braugher's career. His film credits are impressive, including the title role in *The Court-Martial of Jackie Robinson*, Spike Lee's *Get on the Bus*, *Glory*, *Primal Fear*, and, most recently, *City of Angels*. It is especially easy within the confines of a TV series to become complacent about a character, to fill up a niche and then, as if entrusted with a glass brimming with nitroglycerine, be ever so delicate not to spill over and risk immolation. He told *Entertainment Weekly* his nightmare was to end up doing Frank Pembleton movies of the week. But because serial television is so much about marketing, establishing hold over a niche is not looked upon as a bad thing. A series is a living organism, a constant work in progress.

It has a beginning, but no fixed end. Caution is the norm. There is a powerful reluctance to place a lead character in any condition from which extrication may prove impossible. Whatever befalls that character, the producers must be confident they can recover and get back to their familiar place. But *Homicide* is unusual.

Braugher's electric presence caused Pembleton to emerge as *Homicide*'s dominant character. In the debut episode, he gave a tantalizing glimpse of what he could do with intelligent dialogue when caged in the box with a suspect. The tiny set is insufficient to contain his intensity, exacerbating the claustrophobia of the scene. In this instance he confronts a young male prostitute who was the last person seen with an elderly man found murdered in a motel room. Frank leads the suspect to believe the man had died of natural causes so as to elicit an admission that will place him in the room at the time of death. Once he has that, he has him pinned to the murder. Bayliss's crisis of conscience concerning the falsehood that had forced the confession only moves Frank to rage against the rookie.

It wouldn't take Bayliss long to succumb to the compromises of the job. Lying to suspects is standard operating procedure. Tightroping that thin span between convincing and coercing is all part of the acrobatics of police work. Bayliss would become his partner's equal if not in finesse, in tenacity. The Adena Watson case matured — or corrupted — him quickly. Once that murder infected him, Bayliss was immune to the courtesies of legal formality. He could even be moved to roughing up particularly vile creatures.

Pembleton has a complex moral center of gravity. Classically educated by the Jesuits, he is a Catholic, of which he says there are two kinds: "devout and fallen." Though he admits to having fallen, one never ceases to be Catholic. The agony he suffers over his crisis of faith is wrenching. He doubts God's existence for having witnessed evidence of the very thing that confirms Him: God must exist because pure evil exists. What tortures Pembleton is the predominance of the evil. Why are we not more inclined to pure goodness and left to imagine evil, instead of vice-versa? True religious faith wards off too close an examination of why evil so often triumphs over good. A homicide detective is exposed to so much that is sinful and so little good, so much punishment and so little redemption, so much pain and so little joy, that faith wanes. Frank was deeply affected by the serial killing of three good Catholic women, whose bodies were left in dumpsters behind churches around Baltimore (three parts to open the third season: "Nearer My God to Thee," "Fits Like a Glove," and "Extreme Unction"). He is overcome by his inability to reconcile these women's well-meaning lives with the injustice of their deaths. His interrogation of the schizophrenic killer, Annabella Wilgis (Lucinda Jenny), is a breathtaking confrontation/flirtation that has him pinballing all over the emotional scale.

His faith is so badly shaken that he doesn't even want to have his daughter baptized. His wife, Mary (real-life spouse Ami Brabson), who has exhibited such patience and dignity in the face of a hard man that she loves, is compelled to leave him over this issue. They were estranged for a while, but would reconcile and his commitment to his family would become an increasing source of strength for him.

It was this case that called into question his certainties about policing, as well. During his interrogation, Annabella's seven-year-old alter ego mimics everything Frank does. He tests her by holding a match to his wrist until the skin burns. She does the same. Annabella subsequently sues the city for abuse, naming Frank. Rather than proceed with the case, the city settles. Pembleton is distraught at the decision and how it reflects on his reputation.

"I thought I had resolved all of this for myself when I first put the uniform on," he laments. "You do what you have to do to get to the truth."

His two paths to the truth — the police force and Catholicism — were brought into disrepute. This marks a basic philosophical premise for the show: police work is a search for truth. The Bible promises that in truth is to be found freedom.

There is a paradox in the fusion of justice and Catholicism. The latter is based on faith without proof, the former upon proof and precious little faith. In the season-six episode

"Mercy," Frank and Tim investigate a complaint alleging that Dr. Roxanne Turner (Alfre Woodard) is euthanizing terminally ill patients. Bayliss is sympathetic to the doctor and essentially leaves Frank to confront her alone in the interrogation room. She argues that her efforts to ease her patients' death are more legitimate than prolonging their lives and, hence, their suffering. Holding to the argument that any human intervention in the death of another constitutes murder, Frank argues for the sanctity of life and denies her the right to decide upon death on behalf of anyone. With passion, she counters that she is with her patients when they are suffering the agonies and indignities of prolonged illness. How dare he, she asks, come along and assume their best interests after they're gone? How dare she, he counters, assume their best interests at the most vulnerable stage in their lives? There's no answer, no right. Only the futility faced by the detective, who can merely avenge the dead after it's too late, and the doctor, for whom there is no more healing to accomplish.

Pembleton in the box has become *Homicide*'s trademark, its go-to move. Having a gun on his belt isn't what closes cases; intellect, wit, and verbal acuity are his arms. Over the first four seasons, he engaged in several defining sparring sessions. One of Braugher's favorite episodes is that in which detectives Bolander, Felton, and Howard are shot and the subsequent hunt for their assailant. This case culminates in his interrogation of racist underachiever Gordon Pratt, played with all the wounded malice of a stray mongrel by Steve Buscemi ("End Game"). Pembleton ridicules Pratt's pretensions of grandeur, his pseudo-intellectual misinterpretations of the great philosophers. Holding up Pratt's own copy of Plato in the original Greek, Pembleton urges him to regale him with a passage. Pratt demurs, on the grounds that a black man wouldn't be able to comprehend anyway. Finally, he succumbs and gives an infantile précis bearing no resemblance to the actual text. Pembleton leans over Pratt and says quietly, "Let me show you what the Jesuits taught me," and proceeds to translate for him.

For all of that, Frank is not infallible. In a scene from "Kaddish" (season five), he is pile-driving his way through an eloquent, histrionic interrogation, convincing a suspect that he had shot Johnny Abernagi during a pharmacy holdup. He is forceful, confident, totally assured that he has the right man, until Howard interrupts him and points out a man who has turned himself in and confessed to the killing. In his possession were the murder weapon and the cash from the robbery. Without a word of explanation, Frank goes back in the box and tells his suspect, "Go home."

Another favorite of Braugher's is "Every Mother's Son," a powerful episode in which Ronnie Sayers (Sean Nelson), a fourteen-year-old boy, is arrested for the shooting of another child. Ronnie is a serious hardass who readily confesses to the shooting, thinking that because he shot the wrong kid (he had actually been gunning for another boy) he is guilty only of a mistake. He equates what he did to a car accident. "Car accidents kill innocent people all the time. How's this any different?" It takes a night in jail before he realizes what he is in for, before the fear takes hold. A fourteen-year-old convicted of murder in adult court isn't sent up for rehabilitation; he's up for a vicious hardening. Before Ronnie is escorted from the courtroom, Frank gives him his card and invites him to call anytime. It's a generous attempt to give him something to hold on to beyond the cage he's to be penned in. For Frank, it's holding out some hope of redemption, some hope that against all odds a child can be salvaged from the wreckage of a system that no longer sees the trees for the forest.

Interrogation scenes worked for Pembleton and they worked for the show. Unfortunately, after four years they were no longer working for Braugher. He had done these scenes, knew he could do them, and was becoming bored. He needed to be rejuvenated with a new creative challenge.

Tom Fontana had an idea. "I wondered what it would be like to take the most articulate character and remove his ability to articulate. I wanted to return him to zero and see how he'd come back, what he'd learn about himself."

In the finale of season four ("Work Related"), Frank suffered a stroke right in the middle of one of his patented interrogations. He grabbed his head and dropped to the floor in convulsions. At the time, real-life rumors that Braugher wanted to leave the series were swirling about, adding to the tension that perhaps he was being written out.

No such thing was to happen. Fontana had come up with the idea of afflicting Pembleton with the stroke. Braugher was intrigued at the possibilities it presented. "The only problem I saw was that this show is about talking. There's only so many times we could see Frank sitting at home waiting to get better. So we had to rush the recovery somewhat."

Fontana wanted the audience to feel the frustration from the stroke victim's perspective. "Commercially we shot ourselves in the foot, but creatively we were thrilled."

It was a brilliantly fearless direction to go, perhaps the most courageous move in the history of prime-time television. In essence, they took a star vocalist and cut out his tongue. They stripped away what he was made of, sloshed his brain into a pulp from which he would have to rescue his personality. He was robbed of his confidence, incapable of speaking without stuttering, unable to stay focused long enough to complete a thought, confused, slow, impotent. He was no longer Frank Pembleton.

His return to work was a moment of sheer anguish. He stands on the street outside headquarters staring up at the entrance for an eternity. He is being torn up by jumbled memories of who he was and terror about who he has become. An uneasy compact between those two parts of himself is the best he can foresee. To the melancholy, shimmering strains of Cowboy Junkies' "This Street, That Man, This Life," he cautiously mounts the stairs.

Braugher's ability to wear Frank's suffering was astonishing. Watching him, you feel his pain and his desire to break the constraints imposed by his affliction. But a television audience is a strange beast. Rather than being excited at the prospect of witnessing something new, reaction to Frank's condition indicated a consensus that he get well quickly and revert to the Pembleton of old. As a result, his recovery was far swifter than would be the case in reality. No matter. That it took nine episodes before he handled his first case as primary — the shooting of state's attorney Ed Danvers's (Zeljko Ivanek in a recurring role) fiancée in "Blood Wedding" — was astounding. There is no denying the success of bringing Pembleton to a whole new plane.

To Braugher's dismay, Pembleton's return to form marked a return to his tried and true moves.

"Last year (season five), Bayliss and Pembleton solved every case. We always think of the right thing to say, we always get our confession," he says. "Eventually that becomes false, because in life, so many cases aren't put down. Our failure in the Adena Watson case was the best thing that ever happened to us."

"I feel as though I've taken Pembleton as far as I can within the context of this series," admits Braugher. "Right now I'm confined with this character."

He confirmed that season six was to be his last on *Homicide*. Pembleton was to succumb to the waste laid upon his spirit by the job. The ultimate cynic awoke to the toll and, ultimately, did become human. In the season-ending episode, writer Joy Lusco succeeded in tying up his character and gave him an appropriate departure. In one of a series of raids to shut down the Mahoney drug organization, shots are fired. Frank gets one suspect in his sights, but freezes rather than shooting. Bayliss, seeing the suspect turning on him, moves to push Frank out of the way and, in the process, is shot and grievously wounded. As Bayliss lies in hospital, hovering closer to death than life, Giardello assigns Frank to interrogate Kellerman and get to the bottom, once and for all, of the shooting of Luther Mahoney, the family kingpin.

It was classic Pembleton. He hits Mike with the worst allegation possible, accusing him of shooting Luther unarmed and then planting a weapon on him. Though Luther in fact had a gun, it was pointed down at the moment Kellerman shot him. When Kellerman comes clean about this in the box, Frank has to ask him for his badge. Having been ordered to do the job, Frank tells Giardello he intends to write it up straight and leaves it to him what to do with the facts.

Faced with guilt concerning his hesitation and Tim's wounds, the pain of what he did to Kellerman and Giardello's reluctance to charge him, Frank quietly says, "I'm done."

Speaking to Mary as much as to Giardello, he says, "There's no truth for me anymore. Not anymore. I can't be out on the street. I'm never going back in that box ever again. It's done. I'm finished."

"This has been a significant part of my life," Braugher says. "I've grown up a lot with this show. And part of growing up is moving on."

Any actor with vitality is curious about who he or she can portray. The art is in making a character real. Once that has been achieved, the creative fire eventually burns down. To see just how gifted Braugher is, look beyond the interrogations or even the stroke, where he is the centerpiece. Watch him when he's a secondary player. Watch him in "A Doll's Eyes"; his discomfort during the hospital scenes, when he has to deal with the parents of the child left brain-dead by a stray bullet — how he recoils when the mother touches him — is so apparent it makes you want to squirm. His every gesture tells you just how badly he wants to run away from these people. He's not forced to speak, because anything he'd say would be trite.

It's only natural that six seasons of Pembleton would leave him hungering for new experiences.

"Virtue isn't virtue unless it slams up against vice," Frank scolds Bayliss, advising him to embrace his own dark side. On an earlier occasion he had pronounced that he didn't think Bayliss could make it as a detective because he wasn't capable of getting inside the mind of killers and thinking as they do.

Part of the cop mystique is how the job eats its own. It takes a well-meaning kid from the middle-class suburbs who has a notion about helping people, a sort of fetus-like thought that has no obvious form, and turns him into someone who can stir up the ghetto mix as if he's got the only spoon in town. The process is gradual. At first, a rookie feels unsure, overwhelmed even. It's similar to the sensation of a new teacher in the classroom. What if he issues a command and it isn't obeyed? What if he has to take disciplinary measures, and isn't heeded? What if he becomes the object of a test and fails? What if he's challenged and can't respond?

Much to the rookie's amazement, his commands are obeyed, for the most part. When they aren't, an unwavering eye, a stout nightstick, and backup are enough to reclaim a post. Gradually, once-astronomical aspirations plunge. His eye becomes jaundiced. Everything he deals in is tinged with tragedy, from loss of life to the loss of prized possessions, from loss of dignity to loss of hope. Initially, he responds with heartbreak; soon he responds with humor. Eventually his threshold for tragedy soars. Not every dead body is worth pitying. He hoards his emotions like a rare commodity. This guy looks like a junkie — fuck him. Another unmourned prostitute. Damn, here's one more filthy homeless stiff. Until along comes a little girl whose death no one but a stone killer could look upon without emotion.

Kyle Secor has a boyish, softspoken demeanor and kindly eyes that give him a gentle look. He's one of those people you take to instantly. These natural qualities made him ideal for the role of Tim Bayliss. Six seasons ago he was the earnest new member of the squad who had never even seen a dead body before. His intention was to treat suspects humanely, as innocents not yet proven to be guilty, entitled to their rights. He was, in other words, much like many of us would be if we suddenly found ourselves as murder police.

When first given the opportunity to join the *Homicide* cast, Secor balked.

"I never meant to do TV," he allows. "I had always appreciated the short, intense bursts of film work, where you put everything into a character for a few months, then go on to something else."

He has appeared in several movies, both feature (including *Sleeping With the Enemy, City Slickers, The Doctor,* and *Drop Zone*) and made-for-TV (*In the Line of Duty: Standoff at Marion, Inherit the Wind,* and *Trauma*). Fontana was familiar with him from his recurring role as an AIDS patient during *St. Elsewhere's* final season.

When Fontana sought him for *Homicide* to play Beau Felton, Secor was in Germany studying acting. He wasn't prepared to abandon his courses, so he turned the role down, even though he was told that it might not wait for him. The part of Felton went to Daniel Baldwin. When Secor returned to the United States, Fontana was still interested in him, only now for the Bayliss character. Still, Secor was hesitant about the long-term commitment a series would demand.

"I read the first script and my reaction was that it was so good, it couldn't possibly last five years. I read the book and I was intrigued by how it got behind the newscast façade and TV stereotypes of police. Then, Tom described the sixth episode ("Three Men and Adena") and I signed on immediately."

In the Baltimore homicide unit, the primary detective on a case is whoever happens to answer the phone when the call comes in. It's a system of calculated randomness, relying on the law of averages to give each detective the same chance of riding a simple domestic with an easily identifiable suspect to a rapid clearance — known as a dunker — or being saddled with an anonymous body dumped in a vacant lot — a genuine whodunit. Over time, everyone gets their fair share of each. Bayliss took the call for a victim in an alley at the end of episode one. It could have been some unlamented hobo or a deserving dealer. Anyone but who it was: a little girl, Adena Watson.

Bayliss would struggle with, and be defined by, this investigation. Indeed, as recently as the third-to-last episode of the sixth season, he was still haunted by nightmares of Adena. He shed all clinical pretense over her and bared his heart. The body wasn't just a lifeless piece of physical evidence — it was a person robbed of her soul. He vowed that if he couldn't make it as a homicide detective, he'd quit the force, because he would never be able to do anything of equal importance. Whether he could make it in homicide was inextricably tied to this case.

"The scene where I came upon Adena's body wasn't about me. It was about the girl. It was about taking the emphasis off myself and putting it on the wider setting,'' explains Secor.

Uncertain as he was about his own abilities, unwelcome as was the interference of so many other detectives, Bayliss would carry the responsibility for avenging Adena. That weight would never lighten. From the moment he first saw the body, Bayliss was grief-stricken. Sorrow fueled his obsession with the case. Inexperience, fatigue, nicotine, caffeine, disgust, fever, and a severe cough all took their toll.

It would require five episodes, but the investigation would convince him that Risley Tucker (Moses Gunn) — one of the itinerant peddlers who sell fruits and vegetables from a horse-drawn cart, known as Arabers — was the killer. Pembleton had dismissed him as a viable suspect at the outset of the inquiry, but all other avenues had brought them to dead ends. Once the smudges on Adena's clothes were identified as soot, matching the debris from a fire at the Araber's barn, there was sufficient evidence to get a warrant and bring him in for questioning. In the meantime, as Bayliss is further and further consumed with Adena, all the other detectives are detailed to other cases and preoccupied with their own problems. One of the television conventions *Homicide* was visionary enough to violate was that only one major event be handled at a time. It was in the midst of the Watson case that Thormann was shot, for example. One crisis doesn't hold off just because of another; they simply pile up, with the newer moving to the top of the heap. Mayhem, in Baltimore, waits for no investigation.

''Three Men and Adena'' was the climactic confrontation with the Araber. There was not enough physical evidence against him to justify charges being laid. Nothing short of a confession would suffice. Fearing that he might have grounds for a harassment suit if he was brought in again, this would be their last go at him. And they would be working against the clock; precedent says that any confession elicited after more than twelve hours of questioning would be unacceptable to the court. For the entire episode, Secor, Braugher, and Gunn breathed each other's air in the confines of the box, a room that is much smaller in life than it appears on-screen. Claustrophobia — or perhaps it was Adena — was so tangible as to be like a fourth character, constantly jutting into, and cutting off, the space of the other three.

Bayliss is aggressive, going at the Araber straight on, pounding him on the minutest details of his alibi. Throughout, he sustains a single-minded, anguished rage. Pembleton, on the other hand, is patient, commiserating, cajoling, flattering, insulting. It's classic good-cop/bad-cop. The Araber is, by turns, cooperative, defiant, self-pitying, assertive, confused. Gunn's portrayal is masterful. He never strays from the perfect center of that gray zone between guilt and innocence. Watch him and you come away uncertain as to which he holds in his heart.

You can't come face-to-face with his resistance and his own sorrow and not have doubts. The Araber's life comes apart before his interrogators: his alcoholism, his failures, his loneliness, his love for Adena, which under the circumstance is perverse. So, too, do the lives of the inquisitors. You don't pry into another person's life without having something of your own come out. Through all the badgering and threatening and repetition of the accusation, the Araber holds firm. Pembleton emerges from the box positive of the Araber's guilt; Bayliss says he's no longer certain.

This episode is *Homicide*'s tour-de-force. Normally, crime filtered through a cathode tube is cleansed, the sludge of pain is excised from the event. "Three Men and Adena" was painful to watch because the hurt in all three men, as well as in the memory of Adena, was so obvious. There was so much suffering caged in that suffocating box.

Ed Burns said to me about the price in sensitivity exacted by the ghetto, "The more humanity you feel, the more you suffer." The reason you suffer with "Three Men and Adena" is that it brings the humanity of the situation directly to the fore, without the slightest effort to blunt it. No one even pretends at dispassion. The Araber arrives with stoicism, but that quickly gives way to floods of heart-rending emotion. Bayliss holds true to the tearful countenance that had once stood over Adena's casket.

Burns referred to what goes on in the inner city as "a holocaust in slow motion." It's an interesting notion. It demonstrates how effectively most of us have been dulled to suffering. Bodies can be stacked like cordwood and we barely look up from our dinner. Only when a single life is imbued with humanity do we take notice of the loss and despair. Adena's was that single life.

Screenwriter Fontana was paid the ultimate compliment by Tom Pellegrini, who asked if he had ever participated in an interrogation. He hadn't.

"I didn't find it that difficult to write. I found that each answer led to a question." He goes on, "I start with a character's heart, mind, and balls. If I can find those, I can write them in any environment. The first question is always, what does this person care about in this scene?"

As for acting what was, in effect, a single extended scene, Secor says, "It was utterly draining, but absolutely exhilarating. That," he adds, "is where we're different from the real cops. We emerge exhilarated because the outcome is not of consequence, while Pellegrini came out of the real interrogation completely disappointed."

"Bayliss keeps moving away from naïveté to continue being the man," Secor says by way of explaining the character's growth. He would toughen in the wake of the Watson case, but the wound she inflicted has never been expunged. That her memory has continued to torment him is tribute to his inner strength. When Tim learns that the Araber has passed away (during season four, "Stakeout"), he must, once and for all, admit the case will remain forever in blood red. He is still moved to tears at the thought of Adena, so much so that he contemplates quitting the force.

"I try not to care," he whispers. "I can't not care, because if I actually do stop caring, then I just stop being who I am. No job's worth that."

Bayliss hadn't faced his own darkness because — as is natural for caring people — he deluded himself into believing he could be the illuminator. After Adena, he was disabused of that conceit. He began to realize that the darkness wouldn't go away, that it was part of all things, and therefore part of him.

As a murder police he would have more opportunity than most to come to terms with this fact.

He began a journey of sexual awakening in year two with the murder of Angela Frandina, a girl with a leather fetish who gave phone sex ("A Many Splendored Thing"). Bayliss becomes increasingly agitated as he and Frank delve into her associates in Baltimore's S&M underground. As it turned out, she was killed by her neighbor during a session of rough sex. To thank Tim for solving the case, Angela's friend presents him with a black leather jacket. In the episode's final scene he is shown, uneasy and flustered, on the notorious Block, sporting his new leathers.

During the following season ("A Model Citizen"), he would fall passionately for Emma Zoole (Lauren Tom), a sexual siren with the quirk of sleeping in a coffin. They have a brief erotic union that ends when she dumps him for confronting her boyfriend — a county cop — who had hit her upon learning of her relationship with Tim. Distraught, Bayliss stops on his way home at a convenience store for cookies and beer, but comes up 11 cents short. In a scene that is a fine balance between humor (the clerk insists on voiding the sale: "I've already punched it up") and explosive insanity, Tim goes ballistic and pulls his gun, at which point the clerk relents and hands over his package. Tim then picks it up and goes to sit in the parking lot, waiting for the police. Pembleton is called to the scene, and only by volunteering Bayliss as a night watchman does Frank succeed in rescuing him.

"Closet Cases" (season six) has Tim and Frank investigating the murder of a gay man found in a dumpster behind a restaurant frequented by gays. As they move through the gay community in search of witnesses and suspects, Tim finds himself becoming increasingly curious. So much so that he accepts a dinner invitation from the restaurant owner (Peter Gallagher) who helps them navigate through a community notoriously suspicious of police. In a later episode he would confess to Det. Laura Ballard (Callie Thorne) that he was, in fact, bisexual. This represented a tremendous step from a man who once found it difficult to empathize with a victim who was beaten to death by skinheads who mistook him for being gay ("Hate Crimes").

Following on Adena, there would come two additional child murders to investigate. Each would take a further toll on Tim.

"Tom (Fontana) and I began to think about why Bayliss was so obsessed with these child murders, as well as why he couldn't have a successful relationship," according to Secor. "I was prepared to do anything with the character, so long as it was exciting to act."

What they did was have Bayliss reveal to Frank, in season five, that he had been sexually abused by an uncle from the time he was nine years old. The revelation comes after they handle the murder of a little girl whose beaten body is discovered by the side of the interstate. The partners had been uncharacteristically out of sync during an interview of the girl's mother, with Frank trying to soft sell her, and Tim intimidating her and accusing her of failing to protect her daughter. After the state's attorney accepts a plea bargain to manslaughter for the mother's boyfriend, Tim is disconsolate.

He tells Pembleton, "Every murdered child, every abused child, I understand because all those children are me." It was a gutsy performance, destined to draw the character down new avenues, including the reestablishment of a relationship with the abusive uncle. Eventually Tim no longer fears his dark side, but recognizes its role in his personality.

AL GIARDELLO

A businessman heading home drunk from a friend's wake stumbles across a dead body in the parking lot of a commuter train station. The uniforms have him wait for detectives in a radio car. Because the squad is shorthanded, Lt. Al Giardello has taken the call. He questions the man for a precise account of what he saw. The man is cooperative, if a bit fogbound. As if struck by a sudden revelation, he looks closely at Giardello and says, "You're really frightening." And that he can be.

Yaphet Kotto is a man of prodigious proportions. Shake his hand and you know what it's like to fall into the thick, muscular grip of a python. His deep ebony skin nearly shines. The most effective weapon in his arsenal of communication is his eyes, which dance from mischievous mirth to murderous glower. His expressive baritone fills a room. An interview with him is not the standard Q&A, but a philosophical exchange. Unafraid of being challenged, he is uninhibited about challenging.

"The only reason you're writing books about *Homicide*," he chuckles, "is that we have no great wars or issues to deal with. We have nothing significant to talk about, so we analyze TV programs. To apply some sociological meaning to entertainment is a disservice. There's nothing to be drawn from this."

This is not a man overly affected by what he does. In fact, he seems impatient at times when discussing *Homicide*, preferring to converse about conspiracy theories. Not just *a* conspiracy theory, but conspiracy *theories*, which swirl, separately and in concert, to explain much of his worldview. Or his personal spiritual journey, which has returned him to the practice of Judaism. "I've learned how to step back from everything and recognize potential for change. The past, present, and future are enigmas about which we worry too much. We need to seek out equilibrium for ourselves."

Part of his journey has been to delve into his past, which is rich and royal. In his recently published autobiography, *Royalty*, he traced his family's roots back to Britain's Queen Victoria and the Royal Bell family of the Doualla tribe of Cameroon. He brings the cultural breadth of his own multi-ethnic heritage to the character of Giardello, who is a comfortable blend of African-American and Sicilian.

Not that Giardello's unique ethnic mélange was preplanned. Initially, all the actors reading for the part were, in the words of Fontana, "old, white, Italian guys." Once Kotto was auditioned, he was certain the part was for him.

"We weren't aiming to match an actor to a predefined character," Fontana explains. "We had a general sense of who the characters were, and stayed totally open to adapting the character to the best actor."

Kotto's professional background is distinguished, if under-rated. He made an auspicious theater debut, playing *Othello* at the tender age of nineteen. He has graced the stages of Broadway (as Jack Johnson in *The Great White Hope*) and London (*Fences*). His film credits are legion, including *Alien* (he was the first victim of the gut-busting creature), *Live and Let Die*, *The Thomas Crown Affair*, and *Report to the Commissioner*. For the horror film *The Virgin*, he assumed the roles of producer, director, and star. His portrayal of Ugandan dictator Idi Amin in the TV movie *Raid on Entebbe* earned him an Emmy nomination.

Kotto is the only cast member to write for the series, first with "Narcissus" in season five. A murder suspect flees police to the headquarters of a militant group called the African Revival Movement, headed by ex-cop Burundi Robinson (Roger Robinson). A witness from the scene is not only prepared to tell what he saw, but to wear a wire and try to get Robinson to admit to planning the murder of Kenya Merchant, who wouldn't abide Burundi whoring girls from the Movement. Robinson not only refuses to surrender, but it becomes evident that he retains some sort of pull within the department. Captain Gaffney and Colonel Barnfather are both prominent on the scene. When an attempt is made to arrest Robinson, he barricades himself inside the ARM bunker and a police blockade is established. After Deputy Commissioner Harris gives the order to take Robinson out, Giardello insists on going in and speaking with him to try and avert bloodshed. Robinson reveals that, years earlier, he had taken the fall for Harris on some heroin he had pilfered from evidence control. Harris was still paying off that debt by interfering with this investigation and tipping Robinson off to the police's source. When police finally go inside, they find Robinson and his followers have all committed suicide. Giardello vows to bring Harris down, but for some reason this potential plotline isn't followed. A high-level investigation is, however, promised in a following episode and Harris disappeared from the series.

Kotto also wrote season six's "Secrets," wherein the coincidental suicides of two prominent members of Baltimore's financial community, who also belonged to the same private club, are too striking to go unchecked. It turns out that each had been involved in illicit affairs and faced the threat of exposure. Their blackmailer, fellow club member Rutherford Hill (Remak Ramsay), was not demanding payment to guard their secrets, but intended to expose them as a means of urging their repentance. Hill proudly boasts of having exerted the same pressure on several other members, with the happy result that they'd elected to change their ways. In the end, the photographer he enlists to take the incriminating photos shoots Hill for he, too, has a secret about which Hill has become wise.

"I play Giardello as a man trying to find a balance, to make clear and judicious judgment," Kotto explains of his character. "He's a CEO, taking a corporate approach to policing."

There are marvelous layers to Giardello. Yet Kotto complains that he has not been fully developed enough.

"If we are to understand how this man leads other men, we must understand him. But we don't. He is an enigma. I don't know this man any better than do you from watching past shows."

But on that basis we do know much about him. We learn during season six that in his shadowy past was some intelligence work and a spell as a prisoner of war in Hanoi ("Lies and Other Truths"). He calls upon an old contact, a Soviet defector, to help Frank and Tim sort out the doings of a bizarre group of amateur spooks who appear to have murdered one of their own during a "training exercise." When pressed about his experiences, Giardello demurs, preferring not to talk about such matters.

We know that he is a widower and is still in mourning, though somewhat reluctantly. After he kills Raymond Desassy ("The Wedding"), who had fired on him and Howard when they were trying to bring him in for questioning, he recalls to Kay the only other time he had shot a man. He concludes simply by saying, "I miss my wife." This is a man acutely aware that there's nobody waiting at home to console him.

We've seen him out on one date — although there have been allusions to the occasional woman in his life — when Megan introduces him to a friend of hers. All appears to go well and Al wants to pursue her, but she has told Megan she really isn't interested. Upon learning this, Giardello concludes that women like her — educated, sophisticated, light-skinned African Americans — are uninterested in very dark-skinned men like himself, that they consider him beneath them. He discusses his experiences of racism at the hands of his own community, how subtleties of skin tone can have such significance. His anger and hurt is more profound than had he been rejected by a white woman.

His three grown children don't call him often enough. We've seen his daughter Cherisse, who marries in San Francisco. Al is hesitant to attend the wedding because he's never even been given the opportunity to meet the man. He regrets how far removed he's become from her life, how incidental he is to her.

His is a life of isolation. In an early episode, he tells Bolander, "Right now, I want to tell you, I hate myself. I don't have any friends to speak of. All I have is this job, and it disgusts me."

He's a commander who is savvy enough a lieutenant to hold his own, but not agreeable enough a compromiser to ensure favor with his superiors. His subordinates, however, appreciate how he keeps the braids at bay while they do their jobs. If necessary, he'll step well outside the bounds of office. For instance, there was the time when Kellerman and Lewis were obstructed from investigating a murder in a housing project by Black Muslims, who held a contract to provide security on the property ("Scene of the Crime"). The Muslims refuse to cooperate when questioned. Mike gets heated and one of the Muslims responds by shoving him, which brings him a charge. Colonel Barnfather, arguing that the Muslims hold a certain political sway within the community, orders he be released. Indignant at such blatant interference, Giardello calls the *Sun* and is the anonymous ranking officer who leaks a story about the Muslim security agents being prime suspects in the murder. That morning, Barnfather has a change of heart, ordering that any and all avenues of inquiry be pursued. Giardello heartily agrees.

Leaving Gee's office, Barnfather says that if he ever finds out who leaked the story, that person will be walking a foot post through Baltimore's nether regions. "That goes without saying, sir," Gee cheerfully replies.

Many's the time he's gone out on a limb for his men. When asbestos was being secretly removed from the building, he demanded they be informed and protected. He tries in vain to save Kellerman from the bribery investigation of the arson squad in which he has become entangled. When rebuffed by the deputy commissioner, he sadly asks of himself, "When a commander can't do right by his troops, what good is he? In any man's army, what good is he?" At the same time, he recognizes when not to step to that unstable outer branch. When Frank gets jammed up because of his investigation into Congressman Wade's false kidnapping report and is suspended, he looks to Giardello to bail him out. "You told me this was about parking tickets, Frank," Gee shrugs, reminding him that he hadn't seen fit to let him in on what the matter really entailed.

Too often, commanders are portrayed in a constant state of righteous indignation. This is not Giardello. He is sometimes moved to rage, often frustrated, but frequently just bemused. He can scold more quickly than he can comfort. He has that strength — all too rare in a commander — of knowing his people and being able to draw from them their best qualities.

MEGAN RUSSERT

Appearing in *Homicide* for season three, Megan Russert (Isabella Hofmann) boasted the kind of fabricated background commonplace on other TV shows, but totally out of place on *Homicide*. From the outset she struck me as superfluous, a blatant attempt to concoct a certain *type* for the cast.

During its inaugural season (episode seven, "A Dog and Pony Show"), Gee's friend, Lt. Jim Scinta (Michael Constantine), commander of the other homicide shift, had his retirement party. The two found themselves coming to terms with being of a generation fast becoming obsolete in a police force seeking modernization through some ill-conceived new breed, one more clearly defined by what it isn't than by what it is. Scinta was of the old Italian ruling order that had once pulled the force's levers. Giardello, though of the old school, is of the ascendant African-American clan, whose representation had been improved over the years.

Russert is whatever that new breed is supposed to be. Female, in the first place, giving her an affirmative-action advantage in a profession where women are still underrepresented. Her career rode a somewhat Biblical trajectory: from lightning ascension to fall from grace. This suggests that the producers never really decided what to do with the character. Her résumé was nothing short of astonishing. Graduating third in her class at Annapolis, she went on to distinguish herself in naval intelligence, then on to the police and undercover narcotics before being promoted to lieutenant in homicide. All of this and not a day over thirty-five.

In her first week as shift commander, Russert was initiated by fire with the murder of Baltimore's Samaritan of the Year ("Nearer My God to Thee"). The men under her could barely contain their resentment, and those above could hardly keep secret their uneasiness at her inexperience. Roger Gaffney, then a mere detective, was the primary. He came close to sabotaging the investigation before it even began through his sloppy processing of the crime scene. Russert responded by removing him from the case. When he lashed out at her with insults and insubordination, she transferred him out of homicide. He'd be a vindictive enemy later on.

After Giardello exposed Granger's misdeeds and Barnfather made colonel, he had every reason to expect promotion to captain, but was passed over in favor of Russert. She wouldn't last long. Only a season and a half after her arrival as lieutenant, Barnfather would find her handling of the sniper incident wanting. Nine people were randomly gunned down in a series of attacks. A suspect, William Mariner, was finally identified and police were dispatched to his home, where he was cloistered behind the closed door of his study. While Bayliss tried to talk him into surrendering and QRT stood by, Mariner killed himself. The colonel used this occasion to demote Russert back to lieutenant. When she questioned his motives, he busted her all the way down to detective. To everyone's surprise — and disgust — Gaffney was awarded the captain's rank.

Russert spent the rest of the fourth season as a member of Giardello's squad, and was then summarily dispatched to Paris following a whirlwind, off-season romance with a French diplomat. She made a guest appearance at the conclusion of season five, drawn back to Baltimore by Felton's death.

Supervising producer Jim Yoshimura admits, "I failed Russert. I never developed a proper ear for the character." He insists that this is no reflection on Hofmann, whom he praises as a wonderful actor. Russert was too much neither here nor there; affecting to be one of the boys on the job, somehow not quite a boss, yet clearly anointed for high office. Contrast her with Pembleton, who expressly rejected promotion, yet is comfortable being anything but one of the boys. Or Kay, who struggles with being too much one of the boys, and makes no bones about being aggressive and ambitious.

Given the opportunity to stand up for other cops when they faced difficult situations, whether risking a fall on their behalf or just looking the other way, Russert invariably blinked. In the civil suit filed by Wilgis against Frank and the city, Megan was called to testify because she had been the lieutenant on duty. At the time, she had refrained from halting the interview only because Giardello had insisted Pembleton be allowed latitude. Her testimony exhibited only halfhearted support for his conduct.

On another occasion (year four's "Scene of the Crime"), after she had been busted back to detective, Officer Stuart Gharty (Peter Gerety, who would bring this character into the homicide unit as a regular cast member for season six), potbellied and well past his charge-into-the-action prime, was sitting in his radio car contentedly contemplating a sandwich, when he was called to respond to shots fired in a high-rise project. Where adrenaline, the wail of a siren, and the pulse of blue and red lights will carry the younger man, second thought will hold back the older. By the time he dragged himself to the scene, both shooters were dead; in the sage-like summary of Munch, "Shlomo shot Shlomo." Russert's investigation showed that Gharty had been less than enthusiastic about intervening. His time of arrival didn't correspond with his last radioed position or when he put in a call for detectives to come to the scene. A half hour had passed and he never even requested backup. Munch was prepared to let it ride, unwilling to ruin another cop's reputation over drug dealers erasing each other.

Under questioning from Russert, Gharty readily admits, "I pulled up to Boston [Homes], I heard gunfire, and I waited until it was safe to go inside." He's nonchalant about it. Russert is accusatory, telling him he could have stopped them.

"Stopped them, how? Just me and my 9 mm, I might as well go in waving a white flag," Gharty says, incredulous. "I'm fifty-four years old, Detective. Six months away from a nice, cozy desk job. What are my options? I step inside that building, they shoot me, then finish each other off. Or worse, I kill a kid. What then? He's black, I'm white. His mother points her finger. The whole neighborhood's raging against me, my face is on the front page, my family's dragged through hell. I can't take that risk. Why should I?"

Russert had the choice of charging him for dereliction of duty or protecting him, letting the time discrepancy slide. She elected to follow the former course. In the end, he was absolved by the disciplinary board (D'Addario, in the role of Lieutenant Jasper, chaired).

In both of these instances, she did what had come to be expected of a Barnfather or a Gaffney. Giardello would have stood beside his men, giving them at least the benefit of the doubt. But Russert was never quite one nor the other.

The relationship between Russert and Howard — women in a commander-subordinate position — was interesting. It raised issues that are non-issues when men command other men. Kay was as giddy and flustered as a schoolgirl when she initially met the first female shift commander in department history. She gushed out her congratulations and blushed about what an honor it was to serve under her. Russert's response was steely, thanking her but suggesting she get back to work. Howard quickly regained her composure, muttering under her breath, ''Bitch.''

Things never really improved. Howard would be subjected to a lecture about how self-defeating it is to think in terms of being a female cop, as opposed to just being a cop. Russert implies that such thinking erects barriers as much as do male attitudes. It appeared as though peace was in the offing after Howard was shot, but that was merely a function of her being severely weakened and Russert feeling a wave of sympathy.

The very day Howard was presented with her sergeant's badge, she assumed a proprietary interest in the activities of her former colleagues. To say that she came on strong is to give her too much credit. Russert called her aside and invited her to dinner for a heart-to-heart on interpersonal skills. Asserting that she could handle her new responsibilities just fine, Kay rejected her overture. Since Megan was demoted soon after this exchange, this element of their relationship was not explored further.

KAY HOWARD

Joseph Wambaugh includes Kay Howard when he lists the elements of *Homicide* that flout Hollywood convention. Not since Betty Thomas gave us Lucy Bates in *Hill Street Blues* has there been such an authentic representation of a policewoman. In other cop series, women are inserted as obvious sexual diversions. If not drop-dead gorgeous, they exude a certain *Ilsa: She-Wolf of the SS* quality, what with the leather holster and all. Often they amount to little more than *Baywatch* in street clothes.

Although far from unappealing, with her wildly flowing red curls, Melissa Leo placed Howard in an ongoing struggle against exhibitions of femininity. Whenever these qualities threatened to crack through, she dug down for another coat of toughness. Though she never looked like she was primped for an evening out, for the first few episodes she was always seen with makeup. Soon she went au naturel, presumably because police work is no dinner party.

It's hard enough for a man to live up to the exceedingly macho standards of posture demanded by police work; it's nigh on impossible for a woman. Howard doesn't rebel against the conventions of the force, she takes them for her own. Conforming to, rather than changing, the male attitude is her way of subverting expectations. And she does it splendidly, boasting the highest clearance rate in the unit, better even than the more flamboyant Pembleton.

Still, every so often she lets off a flash of vulnerability, as if suddenly concerned over what she's allowed herself to become. Defying an unspoken agreement she had with Felton, she quizzed him about whether he found her attractive. His obvious discomfort failed to dissuade her. It wasn't that she was trying to manipulate her partner into an affair, merely that she wanted to know that she was a woman in his eyes.

What affairs Kay has had have been conducted largely off-screen. She admitted to Pembleton that she had had an affair with Lieutenant Tyron, the suspect in his police-involved shooting investigation. There was a brief romance with Ed Danvers, but it was very peripheral. Again with Frank — the one colleague in whom she'd confide — Kay bragged about the sex as would any self-respecting man in a morning-after locker-room setting ("Ed Danvers is a man among men," she positively cooed).

During a sensitivity counseling session, she revealed why she had difficulties with her social life. "Most of the people who kill are men. And most of the people who get killed are men. I'm surrounded by men solving crimes by men against men. . . . Then I'm supposed to date one of them, have a relationship," she scoffs. "I look at Ed and I think, is that you? Could you knife someone in cold blood over the Super Bowl?"

This predicament may well plague real female cops. However, to depict it in the series is to resist opportunities to toss the female lead into sexual situations with a variety of partners. And, then, what good are they?

So why does she do it? Why is Kay a murder police? "I love getting to the truth," she shrugs.

One entire episode was devoted to Kay's personal life, "The Last of the Watermen" in season three. Burned out and more repulsed than usual by a murder — an old woman was beaten to death and had her tongue cut out while in her own kitchen — she takes some vacation time to visit her family in a small Chesapeake Bay oyster-fishing community. We join her as she catches up with her father, brothers, an old flame, and the other people from her youth who have been content never to move away. Howard has become just a little too street-hardened for the small-town upbringing. The community experien ces its first murder in a half-dozen years during her holiday. Not one of the more memorable episodes; she didn't show much that hadn't already been revealed on the streets of Baltimore.

We get to meet her sister from Florence, Carrie, when she visits Kay at headquarters on the day of Lewis's wedding ("The Wedding"). Carrie is Kay's complete opposite, a giggling coquette whose every gesture is prelude to seduction (in an uncredited role, Leo did double duty, playing Carrie alongside Kay). Kay tries to discourage Bayliss from pursuing her on the grounds that she's crazy. When he presses her about the basis for the diagnosis, Kay replies, "Carrie just sees life as a game. She who has the most fun wins." He's all for that. Life's a more serious matter for Kay.

Michelle Forbes praises Howard for being "one of the most important female characters we've had on television," and lauds Leo for the "extraordinary courage she brought to the role." The writers offered Howard a shot at complete equality and Leo had the confidence to play her as an equal. There was nothing given to the male cops that she wasn't allowed to take, as well.

When she, Felton, and Bolander entered the apartment building for the ill-fated arrest during which they would all be shot, she had prevented Felton from going in first. She was the primary on the case, and the primary always goes through the door first.

Her interrogation style is no less confrontational than the men's. At no time has she been coy. She's not flirtatious, unlike Frank, for example, who was very nearly dirty dancing with Annabella Wilgis. Kay Howard is not one to sweet-talk. She can browbeat the toughest of them. The key to intimidation isn't physical size; it's a relentless, uncompromising drive-for-the-net onslaught. Pulling her weapon to make an arrest, she is every bit believable. In all respects, she is as much cop as her male colleagues. Hers was the type of role actresses clamor after.

When Howard made sergeant, a new dynamic was created; it never quite gelled. In the real Baltimore homicide unit, the lieutenant commands a shift made up of several squads, each headed up by a sergeant. The sergeants will go out on calls to back up the primaries, but they don't lead investigations. Much of their day is spent in the office supervising and administering. There really isn't much space on *Homicide* for that role, seeing as Giardello is pretty well office-bound. That's why the sergeant was disposed of when the TV squad was composed. With nowhere to take the position, Howard was written out for the sixth season.

STEVE CROSETTI

One of the skills that all members of the *Homicide* cast have exhibited — and the hallmark of ensemble acting — is to melt into the background when they aren't the focus of a scene as well as they take command of the camera when at the fore. The mark of the great character actor is the ability to play low-key, to know his or her place in every situation. Veteran Jon Polito is exemplary at this craft. Despite having spent just two attenuated seasons on the show, he made Steve Crosetti an enduring figure. Easily excitable, Crosetti was always struggling to talk and breathe at the same time. Overweight, a smoker and a drinker, he looked like the national poster boy for the Heart and Stroke Foundation. You couldn't help but fear for him lest a suspect run, because you just knew he'd never survive the chase.

Crosetti embodied what middle-aged deterioration does to a man: the enhanced midsection, the diminished hairline, the desultory career, the broken marriage, the alienated teenaged daughter.

Frustrated and distressed over his daughter's intention to sleep with her boyfriend in her mother's home, he reveals to Giardello his simple desires in life: "I wish I had my hair back, I wish my wife still loved me. I wish I could protect my daughter." Not too much for a man to reach for, but still beyond his grasp.

Without question, one of the most memorable episodes in series history was "Crosetti," in which a bloated, decomposing body fished out of the harbor turns out to be the remains of the detective. Although all evidence points to suicide, none of his colleagues want to believe he took his own life. Hardest hit of all is Lewis, his partner, who is overcome with guilt over not having been sensitive to the signs of Crosetti's distress, over the realization that their relationship hadn't been truly intimate. Once again, *Homicide* debunked the myth of the partner as inseparable bosom buddy, and it dealt with the separation between the work environment and private life that most of us experience.

Lewis is intent on proving Steve was killed. He not only refuses to cooperate with Bolander's investigation, he actively interferes. "He did not commit suicide," he insists to Bolander and Munch, as if the idea were inconceivable. "And you're both sons of bitches for trying to prove he did."

Bolander feels pressure from all sides to write up the death as something other than suicide, but balks. "If he chose to commit suicide, what right do I have to make that go away? I don't agree with what he did, but if that's his final statement, should I wipe that clear just for our peace of mind?"

Each member of the squad has to come to terms with not knowing why this man, who they had seen every day and whose life appeared so closely to mirror their own, had chosen death by his own hand. Bolander has to admit that he never exchanged more than greetings with Crosetti. He reminds himself that he always treated him with respect, as if in compensation for the distance. Breaking down at the confirmation that Steve had, indeed, killed himself, Lewis demonstrates that for all their familiarity with death as a grand concept, loss of life as an isolated event can still be a heart-wrenching experience.

Such experiences are never forgotten. And *Homicide* has a long memory. Its characters aren't constantly reinvented; they live with their scars. Lewis has not recovered from Crosetti's death. During "Stakeout" in season four, he launches into self-examination with Russert.

"I'm open. I'm caring. I'm honest. I'm friendly. So why don't people tell me their life stories on trains? And Crosetti —" he shakes his head, coming to the heart of the matter. "I had no idea that Crosetti was going to kill himself. My own partner and I had no idea that he's in that kind of pain. Why didn't he come to me?"

The brass, of course, are preoccupied with how suicides reflect on the department's image, Steve's having been the fourth in 10 months. Barnfather and Granger refuse Crosetti the dignity of a full honor guard at the funeral. They're prepared to disavow him because suicide opens up so many uncomfortable moral questions. It takes the fallen Catholic — Pembleton — to show him the proper respect. After refusing to attend the church funeral, Pembleton pays homage from the steps of police headquarters, standing at attention in his dress blues and saluting the funeral cortege. It is a resonant moment of forgiveness.

In an exchange adapted from the book, Granger and Barnfather express embarrassment over another cop who shot himself in the head in a hotel on the Block. "What's to get upset about? He knew when he did it we'd find him like that," says Barnfather contemptuously. This was drawn from a brief mention in the epilogue, where D'Addario and Sergeant Landsman were called to the home of a detective who had committed suicide. He was found bent over his bathtub, his blood flowing neatly down the drain. All that would be needed to clean up was to turn on the faucet. Simon referred to it as a "detective's suicide." D'Addario is quoted as saying, "Fuck him. He knew when he did it that we'd find him like this."

This is the only point in the book with which D'Addario takes exception. "I did say it was a policeman's suicide because it was so clean and methodical. But the tone in which Dave wrote it was that I was condemning his suicide, and that wasn't the case. He was a good, decent man, who was having some personal problems."

Police have a higher rate of suicide than the population at large. Whenever a cop takes his own life, it touches other cops deeply. They see someone with whom they can identify and ask why it was that he could no longer cope. It gets them reflecting on their own difficulties in this regard. They begin to consider just how secure is the net that supports them. If only for a passing moment, they wonder whether the tricks they've devised for withstanding the pressures might suddenly lose their magic.

Those close to a suicide have to come to grips with the loss. They may feel anger or resentment that the person chose such an irrevocable course of action. They may disparage the suicide as cowardly. But it seems more an act of self-absorption than of cowardice. When people turn completely inward, they can lose sight of all the things outside of themselves worth living for. In such extremes of loneliness, they have nothing to ground them to this life. That seemed to have been Crosetti's condition to the extent that we knew it.

MELDRICK LEWIS

Meldrick Lewis is all cop swagger and attitude. He's funny and perceptive, aggressive and reflective. Beyond street-smart, he's streetwise. Growing up in West Baltimore's Lafayette Courts high-rise, probably the most violent of the city's housing projects, can do that to a man. Given that background (we learned this in season four; it was an excuse to work in some footage of the real-life demolition of the Courts), we needn't wonder at his unflappability. Kids from such an environment are intimate with crime: they start out weakly as potential victims, strengthen to where they can run with the gang, and, finally, stand up and head straight or sink into the fray. One of the surest ways out is through the police, where early lessons in street tough are a valuable education.

Clark Johnson did not draw on anyone in particular from the book to create Lewis. He had played cops before — notably in the Canadian TV series *Night Heat* — and has obviously given much thought to what makes them tick.

"Cops lead dysfunctional lives. That comes from dealing with mortality. It's a job that takes over, making them emotionally distant. I play Meldrick like a human being who happens to be a cop, and is affected by that. He's not larger than life."

He carries the cop look so well — the former National and Canadian Football League prospect has the size — that it's easy to forget how multitalented a performer, director, and technician he is. As he relates in a story he contributed to the book *Standing Naked in the Wings: Anecdotes from Canadian Actors*, he won his first role in his first audition at the age of 10, for the Toronto revival of *South Pacific*. The adulation of the audience almost caused him to miss his exit. He went on to appear in several other stage shows as a child, later studying and playing football at Eastern Michigan and Montreal's Concordia University.

Though Canada proudly claims him as its own, and he largely grew up and makes his permanent home in Toronto, he's actually a native Philadelphian. He describes his parents as political refugees. His mother, who is white, met his father, an African American, in Paris in the 1950s. A mixed-race couple may not have been a huge issue in Europe, but this was segregated America and they faced hardship at home. Seeking a more tolerant climate, they settled in Canada. Johnson is currently at work on a screenplay about their lives.

His early work in the film industry was as a special-effects technician. Notably, he worked on three David Cronenberg films: *The Dead Zone*, *Videodrome*, and *The Fly*. He went on to direct several installments of the Family Channel's South Africa-based adventure series *Under African Skies*, and has since directed several *Homicide* episodes. His on-screen credits include the films *Colors, Drop Zone,* and *Nick of Time,* and TV's *The Women of Brewster Place, LA Law,* as well as a recurring stint with *SCTV*.

Johnson found himself at the center of an incident that has become part of *Homicide* legend. When you shoot out in the open on city streets, life is bound to imitate art. Rehearsing an arrest in an alley, Johnson and Belzer were standing over a suspect lying prone on the ground with their prop guns drawn. Suddenly a man came tearing onto the scene, but froze in his tracks when he saw the *police* with guns at the ready. He dropped what he was carrying — which turned out to be merchandise shoplifted from a nearby pharmacy — only to realize in an instant that he had been faked out by pretend police. He yelled out, "Munch!" before security guards put the grab on him and awaited the arrival of real police. Johnson admitted he has become so bored telling and retelling this story that he sometimes alters the details just to make it more interesting for himself.

Art imitated life when the event was recreated for inclusion in J.H. Brodie's (Max Perlich) documentary about the unit. Levinson and the crew appear as themselves, filming the show, when Lewis pursues a suspect into their midst. The suspect is rattled at having fled right into the heart of all the commotion that accompanies a film crew and gives up. Meldrick goes all giddy at being captured on camera.

Lewis is a patient, methodical cop who doesn't allow much to escape his eye or his gut. It was Lewis who slowed things down during the Thormann investigation when the case against the original suspect didn't quite hold up. He recanvassed the neighborhood and found an old lady with whom he spoke solicitously. This occurred in an inner-city ghetto where the elderly live out their golden years far more peacefully if they don't hear or see anything, or, at the very least, forget whatever they have seen or heard long before the police come asking questions. But the lady heard what she heard. She told Meldrick that word had it that the young man who suffered terrible migraines had shot the officer. "I don't think people ought to shoot at the police," she tells him defiantly. Charlie Flavin had severe headaches. The old lady also understood that the man's girlfriend had been present. Lewis tracked down her whereabouts and picked her up. She went on to give up Flavin for the attack.

Lewis's sensitive treatment of an eight-year-old girl led him to close the Erica Chilton murder, which had stumped the unit for years. First Crosetti had failed to make an arrest in the death of this young woman, found smothered in her bed. Mercifully, her young daughter had been spared. After his cases were farmed out following his death, it would plague Kay. A stone whodunit with no witnesses and no obvious suspects, it looked to be the stumper that would blemish her perfect solution rate. Any hope of solving the case seemed to have been irretrievably lost when Felton, off on one of his by then customary binges, misplaced a stack of letters one of Erica's ex-boyfriends had sent her. They had been turned in by Tom Marans (Dean Winters), with whom she had been living at the time of her death. Marans, genuinely grief-stricken and openly cooperative, had been cleared as a suspect.

A year after the killing, Erica's daughter was deeply troubled and wanting to play "murder" with her classmates. Her teacher brought her to the homicide unit. Meldrick invites the girl to sit down and talk. She reveals that in her dreams a man with the initials M.T. on his shirt is standing over her mom. M.T./T.M.: Tom Marans. On the presumption that this dream was rooted in memory, Marans was brought in for questioning. Under interrogation, he broke down and confessed to the murder, explaining that he had been driven into a jealous rage by Erica's continued infatuation with the previous boyfriend.

Lewis realizes crime is a fact of life. As he is fond of saying, "I've been a police for a long time." He's prepared to come to a rough truce with the run-of-the-mill doping and assaulting and stealing and — even — killing. After all, it's what keeps him on a payroll. What he hasn't become accustomed to is the excess. Most anything else, he can shrug his way through.

He and Crosetti caught one of the more bizarre murders when they arrived at the library and learned that the victim had been killed following a discussion with a man who had wanted his pen ("A Many Splendored Thing" in season two). No explanation for the crime was apparent, other than that the victim refused to surrender the 49-cent Bic.

"Baltimore, home of the misdemeanor homicide," Lewis quipped.

Once they trace the suspect to his apartment, his landlord tells them he's a quiet, polite tenant who pays his rent. Up in his room, they find pens strung everywhere, like beaded curtains. Just your average, normal, unbalanced citizen. After being brought in, the pen-lover manages to get to the roof of headquarters and threatens to jump. Lewis goes up and lures him down with the promise of yet another pen for his collection.

It goes without saying that Meldrick is baffled by demons that would propel a man to murder for a pen. But he doesn't suffer operatic torment about it the way Bayliss does. He wonders at it, then moves along to the next corpse. This is the source of the fascination Johnson has for his character: a murder police gets no respite; he always moves along to the next corpse.

Partnered with Munch, Lewis leads the investigation into the murder of Monk Whetherly, a member of the Deacons biker gang ("Cradle to Grave"). Monk was shot in the face, then dragged behind a car for a couple of miles just for good measure. Their best prospect for information is Preacher (Timothy Wheeler), the Deacons' warlord. They go to meet him at a Blair Road strip bar.

"I see these women and I just get this urge to take them home, try to talk some sense into them," Lewis tells Munch as a girl bumps and grinds on the stage.

"No sex?"

"Oh, yeah, yeah, yeah, a couple of beers, couple of shots, plenty of sex. But I still want to help them out."

Preacher gets into a "mine's bigger than yours" with Lewis, in the words of Munch, before they succeed in bringing him in. He tells them, cryptically, that Monk died because he loved his daughter. Lewis makes a genuine effort to understand the motorcycle culture, their code of honor, their fixation on independence. An FBI undercover informs Lewis which Deacon killed Monk, whose death was ordered because the gang discovered his wife was the Bureau's source. Monk chose to die in place of his wife so his daughter would have a mother. Meldrick goes to Monk's funeral and, in a truly marvelous moment, silently edges his way through the crowd of leather-clad bikers to leave a picture of his little girl on the casket. It's a movingly understated scene, without dialogue, just the up-lifting chords of the Pretenders' "I'll Stand by You."

Lewis's private life hasn't been looked at extensively. He failed to win the affections of Emma Zoole, losing to Bayliss the opportunity for sex in a coffin. His impetuous marriage to Barbara Shivers was a quick failure. Flirtations with Det. Terri Stivers (Toni Lewis) never amounted to anything. We got a brief glimpse into his family when he revealed to Mike that he has a brother in an asylum who he hasn't seen in twenty years. This after they arrested a powerful lunatic for murdering his parents ("I've Got a Secret"). Seeing this lonely soul, rocking himself back and forth inside his straitjacket, unloved and uncared for by anyone in the world, moved him to visit his brother. But he is rebuffed. Besides that, off-duty, he is usually seen at the Waterfront, which he purchased along with Bayliss and Munch. Essentially, what one sees of Lewis on-duty is who Lewis is.

Like his partner, Kellerman, he was deeply affected by the pursuit of Luther Mahoney. He couldn't disassociate himself from the role he'd played in Luther's death. Prepared though he was to carry Mike's questionable shooting, he could no longer trust him as a partner. Saying only that he needed a change, he asked Giardello to let him work with someone else and spent season six with Paul Falsone. This was no escape. In the season opener he, Stivers, and Mike are each shot at by a mysterious assailant on a motorcycle. It turns out to be Junior Bunk (Mekhi Phifer), Luther's nephew, sending out a warning on behalf of his mother, Georgia Rae (Hazelle Goodman), who took over the family drug trade. Then he was named a co-defendant in Georgia Rae's wrongful-death civil suit. When he confronted her about it and advised that she "stick this where you used to mule crack and skank for the Colombians," she kicks him in the groin, to which he responds by breaking her nose. This earns him a suspension that keeps him on the sidelines through much of the season. Over several episodes he played an enigmatic role in sparking the war that rocked the Mahoney clan and led to that season's climactic finale.

MIKE KELLERMAN

Reed Diamond is the second cast member trained at the famed Julliard school. His credits include big screen (*Memphis Belle*, *Assassins*, and *Clear and Present Danger*), stage (*The Home-coming*, *Peer Gynt*, *Romeo and Juliet*, and *Wait Until Dark*), and television (*Law and Order*, *Hallmark Hall of Fame's Blind Spot* and *O Pioneers*, *Danielle Steel's Full Circle*, *The Other Anna*). Until *Homicide* he had never been a series regular.

It must be a surreal experience for an actor to live in the company of a single character over a long period of years. That character has to be internalized close enough to the surface to be dredged up time and again. Diamond affirmed, "Actors play a lot closer to themselves on TV. There's an adage that says, on TV the character is the actor, in film the actor is the character. The delineations between Kellerman and I aren't all that huge. I bring to him my own fallibility." Playing a cop, Diamond has no problem being the character. He's the only cast member who says he ever actually aspired to be a cop. "Being an actor, I looked up to people like cops for doing something real. I wanted to make Kellerman the cop I wanted to be."

In his third year with *Homicide*, Kellerman is no longer the aggressive, bright-eyed, happy-go-lucky (during his second episode, he tells Frank, "Fun is my God. I worship fun. I live for fun") good cop. Indeed, of the entire cast, his character has experienced the most dramatic transformation. Cocky from the moment he appeared as an arson investigator ("Fire," season four's premier), he clashed with Pembleton over whether a teenaged boy discovered in a torched warehouse was deliberately murdered or accidentally trapped by a profit-motivated or psychologically unbalanced arsonist. When a second warehouse goes up in exactly the same manner, this time with a teenage girl inside, he concedes they are likely dealing with a calculated killing, not a firebug. Once a suspect, dog-owning chemistry teacher Gavin Robb (Adam Trese) is finally brought in for questioning, it's Kellerman who trips him into confessing. Though Robb shows no remorse regarding the dead teens, Kellerman makes him believe a dog died in one of the fires. He finishes his line of questioning and tells Robb he's free to leave. As nothing more than an afterthought, he adds, "Why'd you kill the dog?"

"I didn't know it was there," Robb blurts without thinking. He then admits to both fires, saying the first was set as a cover for the second, which was meant to dispose of the body of Bonnie Nash, who he had deliberately killed. Robb hadn't known there was anyone inside the first building when he ignited it.

The detectives knew Bonnie was a wild girl and had been in Robb's class the previous year. However, in typical *Homicide* fashion, his motive is never revealed. He is proven to be the perpetrator and that's enough. Motive may be forethought for a killer; it is afterthought for detectives.

Kellerman can't understand why this ordinary man went out and incinerated a young girl. Giardello tells him, "You sleep better if you don't know."

At the conclusion of this two-parter, Kellerman transfers into homicide. He is paired up with Meldrick, who has bemoaned not having a regular partner since Crosetti's suicide ("I'm a collaborator at heart," he tells Gee). They have an easy chemistry together. Unlike Pembleton and Bayliss, whose relationship is kept interesting by their differences, Kellerman and Lewis seem like guys who might hang out regardless of their job; they just happen to be palling around at crime scenes.

One of my favorite episodes — and one of Diamond's, as well — was "Full Moon," which aired in season four. Kellerman and Lewis drive out to a murder at a run-down, ex-con haven motel on the extreme western outskirts of the city, the kind of place that nestles hard by the interstate like sun-rotted roadkill. They always advertise their amenities right up front — clean, TV, air-conditioning, telephone — as if anyone checks in because they find it at all appealing. You always speed up just a little to push such places behind faster, maybe wondering, in passing, who does stay here? You shudder at the thought of what might be taking place just the other side of those paper-thin walls, what each muffled sound means. Writer Eric Overmyer filled the New Moon Motel with quirky, vaguely dangerous, marginals. Ninety-eight percent of the guests are found to have criminal records.

The victim, Charlie Wells — an eccentric, aging, abandoned ex-con whose death will go unmourned — is shot in his room. The detectives face the task of going door-to-door seeking witnesses or anyone who might know anything about the victim. The atmosphere is one of confined desperation: rooms that seem overcrowded even when empty; an eerie blue tinge clinging to everything, like the light given off by a TV set that's gone to static in the quiet of the night; the full moon smirking from above; the coldly precise guitar track that speaks more to what has happened than it foreshadows what might come. This being a place where you think twice before you look out the window after gunshots, everyone's got a story, but nobody has any information. The episode runs like a finely crafted play, with characters revealing themselves with just a few well-chosen lines. The Wells murder is never solved; fittingly, for his death is made all the more haunting for going unavenged.

"You tend to write better for better actors," offers Overmyer. "Full Moon" was his first *Homicide* script and he handed the case to Lewis and Kellerman because "I chose characters I believed I had a good feel for." He particularly enjoys writing for the newer cast members because he has more leeway in defining them.

In just three seasons, Kellerman endured immense ordeals. The first was perhaps the most trying for a good cop: he was implicated in a corruption scandal. Along with three other members of the arson squad, he was accused of accepting bribes from a developer who burned his unprofitable buildings. As it would unfold over several episodes in season five, culminating in a grand jury hearing, Kellerman was the only arson cop who refused to take payoffs. However, whether or not he was on the take, there is a larger dilemma when corruption taints a police department: what is the culpability of those who knew of wrongdoing by others, but stood by and remained silent?

He faces the sadly incongruous position of taking the Fifth Amendment before the grand jury to protect himself from incrimination in a crime he didn't commit. The alternative is to snitch out his fellow officers. On the day he is to testify, he tells Julianna, "So I tell the grand jury that I knew that three detectives in my unit were dirty. What happens to me then? I'm gonna be brought up on charges for failing to report the graft. If I manage to keep my badge after that, I gotta walk back in this building. Everyone's gonna look at me and know I gave up other cops."

Mike is given a rather too convenient out when he realizes another cop has lied and included him among the dirty cops. As he heads into the grand jury chamber, he tells the prosecutor he'll reveal everything because he's willing to risk his career to tell the truth. She ends up letting him off the hook because she's so moved, and, besides, she just happens to have enough evidence to get the others, anyway.

The stain of accusation, however, is difficult to erase. Kellerman is tormented, driven near to suicide. With Meldrick as witness in the cabin of his houseboat, Mike fondles his gun, mulling the damage done to his life. The scene is overlengthy and it becomes obvious far before Lewis talks the gun out of his hands that he had no intention of shooting himself.

Diamond lists this episode as one of those he most enjoyed acting. He does, however, explain, "You have to be verbose on television. There's no other way to get deep inside." He says that it was Jim Yoshimura who recognized Kellerman held everything to himself and therefore would conceivably contemplate suicide under the circumstances.

Braugher is expansive in discussing some of the moral short-comings of the Kellerman corruption situation. "He was so concerned about his good reputation that he would consider suicide. But how pure is a cop who sits back and watches corruption going on? What does that say about his moral center?"

It was dissatisfying to have the old blue wall of silence invoked. This is not to say it isn't a factor, but it tends to be overstated. After all, Kellerman's arson bunkies did nothing to free him from the jam even though they knew he was innocent. Perhaps the answer is that he hadn't been such a good cop from the beginning and there's far less nobility in refusing to finger dirty cops than in doing the right thing.

"It would have taken a lot of time to deal with all the issues of Kellerman standing by," shrugs Diamond, conceding that television calls for compromise. "TV gives people what they want. Artistry is a perk, it's not what keeps us on the air.

"Sometimes I get bitter at the conundrum. But, then, look at what we've achieved. This has never been a user-friendly show."

This would not be Mike's last tribulation. He'd come back from all of this edgier than before.

Homicide never had villains. The nemesis has been the crime itself. Murder is villainy. Those who perpetrate it are deceptively normal. They are moved by the most inane passions. Sometimes they're stupid, sometimes mean. Rarely are they larger than life. Luther Mahoney, played to his malevolently cunning hilt by Erik Todd Dellums, would be Homicide's white whale, its Wo Fat.

That Luther headed a drug-trafficking organization was one thing. It's Baltimore, and Baltimore is up to its nose in white powder. There's a demand, so somebody's going to supply. But when the bodies of innocent people began to fall, Luther had stepped beyond the bounds of fair trade. Of course, like any mindful CEO, Luther had gone to great pains to insulate himself from the nastier aspects of his industry.

Mahoney first came to homicide's attention when he initiated a war against Drack, a rival dealer (season five's "Bad Medicine"). After Drack's people hijacked a heroin shipment bound for Luther, his people were dropped off like so many bags of trash. The first murder to really incense Kellerman and Lewis was that of a Korean grocer who had the audacity to shoo off Luther's slingers and reclaim his storefront. An informant who provided information against him "took one for the team," as Munch so quaintly phrased it. Collaborators who couldn't balance the books, too, were casually liquidated. In all, thirteen unsolved murders were tied to Luther Mahoney. Worst of all was his arrogance, how he taunted the police for their inability to pin him to any crime. One evening, after he gets out of holding, he shows up at the Waterfront to buy a round for the house. Lewis faces him down for coming into his place, onto his post. Wisely, Luther leaves.

When a Nigerian drug mule dies in a motel room with packets of Luther's heroin still safely stuffed in his intestines, the cops are presented with a classic sting opportunity. They replace the heroin with baking soda and use an undercover to turn it over to a Mahoney lieutenant, Antonio Brookdale. They then use surveillance and wiretaps to follow the reaction. Luther is enraged at being burned, not knowing whether Brookdale or his Nigerian suppliers are playing him for a fool. He arranges a meeting with both parties in Druid Hill Park. Concluding that Antonio was either negligent in not testing the shipment or is ripping him off, Luther opens fire on him. Police sweep in on the scene, but he manages to flee. Meldrick goes in pursuit, directly to Luther's apartment, where they face off.

Though Luther surrenders immediately, Lewis explains that he's in for a serious beat-down.

"Drugs out there, we ain't gonna win that," he allows. "There's a hundred open-air drug markets in this city and there's 50,000 drug fiends out there. And we are taking on human desire with lawyers and jailhouses and lockups. And you and I both know that human desire's kicking us in the ass. So, what I need to know, Luther, why couldn't you be happy with just the packages? If they were just slingin' drugs, me and you wouldn't be here. Would we? But the bodies. What about the bodies, Luther?"

As he proceeds to lay a major ass-kicking on Mahoney, Luther manages to get Meldrick's gun from his holster. With the fury of a wounded animal, he waves the gun at Lewis, just as Kellerman and Stivers arrive. He hesitates when ordered to drop the gun. Finally, he lowers it and looks at Mike. The gun is off Lewis. Frustrated at his uncanny knack for beating the rap, Kellerman shoots Luther through the heart.

Meldrick agrees to write up a clean shooting. Terri is less certain, but goes along, nonetheless. Kellerman — the good cop who had seen justice served so badly in his corruption affair and whenever Luther was arrested — suffered no qualms over the killing. He had gone into the system one side and come out the other.

Throughout season six, Luther stalks Kellerman from the grave. In the season premier, there's the message delivered by Junior Bunk, the fastest-rolling-over criminal in America. The first time he was arrested, on suspicion of carrying out Luther's command to kill a short-changing dealer, he gave up his uncle in a heartbeat. On this occasion, he rolled on his mother, Georgia Rae, who succeeds in beating jail time. Later, she'll invite Mike to meet her at Luther's grave. There, she lets him know that the apartment where the shooting occurred was rigged with surveillance cameras, implying that she has proof he premeditatedly murdered a man who had surrendered to custody. By the time she admits there was never really any video evidence, his reaction has convinced her that he murdered her brother, and for that she vows revenge. The pressures exerted by these threats push him to a place far to the hellish side of cynical. He pistol-whips a black man on a corner while in the throes of an alcoholic delusion that has him seeing Luther's face. He is outspoken about his lack of concern for finding a solution to the murder of an East-side dope dealer.

The civil suit with which Georgia Rae proceeds appears to have dubious merit. Against all odds, however, Judge Gerald Gibbons, the very same judge who had granted her bail in the Bunk case, agrees to send the suit to trial. Kellerman rightly concludes the judge is on the Mahoney pad. Following a private chat with Mike, Gibbons does dismiss the case. Afterward, he is confronted in the lobby of the courthouse by Kellerman, who loudly informs him that the FBI has him for corruption and that he'd better give up the Mahoneys. Not coincidentally, Gibbons is soon stabbed to death and none other than Junior Bunk is nabbed for the crime.

All the while, from somewhere in the nether reaches of Meldrick's suspension, the Mahoney organization is imploding. It begins with bodies falling on East Baltimore corners. Then it moves up the hierarchy to consume lieutenants and suppliers. Such internecine killings are notoriously difficult to solve. But, more to their suspicion than delight, each detective investigating a Mahoney-related slaying receives an anonymous letter providing enough evidence to warrant an arrest. On the basis that he had been feeding Lewis information on some of the individuals who had turned up dead, Falsone concludes Meldrick is the informant.

Mike's squad-room relationships continue to deteriorate. Though he gets along with his new partner, Munch, there is obvious strain between him and Lewis and Stivers. Meldrick's reaction rankles the most, since it was his having been disarmed while beating down the suspect that had provoked the entire chain of events. His once-promising relationship with Julianna never blossoms. Since his arrival in the squad, Falsone has harbored doubts about the justification for the Mahoney shoot. The officers involved had submitted identical reports indicating that Kellerman had fired because Lewis was in imminent danger. Falsone found the reports a little too identical.

The Mahoney epic came to a climax with the two-part conclusion to season six, "Fallen Heroes." Brought in for the Gibbons murder is a new and improved Junior Bunk. Hardened by prison time, Junior no longer falls to pieces at the prospect of taking a charge. Instead, he continues to spew threats and, when heads are turned and his cuffs are removed so he can make his phone call, he grabs a gun out of a desk drawer and opens fire, killing three uniforms and wounding Gharty and Ballard before being killed in a hail of bullets. This is an irrevocable declaration of war between the department and the

Mahoneys. An all-out offensive is launched to arrest anyone and everyone connected with their organization to avenge the dead police.

Stivers takes all of this hard. She goes to Giardello and admits Luther's shooting wasn't quite right. Frank and Falsone are assigned to find out what really happened. Lewis is first in the box and, while he doesn't say it straight-up, he can't deny that Kellerman's actions were dubious. Called on the carpet, Mike inadvertently reveals that the gun was no longer pointed at Meldrick when he shot. Because Frank won't write it up any way other than as it was given, Gee sits down with Mike and gives him two options: face a charge, along with Lewis and Stivers, which he has a good likelihood of beating, or resign and the case will end here and now. Protecting his old partner, he quits.

In a final private exchange with Lewis, he asks him for his gun and then a moment to himself. Meldrick declines. The man who has prided himself in nothing so much as being a good cop is a cop no more.

JULIANNA COX

In season five a hot Mustang convertible screams down the fast lane of the expressway heading toward the Baltimore skyline. At the wheel a beautiful young woman, confident and in control, her short black hair flailing against the wind. She slows down only long enough to take a speeding ticket, before peeling back down the track. Meet Dr. Julianna Cox, chief medical examiner.

Many viewers must have thought, "Uh-oh, here comes the token rating-boosting bimbo."

"You know, it's not like I'm twenty-two and buxom," smiles Michelle Forbes modestly. True, but she's got dark, bottom-less eyes and a graceful casualness that radiates sensuality. She also brought strength, independence, and intelligence to Julianna, so much so that you forget her looks and listen to what she has to say. As we've come to know the character, her attractiveness works to make her even more intriguing. What *is* a girl like her doing in a place like this?

Prior to joining *Homicide*, Forbes had accumulated a short but impressive list of credits. Though she winces at the mention of her tenure on the CBS soap opera *The Guiding Light*, she did earn an Emmy nomination for her performance as a schizophrenic psychiatrist. Her film work includes *Kalifornia*, with a then-unknown David Duchovny and lesser-known Brad Pitt, the very underseen *Swimming with Sharks*, opposite Kevin Spacey and Frank Whaley, as well as *Escape From LA*. She guested on several TV series, including a recurring role on *Star Trek: The Next Generation*. Her name appears on a long list of women who've had occasion to dump George Costanza (Jason Alexander) on *Seinfeld*. Tom Fontana noticed her in the NBC movie *The Prosecutors* and approached her to play Cox.

Like Secor, she had reservations about getting bogged down with a series. "I was afraid of playing one person for a long period of time because tedium can set in." She adds, "TV goes week to week and you never know what they're going to hand you, it's all so vague." What convinced her to come on board was that "*Homicide* was the most interesting piece of TV I'd ever seen."

"We wanted to inject a character who would look at the world differently from the detectives, but who wouldn't be alien to their world," Fontana explains.

Medical examiners work very closely with murder police in the course of an investigation. It is up to the ME to ascertain whether a death was caused by human intercession — in other words, whether it is a homicide. The physical evidence they collect is what conclusively proves how a victim died and attests to many of the accompanying circumstances (i.e., was the victim intoxicated, a drug user, or sexually molested; when was the victim killed; was the victim killed where found; did the victim try to defend himself or herself, etc.).

ME characters have recurred since the series' inception. There was Stan's paramour, Dr. Blythe. Ralph Tabakin continues to appear as Dr. Scheiner, the old, crotchety, rather corpse-like coroner. Harlee McBride (Belzer's real-life wife) also continues to appear as Dr. Alyssa Dyer.

In a short time, Cox has developed into more than merely another angle of approach to the detectives. She's made us wonder about what MEs are all about. After all, what kind of person goes through the tribulations of medical school, absorbs all the knowledge necessary to alleviate suffering and cure illness, only to be drawn to the examination of corpses?

Says Forbes, "The way I see Julianna, she was fascinated by death and justice. She has a passion for it, but realizes that on one level there's a futility to it. I think she's such a control freak that she finds it easier to deal with people who aren't talking back to her."

Her research for the role included speaking with members of Baltimore's medical examiner's office. But she's carefully avoided attending an autopsy. "If I thought I could stomach it I'd go, but . . ." She trails off, laughing.

What Cox has ended up giving us is another angle of approach to death. The detectives look at the corpse and analyze it, minutely examine where it fell and collect whatever they can from the scene that will tell them how it ended up in that condition. The ME, very literally, reaches down inside the corpse and explores its most intimate depths. If the cops can sometimes look askance at a corpse as some insane practical joke, Cox sees it as a jigsaw puzzle. Mmm, let's see: bludgeoned, stabbed, strangled, eviscerated. What was the cause of death?

There's no wincing and looking away for Julianna, only closer, more minute scrutiny.

The Baltimore police have a liaison officer posted permanently at the morgue. Upon being transferred from homicide, Sgt. Terry McLarney was given this assignment. Here is a man who has stood over a lot of corpses, but always with the detachment of purpose. Sitting right in the morgue, seeing these bodies stripped of any context, brought an epiphany of sorts.

"You can't look at those bodies and not recognize that something that had been inside of them is gone," he marvels.

Some element that makes us human dissipates upon death.

Cox echoes this sentiment when discussing how she copes with grief: "Maybe our brains know what we need to do in order to survive. If we could allow ourselves to understand that we're not our bodies; we are not that part of us that dies."

It was a surprise when she turned up at a support group for survivors of murder victims ("The Heart of a Saturday Night"). Cox's father had been killed and she was unable to face the loss all on her own. Intimacy with death on a clinical level gives the illusion that the beast has somehow been tamed, so you're unprepared for the emotional impact when it attacks directly. Emotions under such circumstances are an almost pleasant surprise.

Wouldn't anyone forced to stare at ugliness all day want to anesthetize themselves the rest of the time? By the end of the fifth season Cox was a fairly heavy drinker. Of course she'd get drunk, but there's a distinct line between getting drunk and being a drunk. She'd carouse at the Waterfront, unwind. She ended up doing a one-nighter with Kellerman, and was content to leave it at that. He, however, wanted to pursue some sort of relationship, one that could perhaps even have a more enduring basis than sex.

Both Forbes and Diamond were interested in the possibilities presented by having their characters involved, but had reservations about how it might become gratuitous.

"I was very wary about falling into the *girlfriend* role," she explains, "and I fought hard against that characterization."

"We weren't going to do *Homicide Place*," adds Diamond. "Michelle and I wouldn't do the obligatory nude bedroom scene." These comments refer to the nighttime soap *Melrose Place*, in which every action leads to bed, and *NYPD Blue*, with its famous bare-butt sequences.

"What interested Reed and me was to find out why these people were drawn together. I mean, they're hard, broken, fragmented, cynical people. Julianna smells like formaldehyde. Most men would have a serious problem with what she does. She and Mike find themselves drawn together, but neither is really sure how to have a mature relationship. In their case, sex was just an escape, not a logical step in the development of a healthy relationship."

Entering season six they were essentially broken up, but not necessarily for good. About a quarter of the way into the season, she enjoyed a Christmas fling with Bayliss, but broke it off after several weeks. Mike was hardly reconciled to their on/off status.

Midway through the season, Cox was confronted with a life-changing moral and professional dilemma ("Lies and Other Truths"). Enraged at being cut off by Gerry Dietz, who was on his way from lunch with his wife, Eva, the driver of a state road management truck rams their car until the vehicles crash, killing both drivers and leaving the wife paralyzed. Maryland faces the prospect of a massive lawsuit for negligence, unless the autopsy shows Dietz was legally intoxicated. The original toxicology results posted his blood alcohol at .09 percent, only one-tenth of a point under the legal limit. Accounting for the lapse between time of death and testing, there is a margin for some discretion in the determination. Cox's boss more than urges her to up the score. But no matter how she recalculates it, the number comes out the same. She refuses to lie to save the state at the expense of a horrifically injured woman. In a ploy she hopes will serve to ease the pressure, she leaks the test results to the press. The consequence is her summary dismissal. In a wonderfully symmetrical conclusion, she sadly bids adieu to Mike, and is last seen burning up the highway in her Mustang on her way out of Baltimore.

JOHN MUNCH

Casting acclaimed stand-up comic Richard Belzer in the role of John Munch was nothing short of inspired. All the more so when he tells you that the producers had initially sought a Jason Priestley type. Fontana confirms this. Throughout the casting exercise, he and Levinson had promised NBC they'd find an obligatory hunk. Munch was the last character to be cast, and they still had no hunk. Unaffected by network preferences, they went with Belzer nonetheless.

How could anyone as handsome as a Priestley pull off the responsibility of being cynicism's spokesman in the ultimate cynic's lair? How could anyone so young project the wry gleam that beams through Belzer's rakishly tinted glasses? Or master the off-kilter smile, the slightly askew arch of the eyebrows that communicates his bemusement at every situation? No, nobody but Belzer could be Munch. And without Munch, an essential ingredient would be missing from the squad room. Nobody else could hop on stage on karaoke night and belt out a better ''Mack the Knife'' than he did in a first-year episode. He's the counter-cop. An unrepentant, unapologetic, perhaps unre-formed child of the '60s (when he agreed to allow squad videographer J.H. Brodie to stay at his apartment, he warned him *not* to look in the medicine cabinet). His philosophy, as he explains to Meldrick, is that life is essentially an ironic experience. What is the ultimate irony for someone so anti-establishment? To become a police officer, of course. Only once has he had cause to rue his past: when an ex-girlfriend had an exhibition of her photography at a gallery across the street from headquarters. A larger-than-life wall hanging showed a much younger, longer-haired Munch in all his un-adorned glory.

Belzer is a veteran of the comedy-club circuit, having played legendary places like Caroline's, the Improv, and Catch a Rising Star, and, undoubtedly, a lot of places he'd rather not list on his bio. He was in the off-Broadway production of *The National Lampoon Show* with Bill Murray, Gilda Radner, and John Belushi. He's appeared on all the prime late-night TV shows: *The Tonight Show*, *Late Night with David Letterman*, *Late Night with Conan O'Brien*, *Later*, and *Saturday Night Live*. He hosted his own six-part comedy series on Cinemax, *The Richard Belzer Show*. Last year he did an HBO special, *Another Lone Nut*. And he wrote a book about comedy, *How To Be a Stand-up Comic*. His film credits include several dramatic features — *Scarface*, *Bonfire of the Vanities*, *The Puppet Masters*, *Get on the Bus*, and *Girl 6*. Notwithstanding all his film and television

The original cast (from left to right): Richard Belzer, Ned Beatty, Andre Braugher, Jon Polito, Clark Johnson, Daniel Baldwin, Yaphet Kotto, and Melissa Leo. Kyle Secor kneels in the foreground.

Above: Life imitates art imitates life: Reed Diamond, Clark Johnson, Max Perlich, and executive producer and director Barry Levinson look on as a real criminal fleeing real Baltimore police appears on the set.

Below: Kyle Secor and Andre Braugher on the set.

John Munch (Richard Belzer) had a slavish compulsion
for approval from partner Stanley Bolander (Ned Beatty).

Above: Pembleton in the box has always been *Homicide*'s go-to move. Here he tangles with the icy Gordon Pratt (Steve Buscemi), a suspect in the shooting of three detectives.

Below: Tom Fontana: "Pembleton and Bayliss are the greatest love story in television history."

Above: Munch comforts Robert Ellison (Robin Williams), whose wife was shot during a holdup. Williams was nominated for an Emmy in this part.

Below: Reed Diamond reviews a scene with Kathy Bates, who directed the episode entitled "Scene of the Crime."

Above: The Board: Andre Braugher, Jon Polito, Clark Johnson, and Daniel Baldwin consider the tally of open (red) and closed (black) cases.

Below: Peter Gerety, Callie Thorne, Michelle Forbes.

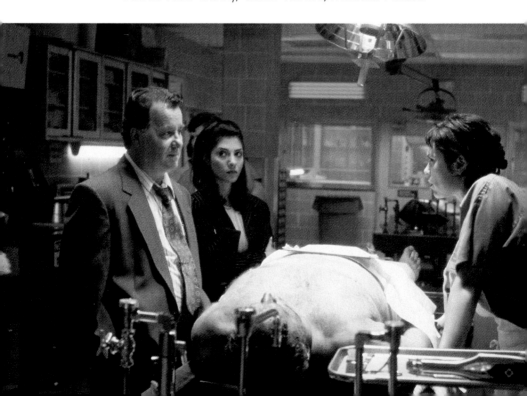

Meldrick Lewis (Clark Johnson) and Mike Kellerman (Reed Diamond) confront druglord Luther Mahoney (Erik Todd Delums).

The Season Six cast (from left to right): Callie Thorne, Kyle Secor, Peter Gerety, Andre Braugher, Yaphet Kotto, Michelle Forbes, Reed Diamond, Richard Belzer, and Clark Johnson. Jon Seda crouches in the foreground.

work, he was invited to audition for *Homicide* because Levinson had heard him doing bits on Howard Stern's radio show.

Who is Munch in relation to Belzer?

"He's pretty close to how I'd be as a cop," he laughs. "I don't have to sit in my trailer for an hour trying to dredge him up before I can come out and perform."

Did he ever think of becoming a cop?

Again he laughs. "You know, I did a ride-along with the Baltimore cops when I got here. I was always afraid."

Wire-thin, packing more muscle in his wit than his body, Munch looks nothing like our image of a cop. His shoulders are barely wide enough to hold up his holster, for heaven's sake. But, he pulls it off, using attitude and sardonic repartee. It's hard to imagine him as a fight-busting uniform — when a fight erupts at the Waterfront, he's the first to hit the floor behind the bar — but he can launch invective blow-for-blow with anyone. A debut episode suspect had no idea what hit him when Munch bellowed, "Don't you lie to me like I'm Montel Williams. *I am not Montel Williams, do you understand?* . . . What, are you saving the good lies for some smarter cop?" (Montel was singled out from a multitude of mediocre trash talk-show hosts because he's the only one from Baltimore.)

There aren't great unplumbed depths to Munch, which doesn't mean he isn't a complex character. He pretty well wears his heart on his sleeve. Until Ned Beatty left the series after three seasons, he was partnered with Bolander. He never hid his unrequited affection for the older detective, nor his puppy-dog desire for the Big Man's approval. After Stan was shot, Munch spent every possible hour by his bedside. He was consumed only with seeing his friend through his recovery. When Stan got out of the hospital and was beset by insomnia, night terrors, and loneliness and wanted a friend to stay with, he turned up at Munch's door, and it was Munch who appeared grateful for the companionship.

When Bolander was off on suspension, Munch called often, only to speak with an answering machine and never to have his calls returned. He invited Bolander to the Waterfront, but

Stan would never show up. He couldn't understand why his efforts to foster an intimate relationship were never reciprocated.

In reality, Belzer says he thrived on the opportunity to work with a man of Beatty's caliber, claiming, "I'm still not over Ned's leaving. I never learned so much as by just being around such a gifted actor. He was tremendously generous, and really expedited my own abilities as an actor."

When Frank returned from his stroke, only Munch refused to treat him as an invalid. He seemed unnecessarily harsh, complaining that if *he* had been stricken, no special effort would have been made to keep him in homicide upon his return. Eventually, it comes out that he had called Frank several times during his absence to check up, but none of his calls were ever returned. Frank says, sheepishly, that he didn't think it mattered whether he called back or not. But John is clearly hurt not to have been permitted to do anything to help Frank through his convalescence.

And let's not forget how Munch is perpetually lovelorn. There were his two divorces, the never seen but oft-discussed Felicia, medical examiner Alyssa Dyer, and any number of other relationships to regret. When he and Dyer seem to be on the brink of something real, with Munch glowing at the thought of having found true love, he arrives at her apartment early for a date and promptly sacks her roommate.

"Oooooohhhhhh," he moans as he struggles to button his shirt, "I am a weak, weak man."

He'll tell Dyer about his lapse and she'll blacken his eye, convincing him that this is a woman worth fighting for. But they would go nowhere together. An inside joke has Dyer confiding to Cox that the experience of dating Munch moved her to swear off cops. Instead, she said, she was dating a stand-up comic.

In "Kaddish," he was conveyed back to his youth when Helen Rosenthal, on whom he'd had a crush in high school, was murdered. The essence of this story was not the crime, but the distance traveled from our youth and those things lost along the way; also those things gained. Munch had been an awkward, nerdy teen, the kind easily bullied in the schoolyard. He blames those attributes for his failure to win her affections. Just maybe it was what he so desperately wanted to shed that drove him to become a police officer. Helen still lived in Pikesville, where they had grown up. Interviewing her acquaintances, he sees people he had known in his youth, which reminds him of who he had been, of the inadequacies of his adolescence. Everyone has a Helen Rosenthal in their past.

"We get older. We forget who we used to be. What we used to believe in," he says with regret for all that's past.

His youth was similarly recalled in "Full Court Press," when he and Gharty investigated the killing of a star high school basketball player. On the surface, the victim was the quintessence of the all-American kid. A deeper look revealed that he was a cruel bully and his death was the result of pushing a weaker kid so far that he felt he had no recourse but to ensure an absolute end to the torment. Munch felt a close affinity with the killer and nearly came to blows with Gharty when he admitted that he'd been a bully as a kid because that's what kids do.

Rarely do inept teens fully get over their ineptitude. They forever carry a certain clumsiness which, in adulthood, can imbue them with a degree of charm. But there's always some remnant that kids can sniff out the way a dog senses fear. In *Homicide*'s twisted take on the annual Christmas show in 1994 ("All Through the House"), Stanley abandons Munch with the son of a murdered street-corner Santa Claus while he fetches someone from child welfare. They put off breaking the news about his father for the social services people. Munch has no idea how to talk to the boy, Fidel, a name Munch might select were he to have a son of his own. When he balks at watching schlock horror movies, Fidel insists on going to a nearby bar/ amusement center where his father is well-known. Reluctantly, John takes him. Fidel insists that Munch take some swings in a batting cage, bragging about his father's baseball skills. Munch is pathetic; his swing would be awful if he were a ten-year-old girl, let alone a grown man. When Fidel ridicules him, all the anger stored up from boyhood pours out. All the abuse he thought he had outgrown has really only been lying in wait for another opportunity to knife through his self-esteem. He would feel the same hurt during the Rosenthal investigation when questioning the bully from his youth. Only, in this instance, he would have the satisfaction of letting him know that he had gone on to become a murder police and had risen above being intimidated. When his tormentor is a child, he has no such ammunition.

Belzer has displayed an excellent touch with Munch. He plays the class clown without being clownish. He's the lyric of a country song played to a sultry jazz beat sung by Leonard Cohen. In every silver lining he can spot the cloud. His expectations of humankind are too low for him to be beaten up by a case. People surprise him when they tell the truth, not when they lie. In his heart of hearts he expects to cheat on his women, the women to leave him, and people to kill each other without reason. Life isn't melodrama, it's tragicomedy. Anything else upsets the cosmic balance.

STANLEY BOLANDER

Stanley is the veteran of the squad, chugging away toward his twenty-five-year pension. Burdened by the loss of his marriage and heavy alimony payments, he admits to having little in his life other than the job. And the job is a hard mistress, demanding far more than it willingly gives in return. It never allows itself to be taken for granted. At every turn, it threatens to let him down and cause self-doubt. Take, for instance, "In Search of Crimes Past" (season three). Bolander is confronted with the prospect of having consigned the wrong man to death row sixteen years earlier. On the eve of his execution, the man's daughter takes Colonel Barnfather hostage and demands the investigation be reopened. When Stan determines that he did, in fact, lock up the wrong man, he begins to doubt the instincts and experience upon which he's come to depend. If he had ever been in jeopardy of succumbing to complacency, this was a wake-up call. In order to get the answers he needs, the detective has to ask the right questions.

Stan's relationship with Munch was one of endless strife. Bolander wouldn't hear of mellowing and letting Munch close enough for something approaching intimacy to develop between them. Not only did he berate Munch, but he assured him that the only man he had ever considered his partner was Mitch Drummond (Tony LoBianco). During the hunt for the shooter of Stan and the other detectives, Mitch, then posted with the bomb squad, volunteered to pitch in and is paired with Munch. Truth be told, he and Stan had fought constantly while working together.

Bolander glided from understanding father figure to no-nonsense disciplinarian when interrogating suspects. He managed to project parental disappointment toward offenders who had probably never had a parent express that much interest. Any of the other detectives might trick you or wear you down, but it was in Bolander you'd most likely confide.

Of all the characters, he was probably most different off the job from on. After his divorce he was reduced to living in what he referred to as "a second-rate building in a third-rate neighborhood." His essence was his solitude. On the job he understood how to behave, how to react to events. Off the job he was all fumbling uncertainty and insecurities, most of which stemmed from his world being turned upside down by his wife's sudden decision to leave him. A confident detective, he was reduced to quivering timidity by Dr. Blythe before, during, and following their dates. He was in much the same state when sharing his love of the cello with Linda, the much younger woman he saw for a short time.

His departure after three seasons left a real void. Without him and Polito, there was no elder statesman, only the superior officer, Giardello. If the latter is like the team's coach, the former were seasoned team leaders, equal to the other players, only with vast reserves of experience upon which to draw. The Big Man brought a certain steadiness to the squad. When Giardello was upset over something, none of the younger men would dare knock on his door and encourage him to talk, or bring him an unwanted sandwich and insist on picnicking on his desk as a means of coaxing him out of his funk. No one

— not Russert or Gaffney as captains, or Howard as sergeant
— has been able to talk to him the way Stan could. There was
a nice quality to having such a veteran presence.

Ned Beatty is a tremendously versatile character actor. On the
big screen he has done everything from heavy drama (*Just
Cause, The Big Easy, Deliverance*) to lighter fare (*Rudy, Hear
My Song, Nashville*). He has also starred in countless made-
for-TV movies and enjoyed a recurring role on *Roseanne* as the
father of Dan Connor (John Goodman). The rumors that
swirled at the time of his departure were that he was not happy
being sequestered in Baltimore for a substantial part of the year.

Having been shot once, Stanley couldn't very well suffer the
same fate again only a few months later. Some more imaginative exit had to be found for the character. Sometimes the
search requires no more than reading the newspaper. During
the show's hiatus of 1995 there had been a police convention
in Washington at which some of the participants had allegedly
rampaged through the hotel committing acts of vandalism and
gross indecency. Bolander — along with Beau Felton — was
simply written into that scenario. Feeling that it might be good
for their recovery after being shot, Giardello sent them off to
the convention. Stan's last act as a policeman was to be seen
running down the hotel corridor with his pants down around
his ankles. The result of their participation was a twenty-two-
week (the number of episodes in a full TV season) suspension.
Stan would quietly retire after serving out his punishment.

BEAU FELTON

At his best, Beau Felton wasn't much of a police officer. He
was sloppy, unimaginative, more plodding than persistent. In
other words, in a big police force, he was like a lot of the cops.
And he was one of those poor performers who somehow — to
the surprise of everyone, not least of all themselves — manage
to make it into an elite unit. To this poor kid from the lower-
working-class streets of South Baltimore, just getting into the
department signaled unexpected success. To be in homicide

was more than he might ever have dreamed. It also proved the bureaucratic axiom that everyone rises one level above their capabilities.

Daniel Baldwin — of the Baldwin brothers movie dynasty — was very good at playing a man who knew he was overmatched and was just short of terrified that someone else might find out. Whatever his shortcomings, Beau wasn't lacking in self-awareness. Marital problems were an ongoing preoccupation. Like so many married people, he acted more out of fear that things were passing him by than any particular grievance with his wife. He had married young to a girl from Boring (the name of a real town in Maryland). He was growing curious about all that was outside his limited experience. His wife eventually left him, taking their two children, and he spent most of his working hours tracing their whereabouts. The rest of his hours passed by in a bourbon-induced haze. Or with his mistress, Russert. When his wife first threw him out of their house, Howard asked him where he was staying. With a friend, he replied. She asked whether this friend was a man or a woman. He came back, "My father always told me never to jump ship without a life raft."

Not the most enlightened of men, Felton's attitude toward African Americans was shaped by the perceptions gained from police work, a warped perspective at the best of times. Police only come in contact with a small percentage of the population, even in high-crime areas. A fact that's easy to forget when everyone you encounter is of an easily identifiable group.

"For an idea to be sustainable, the character has to learn something," offers Clark Johnson. "Felton was a redneck cop, but it was never really taken anywhere."

Felton tried to explain to Pembleton that not everything boiled down to race. True enough, but whatever it boils down to may be rooted in race.

Felton was the least badly wounded of the three detectives who were shot, and was the first back to work. Seeing spilled blood after having his own brush with death was not easy. He was further troubled by the irrevocable destruction of his marriage and the collapse of his affair with Russert. Sickened at the scene of his first murder, and frustrated at his own reaction, Felton makes the huge mistake of propelling a soda can in Giardello's direction. Gee reams into him, "I'm sick of covering for you. . . . Your marriage has been falling apart as long as anybody can remember. You come to work looking as if you'd crawled through every bar in Baltimore. . . . You weren't up to the job before you were shot. That's the point. That's the truth. It's time someone told you." A pretty fair summary of Felton's career.

In any event, his return to the unit would be short-lived. Following three years on *Homicide*, Baldwin reportedly aspired to pursue his career in movies and had lost interest in being tied to the rigors of a weekly series and its eight or so months of shooting. He had landed supporting roles in a number of big-screen movies (*Harley Davidson and the Marlboro Man, Car 54, Where Are You?, Mulholland Falls, Trees Lounge*) and TV productions (*Heroes of Desert Storm, Attack of the 50 Foot Woman, Family of Cops, Twisted Desire*).

He was written out with Bolander, suspended as a result of hijinks at the police convention. This finished him off in body, but not in spirit. Once his suspension had been served, no one seemed to know what became of him. Then, in the concluding episodes of season five ("Partners and Other Strangers," "Strangers and Other Partners"), an apparent suicide, whose face had been obliterated by a shotgun blast, was identified as Beau. Closer investigation would prove that he had been murdered. In fact, he hadn't left the force, as everyone, including Giardello, had been led to believe. He was actually working an undercover operation on behalf of Internal Investigations. They were looking into whether cops were in collusion with a major auto theft ring. Someone had apparently found out that Felton was still a cop and effected his execution.

This incident provided an opportunity for Isabella Hofmann to make a guest appearance as Russert. It also allowed for the introduction of two characters who would remain with the cast for the following season. Gharty, last seen as the timid uniform who hesitated to answer a potentially dangerous call, was the Internal detective running Felton. Paul Falsone was an auto-squad detective with an informant inside the ring.

Baldwin experienced rough times when, on February 2, 1998, he was found in a drug-crazed state in New York's Plaza Hotel. He was rushed to hospital in critical condition, suffering from a cocaine overdose. Though his medical condition improved rapidly, upon release from hospital, he was greeted with a criminal charge for disorderly conduct. In the end, he received a conditional discharge stipulating that his record will be wiped clean provided he stays out of trouble for a year and continues with drug rehab. He was, however, dismissed from *It Had To Be You*, the film on which he had been working.

PAUL FALSONE, STU GHARTY, LAURA BALLARD

To conclude season five, Giardello announced to the troops that the commissioner had decided to rotate officers around the department, as had the real commissioner several years earlier. This foreshadowed significant cast changes for season six. Howard left and three new detectives — Paul Falsone, Stu Gharty, and Laura Ballard — came on board. Gharty is an old veteran; Ballard is a transplanted homicide detective from Seattle. Only Falsone feels the need to prove himself good enough for homicide.

As for proving himself as an actor, where there is no such thing as a true overnight success, Jon Seda is about as close as you can get. In only eight years in the profession, he's appeared in fourteen movies. His big break came as a result of his talent in a completely different arena, boxing. He was runner-up in the New Jersey Gold Gloves when he won a part in the boxing film *Gladiator*. He's been working steadily ever since, including roles in *12 Monkeys*, *Primal Fear*, *Carlito's Way*, and *Selena*. He was nominated for a prestigious Palme d'Or at the 1996 Cannes Film Festival for his part in Michael Cimino's *Sunchaser*. Seda was cast by Levinson and Fontana in the premier episode of their HBO prison series *Oz*, and subsequently brought to *Homicide*, his first regular TV experience.

He admits that fear of being stereotyped is a reason to stay away from television, but intends to continue doing diverse work.

Trying to fit in with an already well-established cast must be fairly intimidating.

Seda, very outgoing and friendly, easily joking with cast and crew between takes, replies, "You can't help but feel like an outsider, because they have such a warm family feeling here. It's like you're afraid to disrupt the flow. But all of that quickly dissipated when I was accepted with open arms."

He had met with members of Baltimore PD's auto squad the previous year when preparing for Falsone's introduction. He deliberately did not talk with any of the homicide cops because he wanted to bring Falsone into the job completely fresh. "I didn't want to know anything about homicide because Falsone didn't know anything. I wanted it all to come to me on the job, the way it would for him."

The three newcomers are all going to commence from the outside looking in. Falsone is paired with Lewis. The first time we see them out together, they are on the receiving end of Junior Bunk's bullets. This motivates Falsone to look into the circumstances behind Luther's death. He starts asking a lot of disconcerting questions. More than that, he goads Mike with his suspicion that something about the shooting is being covered up. In an improbable scene, the two detectives get into a scuffle in a headquarters corridor and end up drawing on each other. They only retreat when someone else comes down the hall.

It's apparent that Seda was being groomed through what was a transitional season to assume a prominent role when *Homicide* begins its seventh season. Falsone was the primary on several cases, including the murder of a teenage model (an episode that crossed over onto *Law and Order*, involving the casts of both shows), the abduction of a little boy from an Inner Harbor playground, and the mauling of an old man by his grandson's pit bulls. Elements of his personal life came into play as he fought for custody of his five-year-old son.

Ballard can boast experience, but no history with her Baltimore counterparts. What she might have done elsewhere holds little weight in Charm City. She is already in homicide when we pick up in season six, and Pembleton and Bayliss are returning from a stint in robbery. She questions Pembleton's presupposition that the Wilson family, prominent members of the black community well-known for their philanthropic work, are not responsible for the death of their Haitian domestic, found dead in the men's room of a luxury hotel during a dinner held in Felix Wilson's (James Earl Jones) honor ("Blood Ties"). Pembleton doesn't appreciate being doubted by anyone, least of all someone he has no reason to take seriously and who has no grasp of what the Wilsons have contributed to the city. After it comes to light that it was, in fact, Felix's son who murdered the girl, he concedes that he shouldn't have been so quick to presume their innocence.

Callie Thorne is probably best recognized for her role in *Turbulence*. Her other film credits include *Ed's Next Move*, *Next Stop Wonderland*, and *Casanova Falling*. She has appeared on the New York stage with the Naked Angels and Malaparte Theater Company troupes.

Peter Gerety's career has been principally on the stage, on and off Broadway and with the respected Trinity Repertory Company of Providence, Rhode Island. He won the 1983 Boston Critics Award for Best Actor for *Billy Bishop Goes to War*. He has appeared in several films (*Wolf, Magic Hour, Montana, Surviving Picasso*) and TV series (*Law and Order, Public Morals, Central Park West, Return to Lonesome Dove*).

His initial appearance on *Homicide* was superb. He imbued Gharty with a humanity that made his fears both realistic and compelling. He begged you to ask the question, at what point do we understand that a human being will place his own safety at the forefront of every other consideration? How much bravery have we purchased for $35,000 a year plus benefits?

Now assigned to homicide, Gharty carries with him bitterness. During the "Blood Ties" investigation, he is very vocal about how much influence the black community of a majority-black city has in a black-led City Hall that runs an increasingly black police department. He more than implies that blacks will be appeased for political expediency. In speaking to Ballard, with whom he is partnered, he accuses Giardello and Pembleton of colluding with the black power structure to protect the Wilsons from a thorough investigation. He is now the oldest officer in homicide, but lacks the credentials to be an elder statesman.

There was an imbalance in season six, as writers struggled to develop new characters and carve out a place for them amid those already established. Adding three new detectives at one time was bold, and created a new dynamic, one that has taken time to solidify. In addition to the new characters, the certainty that Andre Braugher was in his final year, and the possibility the series might be facing termination posed some real problems. Fontana wanted to bring *Homicide* to some conclusion if it was not to be renewed. However, he faced having to write an ending with little advance notice of cancellation. Bets had to be hedged. If it was to continue, the new cast members would carry *Homicide*'s future.

As a result, for example, the mid-season two-hour episode "Something Sacred," about the murder of two priests, concentrated on Gharty. That he was a church-going former altar boy was a key factor in his indignity over the murder of holy men. In the past, it would have been the fallen Pembleton who would have handled such a morally charged case. His part is significant, in that he is called upon to show Roc-Roc, the corner-boy suspect, the true finality of death and the possibilities of life. Ultimately, it is Frank who leads the boy into informing on those in his crew who had done the killings. But, it is the Gharty character that is explored comparably — though not as thoroughly — as Frank's had been in the sequence where Catholic women were hunted by a serial killer.

The cases in season six tended to be more episodic, except for the ongoing Mahoney affair. There was a feeling that certain points had to be made for the purpose of character development, and that the characters could be taken more for granted than in the past. Entering its seventh season, *Homicide* will likely play less to the uncertainty of its fate and feel more confident with its existing cast.

J.H. BRODIE

The short-lived career of J.H. Brodie, the sad sack, marble-mouthed videographer, was another effort to provide a different insight to the workings of the homicide unit. His entire tenure was spent on the outside looking in. Max Perlich (whose filmography includes *Beautiful Girls*, *Rush*, *Drugstore Cowboy*, and *Feeling Minnesota*) brought youth, naïveté, and the occasional surprisingly revelatory flash to the role. For instance, he was the only person in the squad room to pick up that Frank had ceased to take his blood-pressure medication following his stroke. The medication makes it difficult to concentrate and was thus impeding Pembleton's ability to pass the firearms exam that was required before he'd be permitted to return to active investigations. Because his mother had suffered a stroke, Brodie recognized the point at which Frank was better able to focus.

After Brodie was evicted from his apartment, Munch took pity and offered him a place to stay. He soon tired of Brodie's presence and withdrew the offer. This, then, provided a convenient vehicle through which the home life of several detectives could be glimpsed, as he was taken in, in turn, by Bayliss, Lewis, and Kellerman. Not a whole lot was revealed, save that Tim enjoyed watching *Mighty Mouse* in his pajamas while scarfing pizza and Meldrick fought with his wife over an awful velvet print of Teddy Pendergrast that he insisted be hung in plain view in the dining room.

Making his first appearance during season four, Brodie was a film student and TV news cameraman. In "Autofocus," he made it to the scene where an old lady had been shot at a bus stop before the police and may have captured the killers on tape. Though his producer forbids him from taking his film to the police, and the police are reluctant to listen to him, he finally persuades Meldrick and Kellerman to look at what he has. Sure enough, it proves integral to their efforts to identify the killers (the Douglas cousins, who made it easy on the prosecutor by shooting their own video of the murder). For his trouble, Brodie loses his job. The police take pity and hire him to film crime scenes and interrogations. For season five, he would be added to the cast, only to be dropped the following year.

He was given one opportunity to play sleuth during his last season, in "Valentine's Day." He suspected classmate Alan Schack (Neil Patrick Harris) of murder in the case of Nick Bolaentera, which Munch was prepared to write off as a suicide. Schack (who would have thought Doogie Howser could be so convincingly tough?) was a campus dealer and Bolaentera was found all coked out in his apartment. After taking a beating for his snooping around, Brodie comes up with an ingenious way to nail Schack. With some creative editing, he films Schack entering his apartment and inserts the sound of a gunshot. Schack is brought in for questioning and told the film is a narcotics surveillance tape from the day of Bolaentera's death. It appears to prove he was present when Bolaentera died. Schack admits he had induced the other into playing Russian roulette, but had handed him a gun with all six chambers loaded. Bolaentera had been snorting up too much of the profits from drugs he was supposed to be moving for Schack.

"The Documentary" was the on-screen excuse for Brodie's departure. The film he made about the homicide unit and sold to PBS won an Emmy. This news was greeted with the derisive comment, "They'll give one of those to anyone." Emmy winners don't slog out to record crime scenes, and he was summarily dispatched to Hollywood.

F I V E

I S S U E S

VIOLENCE

Murder is a momentary outburst, not really all that interesting in and of itself. Viewers have witnessed it so often and in so many variations that they can sleepwalk through most violence. And most directors can and do likewise. Sure, they throw in the odd novelty: a head exploding like a watermelon when struck by a bullet, an ax, or meat-hook instead of a mere knife, a killer who likes to peel the skin off the corpse. These make us take notice, but they don't require any great thought. But when plots are propelled by dialogue or the psychology of a character, we have to pay attention. After the spasm of violence, what is to be done? What was the impact of this murder? What's running through the killer's mind? Who is grieving for the victim? Where do the police begin their search? The consequences — how it affects people and how people cope — are what make murder interesting.

"I want to know what happens after the body hits the pavement and people have to begin thinking about what's happened," David Simon tells me. "Everything else is just cops and robbers."

No episode looked at the consequences of violence more intensely than "The Subway" (season six). It's an axiom that the victim is an inanimate object by the time the murder police get to the scene. They see the dead, but they don't watch the death. They may speak *for* the dead, but they don't speak *with* the dead. In this particular case, the dead man, John Lange (Vincent D'Onofrio), has been pushed into an oncoming subway, ending up pinned between the train and the platform. That pressure is the only thing keeping his insides from spilling out. He will die the instant the pressure is eased. Everyone is aware he will die. It's only a matter of time before emergency personnel can ready the train so that he can be freed. Pembleton stays with him, first finding out about his next of kin, then getting his account of what happened, finally contemplating the vicissitudes of fate that see a man randomly selected to die violently and purposelessly while doing something as mundane as catching a subway to work in the morning. In contrast with Frank's task, Bayliss has the comfortable chore of questioning Larry Biedran, who, he finds out, had been confined to a mental hospital for shoving someone in front of a subway in Chicago.

"It's not every day you talk to a dead man," Lange chides Frank. No, indeed. Nor is it every drama that has you watch a man die. This isn't the clean, instantaneous, bloodless gunshot death that TV has invented. This is death as full-blown agony and terror and sorrow. James Yoshimura's script is nothing short of brilliant. D'Onofrio is utterly convincing as a man aware he is about to die. And Braugher is incredible, sustaining throughout the look of a man who has no clue what to say next. Gary Fleder's direction holds the tension mesmerizingly in a static situation. More than any other episode, "The Subway" slams home the sometimes forgotten fact that homicide means a person has died.

Investigators accumulate information. Nowhere in the job description does it say anything about action. From Simon's *Homicide*:

> Television has given us the myth of the raging pursuit, the high-speed chase, but in truth there is no such thing; if there were, God knows the Cavalier would throw a rod after a dozen blocks and you'd be writing a Form 95 in which you respectfully submit to your commanding officer

the reasons why you drove a city-owned four-cylinder wonder into an early grave. And there are no fistfights or running gun battles: The glory days of thumping someone on a domestic call or letting a round or two fly in the heat of some gas station holdup ended when you came downtown from patrol. The murder police always get there after the bodies fall, and a homicide detective leaving the office has to remind himself to take his .38 out of the top right desk drawer. Following from this, *Homicide* the series has been more about the consequences of murder than anything else.

A little more than midway through season three, detectives Howard, Felton, Bolander, and Munch were shot at as they knocked on an apartment door to serve a warrant. All except Munch were hit. Howard and Bolander were gravely wounded, Felton less so. Over the course of three episodes, their recovery was held in doubt. This was the first instance in which the detectives had faced direct physical danger, and it was played out right in front of viewers. The earlier incident of a police shooting — when Thormann was blinded — had happened off-screen, so this sequence represented a substantial departure for *Homicide*.

The decision to move in this direction had as much to do with where the series stood with the network at the time as with anything else. *Homicide* was locked in its perpetual struggle to stay on the air; NBC had only committed to 13 episodes, half a TV season. Part one, "The City that Bleeds," was the twelfth episode. Part two, "Dead End," saw the arrest of the suspect the police had originally sought. However, it turns out he hadn't been responsible. A review of the circumstances leading up to the shooting revealed that a clerical error had resulted in the wrong apartment number appearing on the warrant. They then went after Gordon Pratt, the tenant of the apartment to which the detectives had mistakenly gone (part three, "End Game"). This third episode was the first of the new network pact that had *Homicide* completing the season. Hence, all three victims recovered.

Of this plot direction, Levinson says, "We figured — just in case — we'd go out in a blaze of glory in the thirteenth episode by shooting our cast members."

Fontana was initially uncomfortable with introducing such explicit violence, in the event that they were renewed and would have to continue from that point. "Those who favored this course were convinced that it would create an emotional wellspring in which all the characters would be able to participate and from which we'd learn new things about them," he recalls. He ended up agreeing that the possibilities were interesting.

Although he liked the episodes at the time, in retrospect Braugher has mixed feelings about the direction they presaged. "We were sinking neigh unto death when they were shot, and suddenly we got a spike in the ratings. Now we're shooting people every week."

This has been the predicament Homicide has confronted since its inception. In Braugher's words: "If we do what we do, we suffer in the ratings. But I wish we'd just do what we do. Unfortunately our art is part of a business. We have to compromise."

Violence again befell the cast in the second part of "Fallen Heroes," with Bayliss taking a bullet in the course of a running gun battle. Season six concluded with a cliffhanger: Tim lying unconscious in a hospital bed, his recovery not to be determined until the following year.

The question begged: Is violence a necessary selling point for cop shows?

I asked Joseph Wambaugh why he thinks people are fascinated with cops. He denied that this is the case.

"Police work isn't fascinating, per se," he argues. "It's just a convenient outlet for comic-book action, a succession of chase scenes and shoot-ups."

Indeed, ratings make his point tough to refute.

There are two ways of showing violence. That which is favored: stylized and sanitized to the point where it has no visceral impact, where it's made to look as if bullets and blades hardly cause a person to bleed and death is little more than momentary discomfort before sleep. Or, in the fullness of its horror, depicting the massive spillage of blood, the nauseatingly ragged holes left in the body, the ugliness of reflexive vomiting and defecation. Most people find it easier to watch an hour of the carefully choreographed mayhem of a *Miami Vice*, for example, than five minutes of a surgical procedure on The Learning Channel. That's because the former is so blatantly false. If violence is shown from a premise of truth, it is very difficult for most people to watch.

Only cartoonish violence can be used for escapism. Real violence is disturbing; it forces a reaction out of viewers. They must make a conscious decision whether to continue watching or turn away. In either event, it calls for participation that goes beyond mindless gawking. Obviously, there are limitations to how much you want to have shown on television. But let's take an extreme example. No one could possibly accuse the film *Henry: Portrait of a Serial Killer* of glorifying or glamorizing violence. Directed, co-written, and co-produced by John McNaughton, who has directed several episodes of *Homicide*, *Henry* is a savage, chilling, and ultimately disturbing look at the dingy life of a man who casually and voluminously kills for no discernible reason. It is seasick graphic. No matter how many thousands of carefully choreographed TV murders you may have seen, you'll wince at *Henry*. McNaughton's spare, unintrusive style is the reason. You never feel as though there's a protective layer of celluloid between yourself and *Henry*. Compare that with Oliver Stone's more commercial *Natural Born Killers*, with its music-video camera work that reminds you at every cinematic turn you're just watching a movie. That alone makes the violence artificial and, thus, easier to watch and stomach.

"If we're going to show violence on TV, it should be done realistically, in such a way as to affect people," offers Michelle Forbes. "Violence is only gratuitous when it is desensitized, when we make it easy to watch. Close-up, violence is disturbing and will impact on how people react."

Homicide, where it has shown violence, has never made it

easy to look at. When the detectives were shot, you saw the terror, the confusion, the blood gushing profusely from their bodies. With Bayliss, we got a tight close-up of the hole the bullet tore in him. In other instances, you've seen bodies, cut and stabbed, lying in thick pools of coagulated blood. In the cases of the three little girls whose murders haunt Bayliss, you were given close-ups of their lifeless faces, grim recognition that these were human beings that had been destroyed.

"I have a problem when violence is used to tell the story," Levinson states. "It's too easy. I mean, look at *Tin Men*. There are far more salesmen in America than there are killers, but how many movies are there about them? What we deal with, in any story, is human behavior."

Violence is only one part of human behavior, albeit an important one when the story you're telling is of murder police. But, it's only one element of the story. Television is a master illusionist and perhaps its most unreal illusion has been to fool us into thinking that violence is pretty.

INTERROGATION

The verbal and psychological dexterity at the heart of interrogation is the life's blood of *Homicide*. While most cop shows would have it that cases sink or swim on the basis of the car chase and the gunfight, *Homicide* knows that talk is what brings resolution. It's in the interrogation room that the real dramatic action of an investigation plays out. Not only have most episodes revolved around a pivotal confrontation between detective and suspect, but the show used the vehicle of a documentary filmed by Brodie to explore the complex nature of the interrogation as investigative technique. During the quiet of New Year's Eve 1997, Brodie shows the squad the film he has made of their work, *Back Page News: Life and Homicide on the Mean Streets of Baltimore*. Part of the narrative has the detectives quoting a lengthy passage from Simon's *Homicide*, where the author ruminates on the joust when detective and suspect face each other in the box. Most likely, it is here that a case will be made to fly, or deflate like a pricked balloon. The stakes are immense: an individual's freedom.

The greatness of the American Constitution is the protection it accords the citizenry against the legislature and the judiciary. This applies to everyone, equally, without exception. Whatever sociopathic crime you may stand accused of, you are still a member of this society in good standing, deserving of all its rights and privileges. The Fifth Amendment to the Constitution guarantees you the option of not incriminating yourself. In other words, in the event that you are suspected in a criminal matter, you may assert your right to remain silent in the face of a police detective who wants very badly to have a chat with you. Furthermore, you have the right to consult with an attorney and to have that attorney present for all legal proceedings. This attorney, trained in the minutiae and nuance of the law, will work solely on your behalf in the interest of seeing that you get the best outcome the evidence will allow. To make it even easier, if you can't afford to assemble your own dream team of legal experts, a public defender will be at your service free of charge. You might not get Johnnie Cochrane, but you'll get someone who passed the bar. And none of this is a secret. Before you will be asked a single question, the detective will tell you all about these rights. Not only that, he'll give you a piece of paper on which they're all spelled out explicitly and ask you to read each one. Then he'll ask that you tack your initial beside each right, certifying that it's been drawn to your attention and that you fully understand what it means. Could anything be clearer? *You do not have to speak with the police upon being arrested.*

For all of that, the interrogation is the cornerstone of any investigation. Regardless of the conclusiveness of physical evidence, a smart lawyer can often insert some itch of reasonable doubt in the back of the mind of one of 12 jurors. Didn't anybody learn anything from the O.J. Simpson trial? So long as the suspect hasn't done anything stupid like confessing, there's reason for optimism. However, there's not much an advocate can do in the face of a confession freely given.

So, here you are in an interrogation room with a detective.

Your rights have been carefully explained. The police are straight up about advising suspects of their rights. Failure to do so is a sure way to have a confession ruled inadmissible and an entire body of evidence called into question in the minds of jurors. Now, maybe you're no brain surgeon — you have, after all, been caught for your alleged crime — but that doesn't mean you're brain-dead. If you've been given a right, logic suggests it's probably in your best interest to exercise it. Chances are your knowledge of the law doesn't extend to all the fine points and loopholes that could get you out of this jam. And the detective isn't going to tell you how weak a case he has without your cooperation. Only that lawyer you've been promised is going to help you out. Shouldn't you ask for that legal expert and wait for professional counsel before deciding what it would be in your interest to say to the detective?

Well, the detective wants you to know that invoking your rights might not be the best course of action. Once you decline to talk, he's got no alternative but to charge you and lock you up until your attorney arrives. He won't be able to give you the opportunity to tell your side of the story, to explain why you did the killing. Without your statement, all the prosecutor gets is the cold evidence that places all the blame on you. But if there were any extenuating circumstances, this is the time to get it all down on paper so the prosecution has at its disposal the most accurate picture of exactly what happened. Therefore, it really may be to your advantage to speak now, before some lawyer interferes and stops you from telling the truth about the incident. Silence may be your right, but it's gonna get you locked up here and now.

The detective's only ploy for extracting meaningful information from suspects is to convince them to reject the most exacting standard of civil protections known to mankind in favor of the benevolence of a person whose job description includes putting them in jail. In so doing, he becomes, as Simon wrote, "a salesman, a huckster as thieving and silver-tongued as any man who ever moved used cars or aluminum siding — more so, in fact, when you consider that he's selling long prison terms to customers who have no genuine need for the product."

Why does anybody talk? They all want to maximize the prospects of getting out from under the charge. What makes them think that not taking full advantage of every mercy built into the system on their behalf will be of any benefit? Most of all, what would make anyone think that talking to their worst enemy — the person who jacked them up and brought them into custody — would be a good thing?

"Without exception, everyone thinks they can say the right thing, the thing that will absolve them." Simon gives a little chuckle. "They're told that if they don't talk, the cops have no alternative but to lay a charge and send them to pretrial detention. Most of these guys live in the present, they're not thinking about down the road. All they're thinking about is going home tonight, and if they say that right thing, maybe it'll happen."

Harry Edgerton says the suspect needs to believe there's an out. There's a door at the end of the tunnel, and at the top of that door is a window. "Every suspect is reaching for that window, thinking that they can find a way to crawl through."

The out can be anything. That you were provoked, that you acted in self-defense, that the victim pulled a weapon first, that it was an accident. Anything. But none of these outs lead to freedom. All they do is confirm that you did the killing. Remember, the why is unimportant to the police. You did it, you confessed, you're charged. Fine points like motive are the lawyer's domain. Should have gotten yourself a lawyer, bunk.

Donald Worden will tell you that a stone killer won't cop to anything. Fortunately for all of us, there aren't that many stone killers out there. Anyone with a conscience will need to unburden themselves. This is one of the reasons it's imperative to make an arrest as soon as possible: you want them in the box at their most vulnerable, when the remorse is closest to the surface.

Edgerton says the key is in making the suspect forget you're a police for a little while.

"Everyone wants to tell someone," according to Pellegrini. "It's just that you're not the person they want to tell it to. You have to get close to them, make them think that, whatever it is they've done, you've thought of the same thing."

Guy kills his wife, you tell him that yours has made you so angry you don't know how you kept from doing the same thing. Guy rapes and kills a young girl, you tell him you understand what a tease she must have been. Guy beats a child to death, you tell him how you know it's frustrating to come home after a long day and have a kid making all kinds of noise.

"When I first came to homicide, I found it so difficult to lie and be sincere about it." Pellegrini smiles with resignation. "But I ended up mastering it."

Worden recounts one case he worked with Pellegrini in which a child had been killed, wrapped in a fabric, and dumped in a gutter. A suspect was brought in for questioning. How to determine his guilt without a witness placing him at the scene?

"Why did you just throw that little girl's body away?" Worden asked.

The suspect sobbed, "I didn't know what to do with her."

Case closed.

The natural police detective assessed the man as something other than a sociopath. He intuited the wrapping of the body suggested concern for the victim. If guilty, this was the point over which he'd break down. If innocent, he'd protest vehemently. In either event, Worden would have a good idea whether he had his killer.

Talking and listening, that's the murder police. That's *Homicide*. Investigations don't culminate with a shootout, but with an interview. Cops don't go around killing suspects, they talk to them. They confront and manipulate them. An unimpeachable confession brings conviction. Case closed. Rewrite the victim's name from red ink to black.

GRIEF

Murder is a job for the judicial system, a routine occurrence complete with procedures for processing the body, eliciting from it every iota of evidence, and dealing with the perpetrator in the event of arrest. Death, however, impresses far more extensively. *Homicide* has paid significant attention to the mourners. Murder isn't all about the police. To get to the humanity of the story, you must get beyond them. They come to the scene because they're paid to do so. A red ball or a whodunit is overtime in the bank. Neglected and unprepared for how extraordinary a circumstance it is are those who loved the victim. Someway, somehow, they must adapt to a life radically altered. In the days immediately following the murder, the police will be omnipresent, working the case as if no other crime exists. But eventually the buzz will diminish. A suspect will be caught and passed through the courts. Or no one will be caught and the trail will grow cold, until the police become reconciled to its staying red. Either way, it soon becomes jumbled in with all the other uneventful murders that are tallied in the city.

Veteran police have those few peculiar cases that have caused them genuine grief. Child murders are always high on the list, as demonstrated through Bayliss. Pembleton was deeply stricken by the serial murder of Catholic women. Lewis broke down over Crosetti's suicide. Kellerman took personally the killing of the Korean grocer brought about by his eviction of Mahoney's slingers from in front of his shop. Munch had to deal with investigating the death of his high school crush. Giardello had to confront the killer of his friend, the editor of a community newspaper. All of these people know what it is to have a murder hit home. Still, their intimacy with sudden death steels them. No matter what, they'll be back the next day to a new murder, which will be a tragedy for somebody else.

In "Bop Gun," Robert Ellison, whose wife was killed in a robbery outside Camden Yards, is torn up because he failed to protect her. He can't come to terms with an environment in which everyone has a gun, where the unarmed man is at an immediate disadvantage, a weakling. Adding to his sense of inadequacy is the feeling that the detectives are mocking him for not having done something, that because of their familiarity with street violence they look at him and know they would have done better. Bayliss's assurance that this is not so does little to assuage him. For the rest of his life he'll replay that moment, each time changing the scenario ever so slightly, doing something different, acting more reflexively, being braver, knowing instinctively how to defuse the situation and escape unscathed. The torture is that the moment will never be relived. The legacy of an instant that never could have been prepared for will torment him forever.

"I just stood there and watched them kill my wife," he marvels. "I didn't do anything."

He finds himself inducted involuntarily, zombie-like, into a peculiar club of perpetual mourners. "The instant they pulled that trigger I lost my wife, but I joined a club. It's a very exclusive club. But the funny thing about the club is none of the members want to belong. It's like some sort of secret society where only the initiated can recognize the other members."

"Every Mother's Son" is one of those seminal episodes for which *Homicide* will always be remembered. Fourteen-year-old Ronnie Sayers shoots thirteen-year-old Darryl Nawls in a bowling alley. This is less the story of a murder or an investigation than it is of two mothers, both decent, God-fearing women, one of whose children is a killer, the other his victim. What befalls their children is a nightmare for both, equally. Each is in grief, one for a dead child, the other for a boy buried under a life sentence. The two mothers meet in the squad room and share their burdens without knowing who the other is. Their hardships are the same: lack of suitable men, being stuck in bad neighborhoods, keeping their kids safe and off the streets. They're trapped in the same circumstance, only looking at it from opposite ends. They cry the same tears. Both mothers must say goodbye to their boys.

In still another episode, one boy chases another through a shopping mall ("A Doll's Eyes"). Parents are trying to hustle their dawdling son along. Shots ring out. The son falls, leaving a smear of blood on a shop window. Shot in the head by a stray bullet. The parents (Marcia Gay Harden and Gary Basaraba) move through the entire episode dazed, disoriented, trying to cling to reality — discussing parking, whether they had remembered to turn out the lights at home — when faced with the most unreal circumstance that could have befallen them during a normal family outing. They freak out when Bayliss and Pembleton show up and identify themselves as homicide investigators, not understanding why homicide was there when their son was still alive, as if their presence presupposed his death.

"He has a doll's eyes," says Dr. Devilbliss (Sean Whitesell in a recurring role), meaning he's brain-dead.

The parents must decide whether to allow his use as an organ donor. They must choose a moment at which a switch will be flipped and their son will expire. Watching them say farewell is to look in on a moment that deserves privacy. Their tears are the wages of violence.

Baily Lafeld (Terry O'Quinn), the father of the victim in "Hate Crimes," is actually relieved that his boy is dead when it appears that he was gay. He is shocked and angry that his son practiced a lifestyle he finds embarrassing and perverted. He denies it, despite the boy's being killed in a homosexual area of town in front of a gay bar. "If what you say is true, it's better he's dead," he rants. When it's confirmed that Zeke wasn't, in fact, gay, but only in that particular neighborhood, Lafeld breaks down, thanking God. Now he can grieve.

Deep in "The Heart of a Saturday Night," four murders are viewed from the perspective of victims' loved ones participating in a support group. Filmed in sepia tones, parents, a husband, a wife, and Dr. Cox, whose father was killed when his car was run off a road, recount their losses and try to alleviate their sadness and anger. They are all passion and remorse and regret. It is the suddenness of the loss that is so stinging. So much will forever remain unresolved: for the wife contemplating leaving her womanizing husband, who was killed in a bar fight; for the overworked husband, who was at the office when his wife was shot during a carjacking; for the parents who disapproved of their daughter, only to have her found raped and strangled. Peace eludes them all, whether the case has been solved or not. Every one of us fills space in someone's life, if we're lucky, and our unexpected departure opens a void. Seeing what survivors must endure gives a sense of futility to the work of the homicide detectives. They celebrate the victory of an arrest, but it is essentially hollow to those with the most at stake.

PUNISHMENT

The administration of punishment is beyond the scope of the police. As a result, *Homicide* has only sporadically ventured as far as the courtroom or prison. A case is deemed closed as soon as charges are filed. Whether the suspect pleads down from first-degree homicide to involuntary manslaughter is not their concern. If a technicality results in the dismissal of the case, it has still been closed, as a person cannot be tried for the same crime more than once. If a jury acquits, the case remains closed, unless meaningful evidence emerges to suggest that the wrong person had been charged. The police closure rate, then, does not at all correspond with the state's attorney's conviction rate. In 1988, Simon reported, taking into account all the legal permutations (dismissals for lack of evidence, death of suspect, rulings of insanity, cases stetted, etc.), only 60 percent of those cases wherein a suspect was identified resulted in convictions. Toss in all the unsolved cases, and the chance of being convicted for committing a murder fell to just over 40 percent. Lessons to be learned? Well, if you really want someone dead, you've got to like those odds.

One thing you have to appreciate in post-O.J. America is the fickleness of a jury. The old joke about how you wouldn't want to be judged by a dozen people who're too stupid to talk their way out of jury duty holds more than a kernel of truth. Simon assembled the following rules of the jury system:

- To a jury, any doubt is reasonable.
- The better the case, the worse the jury.
- A good man is hard to find, but twelve of them, gathered together in one place, is a miracle.

Reasonable doubt is one of those ambiguous concepts that relies on the common sense of twelve well-intentioned people. Testimony and evidence can be complex and fraught with vagaries that must be carefully sorted through. This requires time and thought, which are the offspring of caring. If those twelve good citizens don't care — and a good prosecutor never assumes they do — they'll suspend all belief in the interest of getting the trial over with.

In Simon's book, the jury in the Gene Cassidy shooting case barely overcame collective indifference to return a guilty verdict. This scenario was appropriated for a different occurrence on *Homicide* ("Justice," in the fourth season). An ex-cop, Edgar Rodzinski, is strangled with a wire coathanger in front of his wife's grave. A suspect, Kenny Damon, is arrested on some solid evidence: the cemetery caretaker places Damon at the scene and testifies they had an argument during which Damon tried to strangle him; the murder weapon and Damon's fingerprints are found when Rodzinski's car is recovered; DNA matches Damon with the scrapings taken from the victim's fingernails. The case is not without complications, but the chain of physical evidence is convincing. Nevertheless, after more than five hours of deliberation, the jury comes back with not guilty.

Lewis and Edgar's son Jake (Bruce Campbell), also a Baltimore cop, catch up with the forewoman to find out what had happened during deliberations. She, along with another juror, was insistent that Damon was guilty. But one man was absolutely adamant that there was reasonable doubt. Finally, she says, "Everyone was tired. We all wanted to go home for the weekend." That was it. Justice and truth were subservient to the press of the weekend. Nobody wanted to be bothered more than that.

Prison is a harsh, brutish place. Regardless of whether inmates get color TVs or telephone privileges or libraries or weights. Fact is, prisons are institutions cramming together hundreds, if not thousands, of violent men left with little more to lose. Packed into cells, all they enjoy is endless time to brood and foster grudges, to brutalize and be brutalized, to fashion crude weapons, to score drugs. When freedom is denied, dignity fades; when dignity fades, self-respect disappears; when self-respect disappears, all bets are off and any horror becomes possible.

Ronnie Sayers ("Every Mother's Son") is all ignorant cockiness when placed in holding to await his hearing. One night is all it takes for him to realize the sorts of predators that would be stalking his young self in the penitentiary. This wasn't the big time of his imagination. This was more mean and cold than anything he could have fathomed. And this was the life he was looking toward.

Frank is more torn up at the prospect of putting this child in prison than he is by the child murders he's seen. After Ronnie's been remanded to custody without bail pending his trial, Frank asks for a moment with him. He whispers in Ronnie's ear that he isn't in the habit of giving advice to killers, but goes on to admonish him, "Keep your ass to the wall. Don't trust anybody. Don't believe anybody. Don't help anybody. Don't ask anybody for anything." He knows what prisoners will do to this boy. He knows his life is over.

To a lot of inner-city kids, prison is a natural occurrence. Most of the people they know — friends, family — have been there. Sometimes they'll find acquaintances on the inside. Often they come home with a better rep than what they left with, just for having been there. It serves as a graduate school of delinquency.

DeAndre McCullough, a low-level West Baltimore dealer who Simon and Burns followed for the writing of *The Corner*, is all of fifteen when he first appears in juvenile court, on charges of auto theft and possession with intent. "I can jail," he boasts to his mother prior to his hearing, dismissive of the worst sanction society has devised. Frightening these kids is no easy task.

Much is made of how the murder police speak for the dead, avenging those who can't avenge themselves. Vengeance comes in the form of a charge and, if all goes well, a lengthy prison term, or even the death penalty. But what of redemption? Where is this to be found?

In confession? Perhaps to a priest, but not to a detective. If you're gonna jail, you'd better harden. This makes you different from who you were when you got there. Understand, you're being incarcerated to protect people on the outside; this ain't a self-improvement seminar. Rehabilitation is an afterthought, especially if you're down for the long count of a murder rap.

You sleep locked in a cage night after night so the rest of us can sleep a little easier behind our dead-bolted doors.

In season five, *Homicide* paid a visit to the state penitentiary at Baltimore to catch up on some of those who had gone away in earlier installments ("Prison Riot"). In the dining hall, a white prisoner (Claude Vetter, who had shot his wife) bumps a black (James Douglas, who had videotaped his cousin, Trevor, in a thrill killing of an old lady at a bus stop). Black prisoner stabs white, a riot ensues. In the melee, black prisoner is killed. Homicide goes in to investigate who killed the second prisoner, albeit perfunctorily. Gee simply wants them to touch the bases and get the paperwork together. They conduct interviews with the prisoners present when the riot erupted and encounter many of the men we've seen them put away over the years. Bayliss is convinced that one prisoner, Elijah Sanborn (Charles S. Dutton), saw what happened.

"I think that he needs to tell me," Tim senses. "I think that Sanborn's looking for redemption."

"You can sit in your living room thinking we're being rehabilitated. But rehabilitated for what? I'm in here forever, Detective. *Forever*," Sanborn says, emphasizing the endlessness and hopelessness of his nightmare, explaining why redemption is of no consequence to him.

Sanborn never gives up the case. It's solved when Tom Marans smashes a pipe over Trevor's skull and admits he did it because Trevor had killed James over a carton of cigarettes. Tom was James's prison wife. Just part of the cycle of prison life, love, and death.

In the end, there's plenty of vengeance, but precious little redemption.

PREJUDICE

Prejudice is always an issue in America. It comes out on some level whenever people of different colors or religions interact, even when they're ostensibly on the same side. Within a police force, race is a touchy and multifaceted subject. Between cops, there are supposed to be no shades of skin, only blue. Rarely are things so simple, however. Attitudes held off the job cannot be discarded on command for a few hours a day. Giardello reminisces about the days when white cops wouldn't let black officers inside radio cars. When the streets of Baltimore were ablaze in 1968, he had to choose with whom he would stand, black or blue. He chose blue.

Few issues are as electrically charged as race. Once someone has been branded a racist, they have been indelibly tattooed. There have been a few squad-room incidents. As already discussed, Pembleton and Felton had some early exchanges in which Beau's attitudes were revealed to be less than enlightened, if not on the cusp of racist. He's not the type to abuse someone because they're black or to not cooperate with a black partner, but he's probably more apt to suspect African Americans or to treat them disrespectfully. He casually refers to them by the police jargon put-down "yo," as in "Yo, how you doin', yo?"

As an issue, prejudice is not confined to race, definitely not limited to questions of black and white. It's far more subtle than that. Really, it addresses all manner of difference between majorities and minorities, including color, religion, and sexual orientation. Sheet-draped cross-burners and swastika-brandishing skinheads are the obvious expressions of small segments of society so consumed with hate that it defines their lives. To them, their racism is a source of pride, not something to be covered up politely. Skinheads were the perpetrators of "Hate Crimes," the beating death of a man they mistook as gay. More disturbing than the perpetrators in this case — because we expect them to behave as they do — is the ambivalence Tim exhibits while investigating the murder. He admits that the case matters less to him because he believes the victim to be gay; he can't identify with the victim. We have reason to expect better of him. Not that he doesn't expend effort in solving the case, or come down hard on a skinhead witness; but he hints that being homosexual somehow means being at fault. This only made it all the more interesting when he began exploring bisexuality several seasons later.

"For God and Country" (season four), one of several cross-overs between *Homicide* and *Law and Order*, introduced a neo-Nazi character more fearsome than skinheads because of his intelligence, leadership savvy, and organizational potential. Alexander Rausch (J. K. Simmons) — West Pointer, decorated Vietnam hero, and covert operator — is suspected of master-minding fatal bombings in a church in Baltimore and the subway in New York, and of murdering the wife of Brian Egan, a jailed associate he feared might expose him. He has the official background and well rehearsed anti-system rap that appeals to a segment of the disaffected.

Under interrogation, Rausch gives Frank the usual "mongrel race," "cancer in America," "decline of civilization because of the amorality of non-whites" spiel of hate mongers in need of a scapegoat for their own inadequacies.

Calmly, with infinite dignity, Frank replies, "You will not make me a martyr because I'm a black American. You will be my martyr for the truth."

However, he is robbed of the chance to parade Rausch's hatefulness when Rausch suffers a fatal heart attack on the tracks at Penn Station before he can be transported to New York to face charges in the subway bombing. Rausch had purposely neglected to take his medication. Frank breaks down in tears, knowing that silence is the ally of injustice. The hate can fester under cover; the best hope to excise it is to expose it.

"I find overt racism less dangerous than insidious racism," offers Jim Yoshimura. "The Klan we can deal with. A more difficult situation exists when a person gives every indication of being decent, but has underlying racist sentiments."

Jim Bayliss (David Morse) — lawyer, homeowner, family man, Tim's cousin, all-around good citizen — shoots down Hikmet Gursal, a seventeen-year-old Turkish exchange student, on his front stoop ("Colors," season three). Gursal, decked out in thick white pancake makeup on his way to a KISS costume party, acting wild and erratic, babbling unintelligibly, had mistakenly gone to the wrong address. Bayliss, feeling threatened, fetched his handgun, and, when Gursal refused to leave his property, fired. Jim seems every bit the decent man who exercised poor judgment under stress. A check of his record reveals that he has been charged with assaulting an Iranian in a bar. His brother had been killed in the Gulf War. Did he react as he did because Hikmet was Turkish? Would he have felt less threatened had the boy at his door been white or speaking English? Was there some underlying anti-Arab sentiment motivating him? Was Jim justified in using lethal force?

You could probably go either way on any of these questions. Then Tim takes him home and Jim sets about hosing the blood off his porch. "Who'd have thought their guts'd be the same color as ours?" he asks in wonderment.

When the grand jury decides not to indict, a standing ovation breaks out in the chamber.

"Jim is worse than a Klansman because at least in their white sheets they're recognizable," Frank concludes. "But your cousin's brand of bigotry is much more frightening, because, like still waters, it runs deep. He doesn't even see it himself." Law-abiding citizens would never have applauded the death of a white child under the same circumstances.

Racial motivations come in all tints.

A woman is killed by a stray bullet in the parking lot of a Fulton Street shopping center that straddles a middle-class, predominantly white neighborhood and the poor, predominantly black projects ("Law and Disorder," season three). The trajectory of the bullet indicates she could have been shot from several hundred yards' distance in any direction. Pembleton and Lewis disagree on how to proceed with the investigation, Frank arguing that probability suggests they begin in the projects, Meldrick suggesting an equal likelihood that the shot originated from the white side of the tracks. They set about tracing every legally purchased gun of the description used in the shooting registered in the vicinity. Lewis objects to Frank's concentration on the black side of town. He thinks Frank is acting on the stereotype that makes violence more likely to come from blacks. It turns out that a gun in the household of a nice, white family got into the hands of their small child.

She fired a shot out the window of their home. It came down through the head of Jean Battisto.

For the most part, police are not racist. As a group, at any rate, no more so than any other of similar demographics. What they tend to be, however, is classist. What that thin blue line really separates are the underclasses from the working and higher classes. Cops develop attitudes based on the districts they work. Those in the black ghettoes will express negative feelings toward blacks. Those in the hillbilly slums will run down "city goats." It's a function of who they encounter on the job. Gharty is a case in point, taking equal opportunity to run down political imperatives he believes are favorable to blacks (in "Blood Ties"), as well as to question the level of variety in the gene pool of the white-trash populace ("Shaggy Dog, City Goat"). Although they deal with only a small percentage of the population, if those dealings tend to be racially homogenous, they'll make the mistake of casting aspersions along general lines. All the while, however, they distinguish between African-American colleagues and taxpayers, and those they lock up.

Simon and Burns speak to the "racial irony" they observed in *The Corner*: how "on the Fayette Street corners today, it's a new generation of young black officers that is proving itself violently aggressive. A white patrolman in West Baltimore has to at least take into account the racial imagery, to acknowledge the fact that he is messing with black folk in a majority black city. Not so his black counterparts, for whom brutality complaints can be shrugged off — not only because the victim was a corner-dwelling fiend, but because the racial aspect is neutralized." It's distressing to think that optics — whether or not brutality may be *seen* to have a racial component — is what keeps a lid on indiscriminate violence.

SIX

AN AMERICAN EPIC

Homicide is, at once, quintessentially American and strikingly universal. The horror of violent death is common to us all. What David Simon drew from his experiences with the Baltimore murder police stirs up emotions we all relate to: fear, hate, grief, relief, compassion. Just as these feelings are within us, so, too, is the capacity for merciless brutality.

A world away from Baltimore, in Johannesburg, South Africa, one of the most violent cities in the world, Rian Malan tried to make sense of his country by sorting through its killings. A former crime-beat reporter with the *Star*, Malan wrote *My Traitor's Heart*, in which he takes readers "to all those extraordinary places" usually open only to killers, their pursuers, and those who recount their stories.

" 'To live in Africa,' said Hemingway, 'you must know what it is to die in Africa.' That made sense to me," Malan reflects. "I was going home to be a crime reporter again, to seek a resolution of the paradox of my South African life in tales of the way we killed one another."

Homicide looks to do much the same thing. As a body of work — both book and series — it is a penetrating exploration of American life through the tales of how we kill each other.

It's surreal that every day a homicide detective goes off to work and will face a dead body, a person whose life has met an unnatural and premature end. For this detective, what should be abnormal is expected. You get up, shower, have your first coffee, look over the newspaper, get in your car, get to the office, have a second jolt of coffee, pick up a ringing phone, go out to stand over a corpse, and set about trying to find out who committed the murder.

"How does someone sustain their own souls seeing that on a daily basis? That's what I want to get to," explains Fontana.

How, indeed, do any of us sustain our souls in violent times? We live in the jet stream of urban deterioration. Every brutality sends out currents that knock our peace of mind off kilter. Every time you reconsider whether it's a good idea to go out for a walk late at night, or worry because your child is half an hour late getting home, you're being affected by the violence in our midst. Make a wrong turn down the wrong street at the wrong time and you could find yourself staring victimhood right in the eye.

Murder mysteries are not morality plays of good triumphing over evil. Because in the real world, evil enjoys more than its fair share of triumphs. No, murder mysteries are horror stories in which adults can invest their complete reservoir of credulity. The traditional Western genre has fallen out of fashion because few of us still believe that good guys can win, if we even believe there are any good guys left. But we all believe in the possibility of suffering a violent death. We've all known the fear of walking by someone or a group that seemed capable of anything. We've all heard footfalls behind us on an otherwise deserted street and wondered . . . .

The popularity of cop shows is that they promise us a weekly dose of urban horror, delivered right to the sanctuary of our living rooms. They give us the opportunity to watch what we fear without risk. They let us see how we kill each other. What does this do to our souls?

David Simon's second foray into yearlong observational journalism was *The Corner: A Year in the Life of an Inner-City Neighborhood*, on which he teamed with Edward Burns. They spent all of 1993 in the fray of the open-air drug markets that pock the corners along West Fayette Street in Franklin Square, and emerged with a book of unnerving force that will rattle even the most steadfastly complacent suburbanites. It shows just how close the ghetto really is to their homes.

Take a ride into West Baltimore some night and you'll find you've descended to a whole other world, a mere 10 blocks from Camden Yards and the glittering Inner Harbor. Here, the street corners hum with a lively commerce, conducted as openly as if the trade wasn't in dope, crack, and weed. Adolescents tout to the passing traffic, looking for prospective customers. This is a world of quick money, blissful stupor, and easy violence.

The corner is *in* America, but not *of* it. Rules that are abided — and make sense — elsewhere don't apply in West Baltimore, or the thousands of urban ghettoes just like it across the country. Disposed of by the mainstream, the residents have embraced drug culture for solace, sustenance, and status. By the mid-1990s, Baltimore had the highest rate of intravenous drug use in the United States. There are an estimated 50,000 heroin and cocaine users in the city. Atlanta is the only major urban center to lock up a greater percentage of its population on drug charges. The explosion of violent crime is traced directly to the advent of crack.

The mean truth of the matter is that addicts will do whatever they must to survive.

"Corner dwellers have adapted to their particular conditions," Burns told me. "You do horrible things to keep breath in your chest."

Adds Simon, "Dope fiends are the hardest-working people in America." From their book: "Every day you start with nothing, and every day you come up with what you need to survive."

It comes down to necessity being the mother of invention. He and Burns write, "When mere vice is sufficient to get the blast, it ends there. But eventually, it's sin that is required, and when sin falls short, absolute evil becomes the standard."

Factor in the striking crush of resignation borne by the youngest children in the inner city and you've got overwhelming and pervasive despondency.

Burns observes, "The corner won't allow you to give of yourself. Anything that isn't bravado is giving an edge to someone else. You end up robbed of the ability to love." The corollary is that you acquire the ability to do violence.

American cities have become overarmed, undereducated, overmedicated, and, generally, neglected as large numbers of taxpayers flee for sanctuary. For the first time, the latest census showed Baltimore County to have a larger population than Baltimore City.

Once upon a time, acquaintance murders far outnumbered stranger murders. In other words, the victim usually had a connection to the killer, whether as lover, business associate, drug seller, neighbor, or whatever else. However fleeting the association may have been, some link could be drawn which lessened the terrifying randomness of the crime. No longer is this the case. More and more killings owe nothing to a relationship. This means any one of us could be the victim. And the more we see ourselves in the role of victim, the more we fear our environment. The stone robber could stick a gun in the ear of anyone who looks like a worthwhile target. They could force their way into your house while you watch TV. Whether or not the victim catches a bullet in the act depends on a mere whim. There are those who want what they can't have, but know only too well that extreme violence allows anything to be had. The junkie in dire straits resorts to whatever needs doing to meet the need. The deranged psychotic evicted from a hospital by budget cuts could attack any passerby, even on the most crowded street. Not to mention the bored and desensitized youth with an existential curiosity about what it feels like to kill someone. Or men whose lust culminates with death. And those who kill out of sheer hate. The point is that the uncertainty caused by pervasive violence puts everyone on edge. Though statistically unlikely, there is an awareness of the possibility of being murdered. Not a constant preoccupation, perhaps, but when you include news reports and crime entertainment, it does occupy an inordinate amount of our time.

"We most want to know what will happen in our lives, but the truth is that everything is transient," offers Kyle Secor. "That's the great paradox of our lives: anything can happen at any time. Life can be snuffed out like nothing at all. Passions, aversions, connections can all carry people away.

"The ego is really the enemy," he goes on. "Ego has its own voice, opposed to that of reason. We show a lot of egos on *Homicide*. We point the finger inward. We really ought to outlaw egos."

Ego feeds that most foolish conceit that we are in control, self-sufficient, that most American of goals. Of course, it's all an illusion. Money makes us feel in control. As does the firmly barricaded door to our home. So, too, does a gun and the readiness to use it. I can jail.

You think so? Tune in to Oz sometime. This is TV too tough for TV. Fontana is the creative force behind this made-for-HBO drama series set in Emerald City, a modern, state-of-the-art, state-of-penal-theory wing of the maximum security Oswald State Penitentiary, known — with intentional irony — as Oz. As with the other Oz, there's no wizard here, either. Unhindered by the sensibilities of network television, Oz is profane and furious. The atmosphere is stifling and enveloping. As tough as it is to watch, you'll be loath to turn away. Spend just an hour in Oz and you come out so relieved to still be in your den that you instinctively hug your mate and cuddle the dog. You've never before had a world so cruel and mean shoved in front of you.

Many of the inmates are familiar from guest appearances on *Homicide*. Lee Tergesen (the blinded Officer Cassidy) plays Tobias Beecher, a lawyer convicted of vehicular manslaughter for killing a child while driving drunk. Weak, soft, totally unsuited for prison life, Beecher is quickly offered protection by Aryan Vern Schillinger (J. K. Simmons, who played Alexander Rausch). The cost for that protection is Beecher's dignity and self-respect — commodities generally in short supply around Oz. He is turned into Vern's bitch, branded with a swastika tattoo on his ass, daubed with makeup, and forced to serve Vern's sexual appetites. Finally degraded past breaking, Tobias lashes out, beating him brutally, tearing out an eye, and shitting in his face for good measure. When he emerges from the hole, Tobias is as pitiless and cold-blooded as anyone in Oz.

Jon Seda was featured in the premier episode as Dino Ortolani, a nails-tough wiseguy. He doesn't go out of his way to beat down other inmates, but is vicious whenever someone gets in his face. Racial distinctions are magnified in prison; everyone moves with their own for security and support. But the Italians are on the wane; still feared, but waning nonetheless. Dino cannot be protected from everyone, and he is dispatched in ghastly fashion. An African-American prisoner bribes a guard to let him into the isolation cell where Dino is held, drugged and in restraints after snuffing an AIDS patient in the infirmary. He is doused in lighter fluid and torched.

There are no good guys in Oz. There is no reprieve from the savageness. Guards are brutal and corrupt, helping smuggle drugs and other contraband into the prison. The reforming Tim McManus (Terry Kinney, who played the ghost-like NSA cartographer in the "Map of the Heart" episode of *Homicide*) is too egotistical to be effectual. One concludes that the system allows no place for decency. A brutal environment brutalizes. A corrupt system corrupts: morally, physically, and spiritually.

Art isn't always pleasant to look at. Nor is it supposed to be. What it is supposed to do is touch us, make an impact on us. It has something to say, an idea to communicate. We depend on art to take us places we've never before been, and show us things as they've never before been seen. It can disturb, provoke, or enrage. So long as it doesn't leave us complacent. This is why escapist entertainment cannot truly be art — it deadens us rather than enlivens us. We turn to it when we want to turn off.

Throughout its run, *Homicide* has striven to be art. It takes us to a Baltimore most of us had never seen. You can substitute pretty much any city for Baltimore and say the same thing. So, in more general terms, it brings us to the American urban experience in an original way. Its perception of murder is in delicate strokes, broadly tragic and extraordinary, while at the same time routine and oddly mundane. It presents the workings of an overburdened homicide squad as it hasn't been shown before. The creative minds that devised the show recognized that realism was not incompatible with entertaining and that being interesting didn't mean surrendering to oversimplification.

The characters that populate the show are nuanced and hold our interest. They can be patient or petulant, concerned or callous, benevolent or bullying. We don't always agree with them, but we always care about their motives.

Homicide's hallmark is honesty; it tells stories with integrity. Over time, it has ventured away from Simon's book to find its own source of truth, give its characters their own place in the world. Needless to say, not every episode over its six-year run has attained the same standard. A TV series is designed by committee, on tight deadlines and strict budgets. And it is a volume business. Different writers come along with different words for actors to speak. New directors inject their visions of how they see characters reacting to situations and how to capture it on film. And the actors bring their intimacy with the character and emotional read into each scene. Meanwhile, the network is arguing for accessibility and resolution in each episode. Finally, everything is informed by the spirit of truth extracted from how real police deal with situations and investigate crime.

Through it all, what is there to be learned about American society from how we kill each other?

America has embraced a culture of violence. Not that this is really anything new. The whole notion of the right to bear arms suggests a right to use them. The romanticized figure of the frontiersman is an anti-establishment man of independence, self-reliance, and — whenever necessary — violence. Urban gangsters live in their image. What is more anti-establishment than an economy based on the free-market supply and demand of an illegal substance? Who is more self-reliant than the drug slinger, who imports, packages, protects, and distributes his own product? And all of this with the forces of law and order trying to put him out of business.

Punishment, as opposed to the creation of alternatives, has been society's response to catastrophic crime rates, as if criminals have chosen their lifestyle out of a multitude of options. In most cases, they have been raised too poor, too uneducated, too unqualified, and too harsh for any other life. Murder is often an act of those who steal and con to survive. Or of those in the drug culture who aren't exactly in a position to go to the police when their stash is robbed or a debt has gone too long unpaid. Or of those who have been hardened past the ability to empathize. Or those who have been led to believe that it is the most effective conflict-resolution option at their disposal. Too many people are growing up dispossessed, with no sense of belonging and no stake in society. Alienation makes killing easier because there is no sense of association with one's victim.

Murder is a crime of extraordinary excess. Yet, it has become an ordinary occurrence. We've become used to it. *Homicide* recognizes this fact, but never takes it for granted. It has invited us to outrage at the sorrow, the waste, and the horror. It has tried to shake our apathy by showing us murder from different slants, twisting our perceptions, awakening our sensitivities. It has tried to make us think about what we have made of our cities, and how those cities have remade us. Never has it been tempted to depict murder as anything short of sin and evil.

Knowing that it will never happen, a bitter, exhausted Frank Pembleton begs rhetorically, "One time, one time I'd like to hear about a murder that makes any sense. One time, for any reason."

APPENDIX

EPISODE GUIDE

Season One: 1993

101. *Gone for Goode*

TELEPLAY: Paul Attanasio
DIRECTOR: Barry Levinson
BROADCAST DATE: January 31, 1993

Rarely has a debut episode been so singularly successful in defining the personality of a series. An ensemble of nine distinct characters is introduced and immediately established. Bolander berates Munch for trying to pass off the murder of Jenny Goode as an accident. He succumbs and reviews mug shots until identifying a suspect. Crosetti and Lewis investigate the murder that would lead them to Calpernia Church (Mary Jefferson) and her web of dead husbands. Rookie Bayliss arrives in homicide and ends up paired with Pembleton, the perpetual loner. Together they interrogate the young hustler who killed an old man in a motel room. Felton and Howard have the privilege of arresting Jerry Jempson (Jim Grollman), a murderer stupid enough to leave the body of his victim stashed in his own basement. Guiding these detectives through the unceasing mayhem is Lieutenant Giardello. Most intriguingly, the case that would preoccupy the rest of the first season — the murder of Adena Watson — would only occur in the final minutes of the episode. The signal was that the series was going to be character- and dialogue-driven. These cops weren't going to shoot, they'd talk; this would be no ordinary cop show.

102. *A Ghost of a Chance*

TELEPLAY: Noel Behn
STORY: Tom Fontana
DIRECTOR: Martin Campbell
BROADCAST DATE: February 3, 1993

The investigation that would indelibly change Bayliss takes shape. Kyle Secor moves through the episode as if dazed, playing Bayliss as overwhelmed by the sheer tragedy of Adena's killing. Giardello tactfully leads him without usurping responsibility. The case is one man's obsession; the other detectives have their own concerns. Bayliss looks utterly broken when he stares down on Adena's body at her funeral. The cases pile up; the world doesn't stop for any single murder. Mrs. Doohan (Gwen Verdon in an Emmy-nominated performance) requires two tries before killing her husband, a murder in stark comic contrast to the Watson case. Howard's dreams are plagued by the weakness of her case against Ralph Fenwick in the murder of Agnes Saunders. Occultism contributes nothing, but in an uncharacteristic demonstration of dedication, Felton tails Fenwick until he leads him to the missing murder weapon. Bolander commences his tentative wooing of Dr. Carol Blythe, the medical examiner.

103. *The Night of the Dead Living*

TELEPLAY: Frank Pugliese
STORY: Tom Fontana & Frank Pugliese
DIRECTOR: Michael Lehmann
BROADCAST DATE: March 31, 1993

It was a bold move to produce such a static episode so early in the series. So much so that it was originally broadcast out of sequence. This episode isn't about the act of murder, it's all about the atmospherics and mood of homicide. The Watson case is stalled; Bayliss focuses in on the Araber as the probable killer. This episode is something of a respite from the intensity of previous installments. It's a hot September night shift, the air-conditioning is on the blink, and the city is uncharacteristically murder-free. A cool jazzy-blues track underlies the inaction. The detectives ponder their dead and dying relationships. A candle is mysteriously lit in front of the board in homage to the dead. A suicidal Santa Claus goes missing in the building and the cleaning lady's baby is mistaken for abandoned and turned over to child welfare, before Bolander reclaims him.

104. *Son of a Gun*

TELEPLAY: James Yoshimura
STORY: Tom Fontana
DIRECTOR: Nick Gomez
BROADCAST DATE: February 10, 1993

Crosetti's friend, Officer Chris Thormann, is shot in the face while making an arrest. Crosetti begs his way onto the investigation. Charlie Flavin (Larry E. Hull) offers himself as a witness to the shooting. A raid on one of the row houses adjacent to the alley where Adena's body was found uncovers no evidence. The squad is burdened by simultaneous red balls. Tough investigations, not easy solutions, follow. Howard and Felton investigate the murder-for-hire of a man because he opposed the placement of a bust of Spiro Agnew in the capitol. Bolander, so cantankerous on the job, shares an intimate conversation with his lovelorn, woodworking neighbor, who later commits suicide. Calpernia Church is brought in for the string of unfortunate deaths that have befallen close relatives in whose insurance policies she is named. A delicate balance is struck between tragedy, comedy, and pathos.

105. *A Shot in the Dark*

TELEPLAY: Jorge Zamacona
STORY: Tom Fontana
DIRECTOR: Bruce Paltrow
BROADCAST DATE: February 24, 1993

Bolander and Munch arrest an overzealous bodyguard who killed his employer so as to get a clean shot at the man who was assailing him. Captain Barnfather's politicking — a speech before a community meeting — leads to the exposure of key information on the Watson investigation. Bayliss's health suffers from the stress. At the same time, he is hardening. The hunt for a repossessed car that had been parked in the alley where Adena was found leads Felton and Pembleton nowhere. During their wanderings, they debate race. Miraculously, Thormann awakens from his coma. Dogged work by Lewis results in Flavin being nabbed as his assailant, after the wrong man has been arrested on the strength of Flavin's witness statement. This was the episode where Lewis came into his own as a detective. It concludes with Munch's spirited rendition of "Mack the Knife" on karaoke night at the Wharf Rat.

106. *Three Men and Adena*

TELEPLAY: Tom Fontana
DIRECTOR: Martin Campbell
BROADCAST DATE: March 3, 1993

The definitive *Homicide*. In its entirety, it is the interrogation of the Araber. Just Pembleton, Bayliss, the suspect (Moses Gunn), and the box. Brilliantly written, intensely acted, claustrophobically staged. Bayliss goes in convinced of the Araber's guilt, but emerges with doubts. In the end, the Araber steadfastly maintains his innocence. The Adena Watson case will stay in red. Where most TV aims for the quick, easy, and satisfying conclusion, *Homicide* accepts ambiguity, demands patience and embraces irresolution. It's a mark of the series' honesty and self-confidence, its unwillingness to compromise integrity or the place of truth from which it originates.

107. *A Dog and Pony Show*

TELEPLAY: James Yoshimura
STORY: Tom Fontana
DIRECTOR: Alan Taylor
BROADCAST DATE: March 10, 1993

Back in the rotation after the distress of the Watson investigation and failure to obtain a confession from the Araber, Bayliss's first case is the apparent murder of a police dog. His partnership with Pembleton begins to gel and take form. In a hilarious sequence, Bolander brings Dr. Blythe's son on a ride-along. The spacey teen questions Stan on his relationship with his mother. Giardello bids farewell to his friend, Lieutenant Scinta (Michael Constantine), who reluctantly takes his retirement. They share a touching moment between old soldiers in Little Italy. Felton and Howard take down Pony Johnson for the murder of his girlfriend and stash-holder, Ida Mae Keene. Howard shows her chops in the box, interrogating William Lyness, whose mother was also killed by Pony. Thormann isn't forgotten just because his case is put down; his recovery continues and Crosetti pays him a visit.

108. *And the Rockets Dead Glare*

TELEPLAY: Jorge Zamacona
STORY: Tom Fontana
DIRECTOR: Peter Markle
BROADCAST DATE: March 17, 1993

Crosetti and Lewis catch the murder of a Chinese student and learn that it was likely politically motivated. They road-trip to DC to interview someone at the Chinese embassy. Needless to say, they get nothing, thanks to the protections enjoyed by diplomatic personnel. The Secret Service, however, lets them know the killer was probably a girl they had spoken with at the scene. The visit gives Crosetti the opportunity to visit Ford's Theatre, the culmination of his preoccupation with the Lincoln assassination. Munch exhibits an astounding knowledge of marijuana cultivation at the scene of a drug murder. Pembleton is approached by the brass as a viable replacement for Scinta and gets his first lesson in political cold-bloodedness when Giardello is informed of the approach by the very bosses who had instructed Frank to keep the matter absolutely confidential. Pembleton confesses to him that he really doesn't want to do the job of a shift commander.

109. *Smoke Gets in Your Eyes*

TELEPLAY: Tom Fontana & James Yoshimura
DIRECTOR: Wayne Ewing
BROADCAST DATE: March 24, 1993

Howard and Bayliss quit smoking, an endeavor that does not go over well with their smoker partners. They sit on a stakeout together discussing the joys of smoking, while Pembleton and Felton sit in another car contemplating giving it up. Bolander uses the electrolyte neutron magnetic test scanner, otherwise known as a photocopier, to convince a member of the Zeff gang that they could read his thoughts and get the information that leads to an arrest in the Percy Howell murder. Howard lets Frank in on the sexual details of her burgeoning relationship with assistant state's attorney Ed Danvers (Zeljko Ivanek), with all the relish of a high school football player in a locker room. Giardello is infuriated after stumbling upon an asbestos-removal operation in the building. Entering a crime scene, Lewis asks Crosetti to let him be primary so he can rack up the overtime.

Season Two: 1994

201. *See No Evil*

TELEPLAY: Paul Attanasio
DIRECTOR: Chris Menaul
BROADCAST DATE: January 13, 1994

Sensitivity counseling is a forum for the detectives to reveal the impact of their job on their relationships. This was one of those episodes to confront a great moral dilemma: is mercy killing murder? Felton begs Lewis to look the other way while he destroys the evidence that proves his friend Chuckie Prentice (Michael Chaban) shot his terminally ill father (Wilford Brimley), who was unable to take his own life. This was Daniel Baldwin's most compelling performance. Lewis reluctantly goes along so the death will be written off as suicide. C. C. Cox, a fleeing suspect, is shot in the back in an alley and all the evidence points to police involvement, even though none of the officers at the scene own up to discharging their weapon. A hostile public and press only complicates the affair. Pembleton is undaunted by the prospect of investigating fellow cops; Giardello is less sanguine about the consequences.

202. *Black and Blue*

TELEPLAY: James Yoshimura
STORY: Tom Fontana
DIRECTOR: Chris Menaul
BROADCAST DATE: January 20, 1994

Pembleton is tenacious in pursuing the police angle of the Cox shooting, and is disheartened at having police lie to him and disavow all knowledge of what happened. Succumbing to Giardello's insistence, Frank psychologically rapes a confession out of a civilian he knows to be innocent. Realizing the confession is garbage, Giardello confronts the suspect in the cells and he concedes that he saw Lieutenant Tyron kill Cox. Bolander meets Linda (Julianna Margulies), a violin-playing waitress at Jimmy's, a Fell's Point diner.

203. *A Many Splendored Thing*

TELEPLAY: Noel Behn
STORY: Tom Fontana
DIRECTOR: John McNaughton
BROADCAST DATE: January 27, 1994

A pivotal episode in Bayliss's development and sexual awakening. He and Pembleton investigate the strangulation of Angela Frandina, a phone-sex provider who was into leather. Tim ventures onto the Block after they solve the case, curious about the S&M underground to which it exposed him. Munch, miserable over breaking up with Felicia and obsessed with uncovering Bolander's new love, crashes Stan's double date with Kay and Danvers. A pen-coveting psychopath kills a man in a library. Lewis laments "Baltimore, the home of the misdemeanor murder."

204. *Bop Gun*

TELEPLAY: David Mills & David Simon
STORY: Tom Fontana
DIRECTOR: Stephen Gyllenhaal
BROADCAST DATE: January 6, 1994

A landmark episode featuring a masterful performance by Robin Williams as a tourist who watches his wife get killed during a mugging by three youths near Camden Yards. The twist is that the shooter was the kid least likely to do a murder: with a clean record, from the suburbs. This troubles Kay until she learns from him that he had asked to hold the gun because he thought he could ensure nobody would get hurt — the shooting was, in essence, an accident. The victim's distress, his failure to find closure despite the successful prosecution of the suspect, are explored. The extraordinariness of his experience runs parallel to the routine business of police work.

Season Three: 1994–95

301. *Nearer My God to Thee*

TELEPLAY: Jorge Zamacona
STORY: Tom Fontana & Jorge Zamacona
DIRECTOR: Tim Hunter
BROADCAST DATE: October 14, 1994

The first of a three-parter, when Andre Braugher definitively asserts himself as the show's star. The body of Baltimore's Samaritan of the Year, a good Catholic, is found in a dumpster behind St. Stanislaus Church, wearing nothing except white cotton gloves. The Jesuit-educated Pembleton endures a crisis of faith resulting from the seeming victory of evil over good he sees on a daily basis. Megan Russert, a rather ill-conceived character, is introduced as the lieutenant of the second homicide shift. Command is concerned about her competence, and Giardello is asked to lend his shift in support. Howard and Russert get off to a bad start, and their relationship won't improve. Beau's wife finally throws him out of the house, after years of therapy, bringing his marriage problems to the fore. He is having an affair with Megan. Crosetti is supposedly off on vacation. Lewis and Munch have begun negotiations to purchase the Waterfront Bar and interest Bayliss in investing with them.

302. *Fits Like a Glove*

TELEPLAY: Jorge Zamacona
STORY: Tom Fontana & Jorge Zamacona
DIRECTOR: Ted Demme
BROADCAST DATE: October 21, 1994

When it's discovered that Roger Gaffney (Walt MacPherson) failed to properly search the crime scene, he's pulled off the Samaritan of the Year investigation, replaced by Pembleton. Before going, he lets Russert know what he thinks of her competence to command a shift. She responds by transferring him out of homicide. A second victim is found in a church dumpster, wearing white cotton gloves. The victims weren't sexually assaulted; these are crimes of faith, not of perversion. A collector of serial-killer memorabilia puts in dibs for souvenirs of the murders, and also provides information that the same killer may be responsible for a series of murders in other states. A gambling indiscretion in Tim's past puts the liquor license for the Waterfront in jeopardy. Beau tells Kay about his affair with Russert. The episode concludes with the discovery of a third victim.

303. *Extreme Unction*

TELEPLAY: D. Keith Mano
STORY: Tom Fontana & Jorge Zamacona
DIRECTOR: Keith Gordo
BROADCAST DATE: October 28, 1994

Annabella Wilgis (Lucinda Jenny) comes forward as a witness in the serial killings. Frank takes her into the box and she reveals herself to be schizophrenic — the killer, herself. During the interrogation, Frank is charming, flirtatious, antagonistic, and finally predatory. Russert fears how far he goes and wants to call him off, but Giardello trusts Frank's instincts and ability. One of Annabella's personalities mimics everything Frank does. He holds a match to his wrist, and she does likewise, burning her own flesh. She had arranged for her lawyer to arrive soon after her. She goes on to confess on TV and seek public sympathy for her multiple personality disorder. The anger Frank directs at God as a result of this investigation would continue to define his character. Beau and Russert call it quits.

304. *Crosetti*

TELEPLAY: James Yoshimura
STORY: Tom Fontana & James Yoshimura
DIRECTOR: Whitney Ransick
BROADCAST DATE: December 2, 1994

A bloated corpse is pulled from the harbor: the body of Steve Crosetti. Despite all the evidence, nobody wants to believe he committed suicide. It is the most poignant of episodes, showing how, immune though they may be to murder, the detectives are still susceptible to the pain wrought by death. Lewis is overcome with grief, a marvelous turn by Johnson. The brass refuses Crosetti an honor-guard funeral because of potential embarrassment for the department. Frank declines to attend the church funeral, but as the procession wends past headquarters, he stands at attention in his dress blues. It's a moving and apt farewell to a respected colleague.

305. *The Last of the Watermen*

TELEPLAY: Henry Bromell & Tom Fontana
DIRECTOR: Richard Pearce
BROADCAST DATE: December 9, 1994

Particularly sickened by the killing of Audrey Resnick in her own kitchen, Kay seizes some vacation time and visits her family in her hometown by the Chesapeake. The plot becomes contrived when the town experiences its first murder in a half-dozen years. The local police request her assistance and she obliges. An oysterman, enraged by the regulations that have put his livelihood, home, and family on the line, murders a state conservation officer. The killer — indeed every potential suspect — is an old friend of Kay's. All the while, Felton and Pembleton continue working the Resnick murder, which was committed by her grandson, who calmly confesses. His motive: she got on his nerves.

306. A Model Citizen

TELEPLAY: Noel Behn
STORY: Tom Fontana & Jorge Zamacona
DIRECTOR: John McNaughton
BROADCAST DATE: November 11, 1994

Whimsical, nonsensical opening has the detectives mourning the cancellation of *Romper Room*. Not a significant moment in series history, but a nice touch. An accidental shooting in a home causes Munch to go out of his way to get the gun out of the house, to no avail due to the nonchalance of the family. It is a rare opportunity to prevent a murder, and Munch takes it to heart. Meldrick experiences love at first sight with Emma Zoole (Lauren Tom), who builds model reconstructions of crime scenes. Frank is incredulous to find himself a defendant in a civil suit launched by Wilgis because she was burned during the interrogation. Russert, as lieutenant responsible for the case, is less than resolutely supportive of Pembleton's methods. Emma doesn't reciprocate Lewis's feelings, but is instantly smitten by Tim. Speaking of whimsy, her bed is a coffin, and she and Tim engage in one of the more interesting sexual encounters in recent TV memory. Meldrick's fury over their affair puts the bar-buying partnership at risk. Beau's wife disappears with their kids, which accelerates his downward spiral.

307. Happy To Be Here

TELEPLAY: Julie Martin
STORY: Tom Fontana & Julie Martin
DIRECTOR: Lee Bonner
BROADCAST DATE: November 18, 1994

Sam Thorne (Joe Morton), editor of a black community newspaper, is executed by a half-wit hired by the Cali cartel to halt his exposé of their movement into the local drug scene. Arthur Balantine keeps his wife's decomposing corpse in the house because he's just not ready to say goodbye. Tim's relationship with Emma goes sour after Tim confronts her boyfriend for having hit her. Distraught, Tim gets drunk and then stops in at a convenience store to pick up some cookies. He comes up 11 cents short and pulls a gun on the clerk. It's a scene replete with black comedy, far enough out on the edge that you're not quite sure how Bayliss is going to walk away from it, a rare quality for a situation involving a series regular. Frank is called and talks the clerk into letting Tim off in exchange for his services as a night watchman.

308. *All Through the House*

TELEPLAY: Henry Bromell
DIRECTOR: Peter Medak
BROADCAST DATE: December 16, 1994

Christmas Ho-Ho-Ho-*Homicide* style. Because of scheduling quirks during its first two seasons, this was its first holiday theme. Needless to say, the cheer is blood-tinged. Bolander abandons Munch in the care of a child (Ryan Todd) whose father, a Salvation Army Santa, had apparently been killed in a mugging. In a twist on the Christmas miracle, Stan was off learning that Santa was alive and well, on a bender somewhere, and the deceased was an unfortunate thief who expected the Santa kettle to be a windfall. Russert accompanies Meldrick to investigate the burning death of an upper-class junkie who was a material witness in another case. Nancy Marchand gives a marvelous portrayal of denial and dignity as the girl's mother. Bayliss seeks a game of hearts, finding one with Giardello, who turns out to be a shark.

309. *Nothing Personal*

TELEPLAY: Bonnie Mark
DIRECTOR: Tim Van Patten
BROADCAST DATE: April 21, 1995

Giardello finally comes around to erasing Crosetti's name from the board and distributing his outstanding cases. The Erica Chilton case, Steve's worst nightmare, goes to Howard, threatening her perfect clearance rate. Russert invites Al out to lunch to introduce him to her friend, Amanda, a light-skinned African American. All appears to go well, and Al intends to call her, but she's not interested. He's convinced she rejected him because he's too black. Erica's boyfriend, Tom Marans, provides a packet of letters sent by her ex-boyfriend that may be a lead, but Beau loses them while on a bar hop. His wife changes her mind about returning to him. The purchase of the Waterfront finally comes through.

310. *Every Mother's Son*

TELEPLAY: Eugene Lee
STORY: Tom Fontana & James Yoshimura
DIRECTOR: Ken Fink
BROADCAST DATE: January 4, 1995

Another seminal episode. Fourteen-year-old Ronnie Sayers shoots down a thirteen-year-old. Each child's mother suffers for the fate of their children. Pembleton, too, is affected by the loss of both lives — one to death, the other to the penal system. The episode explores the impact of murder on all involved parties: victim, perpetrator, their families, and the police who have to wade through the remains. Child murders are hard enough; children murdering children is even tougher. The decency of the mothers is in shattering contrast to the harshness of the environment in which they live. An outrageous Howie Mandel provides a brief moment of light relief as a flamboyant interior decorator working on the Waterfront.

311. *Cradle to Grave*

TELEPLAY: David Mills
STORY: Tom Fontana & Jorge Zamacona
DIRECTOR: Myles Connell
BROADCAST DATE: January 13, 1995

A biker gang, the Deacons, kills one of its own. Lewis comes to the fore as a dedicated, caring officer who genuinely wants to understand the excess of a killing that left a little girl fatherless. Deputy Commissioner James Harris invites Frank out to lunch and asks him a favor, to fix a false kidnapping report submitted by a friendly congressman as a cover for a violent spat with his boyfriend. Harris then disowns the matter, leaving Frank hanging. Frank responds by resigning. Death is never far from the absurd: a homeless corpse is wrongly transported from the scene to the hospital, then returned to the scene, where a uniform repositions it as initially found.

312. *Partners*

TELEPLAY: David Rupel
STORY: Tom Fontana & Julie Martin
DIRECTOR: John McNaughton
BROADCAST DATE: January 20, 1995

The congressman's submission of a false report creates a media firestorm. Though the crime is a misdemeanor, it was committed by a public figure, and his not being charged smacks of conspiracy. In court, Pembleton assumes responsibility for the decision not to lay charges. In effect, he took one for the team. Frank takes over domesticity from his wife, Mary (Ami Brabson). Doug Jones (Robert Clohessy), Russert's friend and new squad member, is beating his wife. Unable to endure any more, she finally shoots him. Bayliss mopes at Pembleton's absence, all the more so after Lewis injures him by literally crashing the car into a crime scene. The Waterfront celebrates its grand opening.

313. *The City that Bleeds*

TELEPLAY: Julie Martin & Jorge Zamacona
STORY: James Yoshimura & Bonnie Mark
DIRECTOR: Tim Hunter
BROADCAST DATE: January 27, 1995

A genuine shocker: serving a warrant, Bolander, Felton, and Howard are ambushed and severely wounded. A clerical error caused them to knock at the wrong door. Thus begins a massive three-part manhunt for pedophile Glenn Holton under Pembleton's lead. Frank is the only detective able to maintain his detachment. A departure for *Homicide* because of the violence, it attacks the subject with customary intelligence, rather than gratuitously trying to glorify and glamorize. Holton is traced to a hole at Penn Station, where a raid is staged, but the suspect evades capture.

314. *Dead End*

TELEPLAY: Jorge Zamacona & Julie Martin
STORY: James Yoshimura
DIRECTOR: Whitney Ransick
BROADCAST DATE: February 3, 1995

The hunt for Holton ends in his arrest. Surprisingly, he turns out not to have been the shooter. Russert acts as the brass's hatchet, investigating whether Giardello should be held responsible for the error on the warrant. Holton is traced to a shipyard where he has holed up on a boat. The arrest is overly theatrical, too much colored lighting, too stage-managed for the purpose of creating dramatic effect.

315. *End Game*

TELEPLAY: Rogers Turrentine
STORY: James Yoshimura & Henry Bromell
DIRECTOR: Lee Bonner
BROADCAST DATE: February 10, 1995

The hunt now turns to the resident of the apartment to which the detectives were wrongly sent. Bolander, Felton, and Howard proceed slowly with their recoveries. Gordon Pratt, a racist gun nut with an assault record, is brought down. Steve Buschemi, compelling, smug, frightened, smolderingly angry as Pratt, is a worthy adversary for Pembleton, who savors tearing down his intellectual and racial pretensions. Their confrontation is one of the series' classics. Pratt is one of the few suspects he fails to break. Pratt walks out of headquarters, only to end up shot in the head in the lobby of his apartment.

316. *Law and Disorder*

TELEPLAY: Bonnie Mark & Julie Martin
STORY: Henry Bromell & James Yoshimura
DIRECTOR: John McNaughton
BROADCAST DATE: February 24, 1995

Bayliss is saddled with investigating the Pratt killing alone, but everyone is overtly disinterested in finding the killer. Every cop in Baltimore is a viable suspect, since he was shot with a standard police-issue Glock. His murder stays red. Better than that, no clue is left with the viewer as to who might be guilty. Felton returns to work, but isn't quite up to it. Pembleton and Lewis clash on how to handle a woman who was killed by a stray bullet — Pembleton wants to focus on the black projects, Meldrick thinks the white area on the other side of the crime scene deserves equal time. Turns out a white child discharged her father's gun accidentally. Munch is humiliated by a larger-than-life nude — painted of him during his more free-spirited days — that is displayed in an art exhibition across the street from headquarters.

317. *The Old and the Dead*

TELEPLAY: Randall Anderson
STORY: Henry Bromell & Jorge Zamacona
DIRECTOR: Michael Fields
BROADCAST DATE: March 3, 1995

Headquarters' plumbing problems lead to Colonel Granger's downfall when Giardello finds out he's been hiring his brothers-in-law and authorizing their double-billed work orders. Barnfather moves up to colonel, opening a captain's vacancy. Giardello had every reason to expect the job, but sees it handed to Russert instead. Stan and Kay get back on the job. A couple of hillbilly brothers have buried their father in the backyard. They didn't kill him, but never reported his death so as to continue collecting his social security. The Warners are beaten to death in their mansion by their grandson, who feels unloved. Bolander, having trouble sleeping, turns up on Munch's doorstep.

318. *In Search of Crimes Past*

TELEPLAY: Jane Smiley
STORY: Henry Bromell & Julie Martin
DIRECTOR: Ken Fink
BROADCAST DATE: April 14, 1995

Michael Bigelow's daughter takes Barnfather hostage seven hours before her father is to be executed for a murder she claims he didn't commit. She demands that Bolander reopen the case, which he had investigated sixteen years earlier. On the same evening Jeffrey Zwick commits suicide. Zwick's note is a signed confession for the murder for which Bigelow was convicted. The victim had been sleeping with Zwick's wife. Realizing his responsibility for the near execution of an innocent man, Stan begins to doubt himself, his ability to ask the right questions. Frank and Tim look into the suspicious death of an old lady in her bathtub. Bayliss suspects her husband was responsible. Turns out he did kill her, to clear the way for an old sweetheart he wanted to marry. Jerry Stiller guests as new Waterfront bartender.

319. *Colors*

TELEPLAY: Tom Fontana
DIRECTOR: Peter Medak
BROADCAST DATE: April 28, 1995

Tim's cousin Jim (David Morse) shoots down a Turkish exchange student who had mistakenly knocked on his door on his way to a KISS party. Pembleton is convinced he was acting out some deep-seated racism. Tim defends Jim as a justifiably frightened home-owner responding to a drunk, erratically behaving youth. The grand jury agrees in not holding him over for trial. Through flashbacks into the stories of all witnesses, the shooting is recreated. Jim's conversations with Bayliss and his wife reveal a man who does harbor racist attitudes. However, he was also genuinely concerned for his family's security. In its best tradition, *Homicide* raises difficult issues and is unafraid to leave them ambiguous enough to allow for interpretation.

320. *The Gas Man*

TELEPLAY: Henry Bromell
STORY: Tom Fontana & Henry Bromell
DIRECTOR: Barry Levinson
BROADCAST DATE: May 5, 1995

Bruno Kirby guests as squirrelly, quick-tempered Victor, who is just released from prison where he's done six years for installing a defective gas heater that blew up and killed a family. He stalks Pembleton, blaming his arrest on a personal crusade on Frank's part. Victor follows him to the scene of Sister Zelda's murder. She was decapitated and her head was dumped in an alley. Victor finds the head and the murder weapon and uses them to taunt and humiliate Frank. He follows Mary and drops hints to her about the case, makes his way into their house and turns on the gas. When he finally lures Frank to an abandoned house and puts a knife to his throat, he finds himself incapable of murdering in cold blood. It's fascinating to see Frank from the perspective of one of his suspects.

Season Four: 1995–96

401. *Fire (1)*

TELEPLAY: Julie Martin
STORY: Tom Fontana & Henry Bromell
DIRECTOR: Don Scardino
BROADCAST DATE: October 20, 1995

Bolander and Felton have been suspended for twenty-two weeks (the full length of a TV season) for indiscretions committed at a national police conference in DC, explaining their absence. Cocky Mike Kellerman of arson establishes his strong personality in clashes with Pembleton over the investigation of a body found in a torched warehouse. The victim was a teenager waiting for a tryst with his girlfriend. Giardello presses Captain Russert for more manpower. Whenever they confronted each other after Russert's promotion, Giardello was overpowering. Howard and Munch wager over the sergeant's exam. Mary Pembleton is pregnant. Part 1 ends with a second fire, where a second body is discovered.

402. *Fire (2)*

TELEPLAY: Jack Behr
STORY: Henry Bromell & Tom Fontana
DIRECTOR: Nick Gomez
BROADCAST DATE: October 27, 1995

The second victim is a teenage girl. Kellerman gets to show his chops in his first interrogation for a homicide, tripping up the arsonist responsible for the murders of two teenagers by playing on his love of dogs, making him believe a dog died in the fires. A classic *Homicide* outcome: the killer is revealed, the motive is withheld. Mike's reward is the offer of a permanent transfer to homicide. Murder police are the elite; he takes the job.

403. *Autofocus*

TELEPLAY: Bonnie Mark
STORY: Tom Fontana & Henry Bromell
DIRECTOR: Alan Taylor
BROADCAST DATE: November 3, 1995

A gas leak causes the evacuation of headquarters and temporary establishment of a new facility. Begging for a new partner since Crosetti's suicide, Lewis is teamed with Kellerman. In a series largely about senseless killing, they catch one of the most senseless ever. A pair of cousins thrill-kill an old woman at a bus stop and videotape themselves in the act for later entertainment. J. H. Brodie, a TV news cameraman, was on the scene before police and got a shot of the killers on tape. His work was instrumental in the identification of suspects, but cooperating with the police got him fired. Howard receives her sergeant's stripes and immediately begins alienating squad members by asserting her oversight prerogatives, particularly annoying Lewis.

404. *A Doll's Eyes*

TELEPLAY: James Yoshimura
STORY: Tom Fontana & Henry Bromell
DIRECTOR: Ken Fink
BROADCAST DATE: December 1, 1995

In one of the most purely tragic episodes, a 10-year-old bystander is felled by a stray bullet in a shopping mall and left brain-dead. Pembleton and Bayliss spend equal time seeking the shooter and consoling the parents. Marvelously understated performances by Gary Basaraba and Marcia Gay Harden as the parents bring the victim's grief to life. There is nothing epic about the crime, it is the personification of mundane: one brother shoots at another over a girl. And the consequences touch no one but the immediate family. But for them, the impact is epic. The moment when they have to decide to turn off their son's life support is agonizing and heartbreaking to watch. Wrenching as it is for Frank and Tim, the case is barely turned to black when they get a call out to the next murder.

405. *Heartbeat*

TELEPLAY: Kevin Arkadie
STORY: Henry Bromell & Tom Fontana
DIRECTOR: Bruno Kirby
BROADCAST DATE: December 8, 1995

It took four seasons, but it was inevitable that *Homicide* would pay homage to Baltimore's most famous literary son, Edgar Allan Poe. This is Munch's finest hour as he haunts suspect Joseph Cardero (Kevin Conway), a small-time drug dealer, failed poet and Poe aficionado. A source leads police to a body that had been bricked behind a wall a decade ago. Prodded by Munch, Cardero hears his victim's telltale heart. Driven mad by the sound, his only relief is to surrender to the fate to which he'd condemned another. Thus does Cardero consign himself to the slow, lonely agony of a suffocating death behind an impregnable brick wall.

406. *Hate Crimes*

TELEPLAY: James Yoshimura & Tom Fontana
DIRECTOR: Peter Weller
BROADCAST DATE: November 17, 1995

A man presumed to be gay is beaten to death by skinheads in a gay area of town. Bayliss is tormented by his inability to identify with the victim because of his sexuality. The victim's father, too, is more upset that his son may have been homosexual than that he was killed. Only later is it conclusively determined that the man wasn't gay. How we identify with the victim is crucial in how we react to the murders we hear of. Such things aren't supposed to matter, least of all to investigating detectives, but they do. Notwithstanding, Tim is brutal in questioning a skinhead with material information on the case, enthusiastically beating on him. The detectives ponder how to spend Thanksgiving. In a rare act of charity, Brodie is brought in and offered a job videographing crime scenes and interviews to make up for his being fired by the TV station. He will be a recurring character through the rest of the season, and will join the cast the following year. Lewis gets a break in the lingering Erica Chilton case that results in the arrest of Tom Marans.

407. *Thrill of the Kill*

TELEPLAY: Jorge Zamacona
STORY: Tom Fontana & Henry Bromell
DIRECTOR: Tim Hunter
BROADCAST DATE: November 10, 1995

An exciting, cinematic-looking episode, with a surprising twist at the end. A thrill-killer (Jeffrey Donovan) makes his way north up the interstate toward Baltimore, murdering every time he stops for gas. There's more here about waiting for the madman to strike than there is investigating. The suspect who is first brought into custody turns out to be the twin of the actual killer. With his brother in custody, the real killer calls in and surrenders after one more murder. A personal element is added as Giardello impatiently awaits his daughter's arrival from Richmond. The later she is, the more anxious he becomes that she may have crossed paths with the killer.

408. *Sniper (1)*

TELEPLAY: Jean Gennis & Phyllis Murphy
STORY: Henry Bromell & Tom Fontana
DIRECTOR: Jean de Segonzac
BROADCAST DATE: January 5, 1996

Jay Leno drops in at the Waterfront. A sniper playing a psychotic game of hangman terrorizes Baltimore as he goes from vantage point to vantage point, gunning down passersby. The detectives try to make sense of it by linking the victims, but come to the conclusion that they were picked off at random. This is Russert's first major case as captain and Colonel Barnfather is not pleased with her handling of it. A suspect, William Mariner, is identified and his home is raided. Isolated behind the locked door of his study, Bayliss helps him finish his game while QRT looks on. Before they can get to him, Mariner shoots himself. Barnfather informs Russert that she's being returned to lieutenant rank. When she attacks his decision, he demotes her to detective. It seems like a desperate attempt to find a place for her. Just as everyone thinks the matter is closed, another sniper fires off the Bromo Seltzer Tower downtown.

409. *Sniper (2)*

TELEPLAY: Edward Gold
STORY: Henry Bromell & Tom Fontana
DIRECTOR: Darnell Martin
BROADCAST DATE: January 12, 1996

Alex Robie (David Eigenberg) goes out of his way to assist police at the scene of the first post-Mariner sniping. He is overly cooperative, talking to reporters, dropping in at HQ. A second sniper attack since the Mariner suicide is also witnessed by Robie. This immediately brings suspicion onto him. He is able to quote chapter and verse from newspaper reports on the first incidents. He's disappointed when the police are finished questioning him. The worst thing they can do is disparage him as boring. Even when invited to leave the interrogation room, he stays. Russert talks to him of her demotion and how she's a nobody. She convinces Robie that as long as the shooter remains unknown, he, too, is a nobody. Fearing that, above all, he confesses his guilt.

410. *Full Moon*

TELEPLAY: Eric Overmyer
STORY: Tom Fontana, Henry Bromell, & Eric Overmyer
DIRECTORS: Leslie Libman & Larry Williams
BROADCAST DATE: April 5, 1996

A marvelously executed episode, one of the most interesting and atmospheric. Lewis and Kellerman go door to door at the New Moon Motel, a dead end, down and out, last chance, no-tell motel that houses an inordinate number of ex-cons. Charlie Wells, an ex-con biker and small time drug dealer is murdered. Everybody and nobody is a suspect. All the residents are so well defined in the briefest of glimpses. The murder, which is never solved, almost dissolves into the sultry background.

411. *For God and Country*

TELEPLAY: Jorge Zamacona & Michael S. Chernuchin
DIRECTOR: Ed Sherin
BROADCAST DATE: February 9, 1996

An episode done in conjunction with *Law and Order*. A gas bombing in the New York subway is tied to a five-year-old church bombing in Baltimore. The mastermind is Alexander Rausch (J. K. Simmons), a former military covert operative, now a white-supremacist organizer. Pembleton and Bayliss's interrogation of Rausch is a great sequence. Though he is arrested for murdering the wife of the suspect in the New York bombing in Baltimore, the court awards custody to New York so that Rausch may be tried there. Pembleton is bent on holding Rausch up to public scrutiny so that his evil will be fully exposed and, thereby, expunged. But Rausch brings on his own death by failing to take his heart medication. He dies on the platform of Penn Station. Munch learns that Lenny Briscoe (Jerry Orbach of *Law and Order*) had slept with his ex-wife Gwen.

412. *The Hat*

TELEPLAY: Anya Epstein
STORY: Henry Bromell & Tom Fontana
DIRECTOR: Peter Medak
BROADCAST DATE: January 19, 1996

A Bob Hope, Bing Crosby, Dorothy Lamour road movie done *Homicide*-style with Lewis, Kellerman, and guest Lily Tomlin as the principals. The boys road-trip to Hazelton, Pennsylvania, to pick up Rose Halligan, who is suspected of bludgeoning her husband. They gab, they bond, they buy her lunch. Until she escapes custody to murder the woman with whom her husband had been having an affair. They easily retrieve her at the scene of the crime. The hateful Roger Gaffney (Walt MacPherson) is promoted to captain over Giardello. A crime-scene video shot by Brodie fails to support the testimony of Munch, thus helping get a killer off on a technicality.

413. *I've Got a Secret*

TELEPLAY: D. Maria Legaspi
STORY: Tom Fontana & Henry Bromell
DIRECTOR: Gwen Arner
BROADCAST DATE: February 2, 1996

Lewis and Kellerman are faced with bringing in a huge monster who killed his parents. The man is committed to a mental institution. Meldrick is sympathetic, and he reveals to Mike that he has a brother who's been committed to an institution. Angel Slayton is found slumped in a car, the only clue being blood in the back seat. The autopsy shows he had been shot sometime before, had received medical treatment, but died of massive internal bleeding. Pembleton and Bayliss check the ER staff to see who had been involved in his treatment. They are faced with having to charge Dr. Kate Wystan (Mimi Kennedy), who had intentionally botched the job. Her husband had recently been the victim of a violent mugging, clouding her judgment. Much to his dismay, Tim has to lay charges against her. Munch is preoccupied with uncovering the secrets of Kay's love life.

414. *Justice (1)*

TELEPLAY: David Rupel
STORY: Tom Fontana & Henry Bromell
DIRECTOR: Michael Radford
BROADCAST DATE: February 16, 1996

Edgar Rodzinski, an ex-cop, is found strangled near his wife's grave. His son, Jake (Bruce Campbell), is a cop and a friend of Meldrick's. Jake, understandably distraught, shadows the investigation assigned to Munch and Russert. He complicates the case by beating up someone he is convinced is a suspect. It isn't until a cash reward is put up that the cemetery caretaker offers up crucial evidence that leads to Kenny Damon (Wendell Jordan). Despite a solid case, Damon is acquitted. This was no landmark trial; the jury wanted to be home for the weekend, and found it easier to agree on a not-guilty verdict. The episode ends with Jake issuing a warning to Damon.

415. *Justice (2)*

TELEPLAY: David Simon
STORY: Tom Fontana & Henry Bromell
DIRECTOR: Peter Medak
BROADCAST DATE: February 23, 1996

Jake is increasingly withdrawn following Damon's release. The day he returns to work, Damon's body turns up in a vacant lot. Kellerman is tasked with looking into Jake's whereabouts while Lewis looks into all other angles. The oddball gun used in the killing points to Jake. His partner crumbles during interrogation and gives him up as the shooter. A great sideline is Tim's torturing Frank after he forgets to bring him a grilled cheese sandwich when making a lunch run. The feud ends when Frank fills his desk with grilled cheese sandwiches by way of apology.

416. *Stakeout*

TELEPLAY: Noel Behn
STORY: Tom Fontana & Noel Behn
DIRECTOR: John McNaughton
BROADCAST DATE: March 15, 1996

The police get a tip on a serial murderer. The killer is out of town, so a stakeout is set up on his residence. The case becomes background as the detectives sit around and muse. The interchange between Frank and Tim mirrors the bad marriage of George and Kathy, in whose house the stakeout is established. Giardello is pressed to catch a flight to San Francisco for his daughter's wedding. Tim contemplates quitting after learning of the death of the Araber, his suspect in the Adena Watson murder. What is so rare about *Homicide* is that the characters are real people; they don't get over traumas in TV time — they endure them in human time.

417. *Map of the Heart*

TELEPLAY: Michael Whaley
STORY: Michael Whaley & James Yoshimura
DIRECTOR: Clark Johnson
BROADCAST DATE: April 26, 1996

A rather confused, convoluted episode about a National Security Agency cartographer who claims to be the biological son of a murdered millionaire lawyer who left no heirs. The VCR Munch purchased from Mike turns out to have been procured from the property room. Kellerman is victimized by the lunch bandit.

418. *Requiem for Adena*

TELEPLAY: Julie Martin
DIRECTOR: Lee Bonner
BROADCAST DATE: March 29, 1996

Bayliss and Pembleton get another murdered child, 11-year-old Janelle Parsons, which vividly recalls the Watson case. To the potential detriment of the investigation, Tim tries desperately to link this killing with the earlier case. Knowing the emotional baggage Bayliss is carrying, Frank asks to work without him on this one. Distrust enters their relationship. Tim retraces some of the ground covered in the Watson case and threatens to sidetrack the inquiry. In drunken indiscretion, Bayliss leaks information to a reporter he picks up from the Waterfront. Comedian Chris Rock makes a rare dramatic appearance as Carver Dooley, Janelle's killer.

419. *The Damage Done*

TELEPLAY: Jorge Zamacona
STORY: Henry Bromell & Tom Fontana
DIRECTOR: Jace Alexander
BROADCAST DATE: May 3, 1996

A drug war erupts when a shipment bound for Luther Mahoney is hijacked by a rival dealer. Mahoney is a slithery kingpin who masquerades as a community leader. Kellerman and Lewis have their first chat with Luther.

They go after Drack (Kevin Thigpen), whose crew is being wiped out. During an arrest attempt, Drack gets the draw on Mike. He has the choice of whether to kill him or not, and lets him go. At a peace vigil in front of HQ, Drack is gunned down.

420. *The Wedding*

TELEPLAY: Henry Bromell
DIRECTOR: Alan Taylor
BROADCAST DATE: May 10, 1996

Brash talk-radio host Kevin Lugo is gunned down on his way home. Pretty much everyone in Baltimore is a reasonable suspect. Meldrick arrives at work and announces he's getting married that night and promptly vomits. He enlists the entire squad to help with the arrangements. With the detectives so engaged, Giardello goes out with Kay on the Lugo case. Attempting to arrest a suspect, Raymond Desassy, Giardello is forced to shoot and kills him. Howard's flirty sister, Carrie, drops by the squad room and causes a fluster, squaring Tim off against Mike. Margaret May, credited with playing Carrie, is in fact Melissa Leo in a dual role. In all the excitement of the wedding, Mary Pembleton goes into labor.

421. *Scene of the Crime*

TELEPLAY: Anya Epstein & David Simon
STORY: Henry Bromell, Tom Fontana, & Barry Levinson
DIRECTOR: Kathy Bates
BROADCAST DATE: April 12, 1996

A drug dealer is thrown off a balcony in the Highland Terrace housing project where Black Muslims provide security. Kellerman believes the Muslims are obstructing his investigation and may even be responsible as part of their ongoing efforts to clean up the projects. Lewis is conflicted, respecting the work they do. Officer Stu Gharty (Peter Gerety) is on patrol outside the Boston Homes when he receives a call about shots fired. Rather than responding, he freezes outside and doesn't put in a call for backup until a full half hour has passed. Russert brings him up on charges of non-performance for his failure to intervene. The episode walks a subtle moral line on both cases: Gharty surely should have responded, but his fears were not unfounded; the Muslims obstruct, but are clearly doing good works within the community.

422. *Work Related*

TELEPLAY: Tom Fontana
DIRECTOR: Jean de Segonzac
BROADCAST DATE: May 17, 1996

Frank and Tim investigate a double homicide during a fast-food restaurant holdup. Piecing it together, they realize that Ian MacKenzie, a wounded witness, was actually an accomplice. In the midst of the interrogation, Frank suffers a massive stroke and goes into a coma. Lewis, freshly back from his honeymoon in Toronto, is teamed with Kellerman to investigate a woman who is killed by a bowling ball dropped through her windshield from an overpass. Meldrick is already experiencing marital difficulties. Russert and Munch step in for Frank and find the other suspect in the robbery-murder, but Eloise Pfeiffer had hung himself before they get to him.

Season Five: 1996–97

501. *Hostage (1)*

TELEPLAY: James Yoshimura
STORY: Tom Fontana & Julie Martin
DIRECTOR: Ted Demme
BROADCAST DATE: September 20, 1996

Frank makes his heroic return to the squad and begins the long journey back from his debilitating stroke. Ami Brabson, as Mary, gets the opportunity to shine during this sequence of episodes. Irritable and angry, Frank's recovery is torturous. Russert runs off to France with a diplomat. Tim catches the murder of Francis Uba, whose body is found in the company of the family's pet pig. He begins searching for her absent son, Jerry (Geoffrey Nauffts). Hostages are taken at a middle school by a lone gunman. QRT's Lieutenant Jasper (Gary D'Addario) is in charge of the operation.

502. *Hostage (2)*

TELEPLAY: Julie Martin
STORY: Tom Fontana & James Yoshimura
DIRECTOR: Jean de Segonzac
BROADCAST DATE: September 27, 1996

The hostage-taker's demand: to see his pig. When his deadline passes, he kills a child then sets fire to the classroom. Only once in custody is he identified as Jerry Uba. His act was utterly senseless. His aspiration had been to die during the hostage-taking. He had shot his mother so she wouldn't have to suffer the pain of his death. The ever-acerbic Munch is hard on Frank. In the final scene, Frank, frustrated at the side effects of his medication, flushes his pills down the toilet.

503. *Prison Riot*

TELEPLAY: Tom Fontana
STORY: Tom Fontana & Henry Bromell
DIRECTOR: Ken Fink
BROADCAST DATE: October 18, 1996

A superb episode. Two murders are committed during a riot at the state penitentiary. The entire squad goes in to investigate, but no one is terribly concerned with finding a solution. Except for Bayliss. He works the children of one of the prisoners, Elijah Sanborn (Charles S. Dutton), for leverage to get him to reveal what he witnessed. But the case actually breaks when there's another assault and the perpetrator is caught. Tom Marans admits he committed the attack to avenge the earlier murder. This episode allowed for several of the people put in jail over the years to be revisited. It is remarkable to see the effect prison has on men who had been citizens before a moment of passion or stupidity put them on hard time.

504. *Bad Medicine*

TELEPLAY: David Simon
STORY: Tom Fontana & Julie Martin
DIRECTOR: Ken Fink
BROADCAST DATE: October 25, 1996

The Luther Mahoney saga commences in earnest. A bad package of dope leaves a trail of corpses across Baltimore. Kellerman upgrades his houseboat; on the very same day he's informed that he's confined to desk duty and under investigation for corrupt practices from his time in arson. He explains that the Roland brothers had the other three detectives in the squad on the pad, but he refused to take their money. It is taken for granted by no one that he is innocent. Lewis teams with narcotics detective Terri Stivers (Toni Lewis). The bad dope is tied to Bo Jack Reed. An informant says Luther aced Bo Jack because he was marketing the dope with Luther's moniker to scare users over to his product. Luther beats the charge. Frank is off his medication so he can better focus and pass his firearms test, a prerequisite to his getting back on the street. He fails by four points.

505. *ME, Myself, and I*

TELEPLAY: Lyle Weldon & Emily Whitesell
STORY: Tom Fontana
DIRECTOR: Michael Fields
BROADCAST DATE: November 1, 1996

Dr. Julianna Cox, the new chief medical examiner, makes a flamboyant debut. The FBI investigation into Kellerman goes on. A hooker is found dead in a park. The uniforms arrest Bob Thompson, a homeless man at the scene, and he confesses to this as well as another hooker murder, which fails to show in homicide's records. Cox discovers that another ME had passed the murder off as an overdose as a favor to Det. Willard Higby (Beau James) of the other shift, who had no leads and no genuine desire to find any. They had both dismissed her death as unimportant because she was just a whore. With Brodie over for dinner, Meldrick and his wife get into a fight over the atrocious silk painting of Teddy Pendergrast he insists on hanging in the dining room. Cox's father dies.

506. *White Lies*

TELEPLAY: Anya Epstein
STORY: Tom Fontana & James Yoshimura
DIRECTOR: Peter Weller
BROADCAST DATE: November 8, 1996

Kellerman awakens to his picture on page one of the *Sun*, in an article identifying cops under investigation. He confronts Mitch Roland (Stephen Legnar) at his office. He admits to Lewis that he knew the other arson cops were on the take. Munch probes the suspicious death of Nina Engle. Her husband Phillip's (Scott Bryce) story of how he found the body doesn't add up, leading Munch to believe he is involved. He pushes and pushes until Phillip breaks down and confesses, only to learn from Dr. Cox that the death was a straight overdose. It's a chilling account of how sentiments of guilt and aggressive suggestion from an interrogator can result in a wrongful admission to something that resembles murder. From his desk, Frank cracks the Allison Lambert case, which has been up in red under Bayliss's name for months. Staring into the box, he relives past glories, frustrated at having lost the man he used to be. Tim blows the interrogation of Samuel Colby, the suspect in the Lambert slaying, failing to draw out a confession.

507. *The Heart of a Saturday Night*

TELEPLAY: Henry Bromell
DIRECTOR: Whit Stillman
BROADCAST DATE: November 15, 1996

Again the gyroscope through which murder is perceived gets twisted. A counseling session for survivors of victims, shot in sepia tones; the grief and guilt they bear provides the foundation for three murder investigations. The comforting filter police work inserts between murder and sorrow is lifted and the hard evil is exposed. The question is how they will come to terms with their losses. A husband is bitter over the carjack killing of his wife. A woman (Rosanna Arquette) deals with the bar-fight death of her cheating husband. Aging parents adjust in the aftermath of the rape-murder of their teenage daughter. At the end of the session, Cox shows up for help in coping with the road-kill death of her father. Giardello, looking for vindication after the Desassy shooting, handles the bar fight and, closing the case, confirms that he is still a police.

508. *The True Test*

TELEPLAY: Noel Behn
STORY: Tom Fontana & Noel Behn
DIRECTOR: Alan Taylor
BROADCAST DATE: November 22, 1996

Bayliss and Lewis investigate the murder of an African-American student at exclusive Larchfield Prep School. From case to case, Bayliss looks harder and harder. Elijah Wood, as the son of Judge Aandahl, is convincingly cruel and manipulative, using his crew of followers to do whatever horrors he dreams up. The political pressure of going after the minor son of a powerful jurist is tangible, even when it comes out that the murder was carried out on his command because the boy had been unwilling to carry through a plot to murder Aandahl herself. Frank finally passes the firearms test and is cleared to return to full active duty.

509. *Control*

TELEPLAY: Les Carter & Susan Sisko
STORY: Tom Fontana & Julie Martin
DIRECTOR: Jean de Segonzac
BROADCAST DATE: December 6, 1996

Frank goes out on his first case, with Bayliss as primary. They handle the brutal killing of a woman and her two children. Frank is convinced her boyfriend, with whom she had a tumultuous relationship, is guilty. Tim, on the other hand, suspects her ex-husband, Alex Clifton (Michael Gaston), a Navy commander based in Annapolis, because of the control he maintains over his emotions, the way all his reactions seem so carefully rehearsed. Their teamwork in the box with Clifton is as dazzling as anything they had ever managed, although Tim feels their rhythm is off and he expresses fear over whether Frank has recovered sufficiently. He still stutters and is prone to confusion, but is on his way back to form. The murder of drug dealer Reggie Copeland is tied by witnesses to Luther Mahoney. Even from lockup, Luther is able to intimidate the prosecution's star, his nephew Junior Bunk (Mekhi Phifer). Bunk recants and, once again, Luther walks. He makes things personal by dropping in at the Waterfront and trying to show up Meldrick. Cox shows up at Mike's boat and they spend the night together.

510. *Blood Wedding*

TELEPLAY: Matthew Witten
STORY: Tom Fontana & James Yoshimura
DIRECTOR: Kevin Hooks
BROADCAST DATE: December 13, 1996

Frank's first case as primary since the stroke is the killing of Ed Danvers' fiancée, a public defender, during a holdup at a bridal shop. There is a certain irony whenever someone familiar with the justice system is victimized, as they face the desensitized machine of the system. Danvers is particularly concerned with Pembleton's residual shakiness. Frank and Tim convince the suspect, Julius Cummings, that there's not a public defender in the city who'd want to represent him in this case. He ends up committing suicide in his cell — whether out of fear or guilt is ambiguous. Kellerman wants his night with Julianna to blossom into a relationship, but she's satisfied with a single night. Giardello visits the arson cops being investigated for corruption and two of three assure him they wouldn't implicate Mike in their testimony. He then approaches Deputy Commissioner James Harris to request his intercession in getting Mike off. Harris reminds him of his reluctance to help out years ago in the Congressman Wade affair and suggests he would be advised never to approach him for favors in the future.

511. *The Documentary*

TELEPLAY: Eric Overmyer
STORY: Tom Fontana, James Yoshimura, & Eric Overmyer
DIRECTOR: Barbara Kopple
BROADCAST DATE: January 3, 1997

During an uncharacteristically quiet New Year's Eve shift, the squad sits around to watch Brodie's documentary about the unit. His film does much the same as Simon's book: it shows the cops in their humanity, flaws and strengths. They joke over bodies, calculate overtime, file perjured accident reports, drink, etc. The case he works his film around is that of a necrophiliac undertaker who kills his neighbors when they threaten to expose his habit of bringing home the corpses of his female clientele for private parties. The documentary also incorporates a take on the incident when a thief stumbled into the filming of *Homicide*. Lewis chases a subject right into Barry Levinson and the real crew, who make a unique on-screen appearance. It is a clever and quirky blend of the macabre and the very blackest of humor.

512. *Betrayal*

TELEPLAY: Gay Walsh
STORY: Tom Fontana & Julie Martin
DIRECTOR: Clark Johnson
BROADCAST DATE: January 10, 1997

The body of Tonya Thomson, a young girl who was beaten to death, is found dumped by the side of the interstate. This is the third murder of a young girl to be worked by Bayliss and Pembleton. Tim goes through the episode in a sorrowful fury, especially when confronting Tonya's mother, who he blames for standing by while her boyfriend battered the girl. While he charges through the investigation like a bull in a china shop, Frank tells the mother he understands how a man can come home from work and beat a child to enforce his need for peace and quiet. It's Kellerman's turn to testify before the grand jury. He elects not to take the Fifth Amendment when he realizes another cop has named him as corrupt. However, he is let off the hook when the U.S. attorney takes to heart his stated devotion to being a cop. Tim reveals that his acute pain at child murders stems from his having been sexually abused by his uncle when he was a child. He informs Frank he no longer wants to partner with him.

513. *Have a Conscience*

TELEPLAY: James Yoshimura
DIRECTOR: Uli Edel
BROADCAST DATE: January 17, 1997

Kellerman is bitter and despondent that his absolution hasn't fully erased the taint of the accusations against him. A Korean grocer is killed after chasing Luther's slingers away from in front of his store. This gives Meldrick and Mike another opportunity to go at Mahoney. Luther taunts Kellerman about his grand jury appearance, a witness refuses to talk after recognizing him from the newspaper, and Gaffney rides on him. Concerned for his well-being, Lewis comes by his boat during the evening and finds him suicidal. Mike caresses his gun during an overlong scene before Lewis talks it out of his hands. It seems as though he ran out of things to say long before it ends.

514. *Diener*

TELEPLAY: Christopher Kyle
STORY: Tom Fontana & Julie Martin
DIRECTOR: Kyle Secor
BROADCAST DATE: January 31, 1997

Carol Bridgewell is found dead in her home. The presence of jewelry and finery indicates robbery wasn't a motive. Frank has Lewis thrust upon him as a partner. The victim and her brother, Matthew, were involved in an inheritance dispute. He is the most likely suspect until Carol's diamond ring turns up missing, making robbery a viable motive, threatening the case against Matthew. Brodie and Cox rig a hidden camera in the ME's office and catch Jeff McGinn (Glenn Fitzgerald), an attendant, taking the personal effects of victims. He confesses to taking the Bridgewell diamond. Mike takes some time off. Meldrick is visibly uncomfortable talking to him in the aftermath of his suicidal behavior. As Frank becomes more involved with his work, he becomes more distant from his family. Mary wants to go for counseling.

515. *Wu's on First*

TELEPLAY: David Simon & Anya Epstein
STORY: James Yoshimura & Julie Martin
DIRECTOR: Tim McCann
BROADCAST DATE: February 7, 1997

This episode follows an investigation into the shooting of a Calvert County cop at a drug corner in Baltimore from the perspective of Elizabeth Wu (Joan Chen), the *Sun*'s new police-beat reporter, as well as from Pembleton. She's sharp and aggressive, gathering information parallel with the police. She's under deadline pressures that have her stories changing as details come to light. She ends up inadvertently setting up her source — who turns out to be the shooter — when the police follow her to a meet. Mike goes bingeing around Baltimore with his delinquent brothers (Eric Stoltz and Tate Donovan), who are on the run from Cleveland bookies. This rollicking sequence really gave Reed Diamond the chance to cut loose.

516. *Valentine's Day*

TELEPLAY: Tom Fontana
DIRECTOR: Clark Johnson
BROADCAST DATE: February 14, 1997

Nick Bolaentera, an apparent suicide, is found in Allan Schack's (Neil Patrick Harris) apartment. Brodie knows Schack as a small-time dealer from university. Suspecting foul play, he snoops around Schack. After Brodie pesters Munch, he is finally brought in for questioning and admits he convinced a coked-out Bolaentera to play Russian roulette, but gave him a fully loaded gun. Ben Roh, the son of the Korean grocer killed by Luther's people, delivers package bombs to all those he blames for the miscarriage of justice that saw no one punished for his father's death. Insights into Frank and Mary's marriage are provided in their counseling sessions. Mary's insistence that Olivia be baptized is a point of contention, given Frank's abandonment of God. His late arrival for her baptism is the final straw, and Mary announces her intention to leave him.

517. *Kaddish*

TELEPLAY: Linda McGibney
STORY: Julie Martin, James Yoshimura, & Ron Goldstein
DIRECTOR: Jean de Segonzac
BROADCAST DATE: February 21, 1997

Munch is transported back to his adolescence when Helen Rosenthal, the object of his high school crush, is found victimized by a serial rapist. A series of flashbacks takes him to his youth as he tracks down her circle of acquaintances, many of whom he had known. Discombobulated by Mary's absence, Frank invites Tim to have dinner at his house. He has to rethink his identity as a homicide detective. He's lost his wife, his child, even his partner. He goes to morning mass. He and Tim get called to the scene where an old lady has been found in bed. She died of natural causes. In the context of *Homicide*, this natural death comes across as a beautiful aberration.

518. *Double Blind*

TELEPLAY: Lee Blessing & Jeanne Blake
STORY: Tom Fontana & James Yoshimura
DIRECTOR: Uli Edel
BROADCAST DATE: April 11, 1997

Charlie Flavin, who had shot Chris Thormann, comes up for early parole after saving the life of a guard during a prison riot. Chris gives a moving victim-impact statement that keeps Flavin behind bars for another five years, minimum. Despite his years of blindness, Chris still misses the drill of being a cop. Tim and Frank work the murder of Franz Rader, whose abused wife readily tells them their daughter shot him after he had dropped to his knees in surrender. Having just been deserted by his wife, Frank can't understand why Lucille Rader stayed with her husband. Tim, the victim of abuse, understands how Franz victimized his family and how they felt trapped by fear. With the daughter in the box, Frank tries to twist her confession into a statement that she feared her father. Lucille recants her original statement and says her daughter acted in self-defense. Kellerman reveals to Julianna that he had been suicidal. Bayliss goes to his uncle's house to confront him and finds a broken old man.

519. *Deception*

TELEPLAY: Debbie Sarjeant
STORY: Tom Fontana, Julie Martin, & James Yoshimura
DIRECTOR: Peter Medak
BROADCAST DATE: April 25, 1997

A Nigerian drug mule dies in a motel before delivering his shipment to Luther Mahoney. The police take advantage of the situation, passing baking soda to him. Then they wait for the fallout that will come when Luther realizes he's been cheated. He goes ballistic, meeting in Druid Hill Park at high noon with the Nigerians and his lieutenant who had accepted the bad package. Luther opens fire on his lieutenant. He flees as police close in. Lewis gives chase and corners Luther at his apartment. As he's laying a beating on Luther, he's disarmed. Luther has him at gunpoint when Mike and Stivers arrive. Mahoney lowers the gun, but Mike shoots to kill nonetheless. This incident would prove pivotal as an ongoing story line in season six. Munch is contacted by one Punchy DeLeone (Lewis Black), who offers to lead him to the body of a Jimmy Pugliese. On his directions, Munch digs up the Pimlico parking lot in search of the body. In fact, Punchy follows Munch until he finds a very-much-alive Pugliese, then he kills him. Payback for his spending ten years in jail for a murder Pugliese had committed. Frank and Tim reconcile, agreeing to partner up again.

520. *Narcissus*

TELEPLAY: Yaphet Kotto
TIRECTOR: Jean de Segonzac
BROADCAST DATE: May 2, 1997

A murder suspect flees the scene to the headquarters of the African Revival Movement, a militant self-reliance community group run by an ex-cop named Burundi Robinson (Roger Robinson). A witness is willing to go into ARM wearing a wire because, he says, the victim was killed because he knew Robinson was whoring girls in the Movement. The brass is all over the investigation. Gaffney demands the name of the witness and speaks privately with the suspect. Robinson is obviously tipped about the wire. Facing an arrest warrant, he barricades himself inside ARM and a police blockade is erected. Giardello goes in to speak with Burundi who reveals that he took the rap for some heroin pilfered from evidence control many years earlier by Deputy Commissioner Harris. This gives him continued pull in the department. Robinson and his people end up committing mass suicide. Stivers has second thoughts about calling the Mahoney shooting clean.

521. *Partners and Other Strangers (1)*

TELEPLAY: Anya Epstein, Julie Martin, & Darryl LaMont Wharton
DIRECTORS: Leslie Libman & Larry Williams
BROADCAST DATE: May 9, 1996

Pembleton goes to the scene of a straight-up suicide that quickly gets turned on its side. In the first place, the victim is none other than Beau Felton. Just as the squad struggles to come to terms with another of their fellows dying by his own hand, Cox's autopsy shows that he was actually executed and then set up to resemble a suicide. Auto squad detective Paul Falsone (Jon Seda) has a source in the Frank Cantwell auto ring Felton had been infiltrating on behalf of Internal Investigations. Stu Gharty (Peter Gerety) is the IID detective who had been running Felton. Megan returns from Paris to contribute to the inquiry. Stivers still can't rest easy with the Mahoney shooting. Julianna and Mike's drinking is getting out of hand. Bayliss is an increasing absentee as he searches for peace with his uncle.

522. *Strangers and Other Partners (2)*

TELEPLAY: David Simon, James Yoshimura, & Tom Fontana
DIRECTOR: Ken Fink
BROADCAST DATE: May 16, 1997

Gharty pairs with Pembleton to solve the Felton killing. Recalling his fears during the project shooting, no one is thrilled to work with him. Falsone is tense because of the implication that the auto ring was being tipped to police operations. It turns out Falsone's source, Eddie Duggan, was IID's source and had introduced Felton to Cantwell. He then set Felton up for murder. The raid on Cantwell's chop shop comes up empty. Maudlin Russert and Howard are assigned to plan Beau's funeral. Kellerman and Cox wake up together with no memory of the night before. They are both on a downward spiral. On a call with Lewis, at the scene of a stabbing, Kellerman loses a witness whom he had been interviewing. Frank and Mary reconcile. The season ends on an ominous note: Giardello announces the commissioner's decision to rotate officers into and out of homicide. This would end up being Melissa Leo's last show.

Season Six: 1997–98

601. *Blood Ties (1)*

TELEPLAY: Anya Epstein
STORY: Tom Fontana & Julie Martin
DIRECTOR: Alan Taylor
BROADCAST DATE: October 17, 1997

Frank and Tim return to homicide from a tour in robbery to find a drastically revamped squad, including Seattle transplant Laura Ballard (Callie Thorne), IID's Gharty, and auto's Falsone. Their absence went strangely unnoticed. Georgia Rae Mahoney (Hazelle Goodman) has her son, Junior Bunk, shoot at Lewis, Kellerman, and Stivers. Falsone puts it together that the shootings were related to Luther. He suspects the Mahoney shooting was something less than clean. Lewis doesn't want to team with Mike anymore, and so is partnered with Falsone. Melia Brierre, the maid of Felix Wilson (James Earl Jones), a local snack-cake king and black community benefactor, is murdered in the men's room of a hotel during a dinner in his honor. Considering his status, Frank is prepared to consider every possibility save that Wilson is responsible.

602. *Blood Ties (2)*

TELEPLAY: David Simon
STORY: Tom Fontana & James Yoshimura
DIRECTOR: Nick Gomez
BROADCAST DATE: October 24, 1997

Ballard and Gharty focus on the Wilson family. Gharty is upset that a black police department in a majority black city seems unwilling to go after this black family. He also feels Giardello's personal friendship with the Wilsons is an impediment. Not surprisingly, this puts him and Ballard on a collision course with Pembleton, who hunts down a lead on Melia's ex-boyfriend. When he is shown to be in jail in Haiti, the investigation turns toward the Wilson family. Felix admits to having had sex with Melia prior to the party. Munch and Kellerman go to Camden Yards to handle a mid-game murder. Falsone continues to dig around the Mahoney shooting.

603. *Blood Ties (3)*

TELEPLAY: Anya Epstein & David Simon
STORY: Tom Fontana, Julie Martin, & James Yoshimura
DIRECTOR: Mark Pellingham
BROADCAST DATE: October 31, 1997

Felix and his son Hal (Jeffrey Wright) agree to answer Frank's questions, but only if they aren't advised of their rights so that whatever they say will be inadmissible in court. Faced with love letters he'd written to Melia, Hal admits to the killing, motivated by jealousy for her affair with his father. Felix affirms that he will take any measures necessary to protect his son. Wilkie Collins, who had given up Bunk, and his wife are killed. Luther's posthumous trail of destruction continues to lengthen. The killer is a narcotics cop who acted on behalf of Georgia Rae.

604. *Birthday*

TELEPLAY: Julie Martin
DIRECTOR: Alison MacLean
BROADCAST DATE: November 7, 1997

Grace Rivera (Alison Follard) is found raped, beaten, at death's door. Lewis and Falsone work with Stivers from sex crimes. Rivera appears to be on the road to recovery when she suddenly succumbs to her injuries. Falsone is emotional. He beats the initial suspect. Finally, the seemingly cooperative bartender at the last place she had been drinking on the night of the assault is matched to the attack. Mary experiences complications with her pregnancy, before giving birth to a son. Frank finally tells her that she and their family are priority, not homicide. Georgia Rae confronts Mike and informs him that Luther's apartment had been wired with surveillance cameras and that his shooting is on film. This is a much embittered, not to mention very worried, Kellerman we see this season.

605. *Baby, It's You*

TELEPLAY: Anya Epstein & David Simon
STORY: Jorge Zamacona
DIRECTOR: Ed Sherin
BROADCAST DATE: November 14, 1997

A *Law and Order* crossover episode. Very JonBenet Ramsey. Brittany Janaway, a teenage model, dies in New York. She and her family split their time between there and Baltimore. Outwardly distraught, her parents launch a PR blitz, leak inside information to the media, and hide behind a lawyer's shield. The infection from which Brittany died occurred as a result of injuries incurred from a rape while she was in Baltimore. Falsone and Munch assist Briscoe and Curtis (Jerry Orbach and Benjamin Bratt, respectively) from the NYPD. The Janaways return to Baltimore. Evidence and signs of past abuse result in her father being charged and going to trial, co-prosecuted by Danvers and New York's Jack McCoy (Sam Waterston). This was one of the few episodes where courtroom scenes are central. The father has an airtight alibi: he was in a hotel room with his mistress on the night the rape happened. In a surprise revelation, it turns out that the mother actually committed the fatal assault.

606. *Saigon Rose*

TELEPLAY: Anya Epstein & David Simon
STORY: Eric Overmyer
DIRECTOR: Nick Gomez
BROADCAST DATE: November 21, 1997

Straight out of the New Orleans headlines. A massacre at a Vietnamese restaurant claims a family and an off-duty cop who worked there as a security guard. Antoinette Perry (Camille McCurty Ali), who arrives on the scene and is most helpful, is another cop who moonlighted at the restaurant. Kids who witnessed the shooting from the kitchen identify Perry as the shooter. She had gone in with her cousin to rob the place and ended up murdering everyone in sight. Digging through the basement in Perry's home, they find the body of her long-missing father. Falsone continues to dog Kellerman. It goes a little overboard when they draw their weapons on each other in the stairwell. Mike confesses to Cox about the Mahoney shooting.

607. *The Subway*

TELEPLAY: James Yoshimura
DIRECTOR: Gary Fleder
BROADCAST DATE: December 5, 1997

In a brilliantly ambiguous sequence, John Lange (Vincent D'Onofrio) either is pushed or falls in front of a subway train. Pinned between the train and platform, the only thing keeping his insides from spilling out is the pressure of the train. As emergency crews try to keep him as comfortable as possible while preparing to move the train, Pembleton and Bayliss attempt to sort out what happened. This is one of the series' truly great episodes. Braugher is outstanding as he tries to keep the victim calm, not to mention keeping his own emotions in check. D'Onofrio is utterly convincing as a man with only minutes to live. James Yoshimura's script captures the moment sublimely, never giving way to the sappy. Gary Fleder's direction is crisp, keeping a static scene interesting. Larry Biedron (Bruce MacVittie), a lunatic who had previously been committed for pushing someone in front of a subway in Chicago, intentionally pushed Lange. There are no happy endings. This is *Homicide*. Lange succumbs on the platform as soon as he's pulled free.

608. *All Is Bright*

TELEPLAY: Raphael Alverez
STORY: James Yoshimura & Julie Martin
DIRECTOR: Matt Reeves
BROADCAST DATE: December 12, 1997

A woman kills the ex-boyfriend who has given her AIDS. Uncomfortable though he is around the suspect, who shows obvious signs of the disease, Gharty treats her as just another suspect. Ballard looks for some way to call it something other than murder. Munch is a source of comfort for his ex-wife Gwen (Carol Kane) on the occasion of her mother's death. Bayliss and Cox hook up at a Christmas party at the Waterfront. On Cox's advice, Mike tells Meldrick that Georgia Rae has a video of the shooting.

609. *Closet Cases*

TELEPLAY: Christopher Kyle
STORY: Julie Martin & James Yoshimura
DIRECTORS: Leslie Libman & Larry Williams
BROADCAST DATE: January 2, 1998

A gay man is beaten and left in a dumpster behind the Zodiac, a restaurant frequented by gays. The owner, Chris Rawls (Peter Gallagher), found the body and is helpful with Tim and Frank. Canvassing the gay area, Tim is impressed by how joyous their nightlife appears. Rawls identifies the victim. They arrest Peter Fields (Brian Van Holt), an Andrew Cunanan-like street hustler the victim had tried to rehabilitate. In the box, he bates Tim, only copping to the murder after Tim says how he wants his young body. It's an intense, embarrassing confrontation, squeezed out for all it's worth by Secor. Cox and Bayliss break off their three-week relationship. Unhappy, Tim accepts a dinner invitation from Rawls at the end of the episode. Kellerman confronts Georgia Rae once and for all to bring her threats to a head. She sends him a video on which she admits having no tape of Luther's shooting, but she promises to effect revenge on him for the killing. Falsone confronts his ex-wife, requesting additional access to their son.

610. *Sins of the Father*

TELEPLAY: Darryl LaMont Wharton
STORY: James Yoshimura & Julie Martin
DIRECTOR: Mary Harron
BROADCAST DATE: January 9, 1998

Martin Ridenour, a white ad exec, is found whipped and lynched in a vacant West Baltimore row house. He is a descendant of Patty Ridenour, a female bounty hunter, legendary captor of runaway slaves and free blacks alike for Southern plantation owners. Lewis is less than comfortable with the Confederacy throwback. Dennis Rigby (Laurence Mason), a black history buff, went out to make him pay for his sins of ancestry. Bayliss is slyly ambiguous about his date with Chris Rawls. He and Ballard flirt. Gharty acts like a jealous cuckold, dropping ugly rumors that Tim is a "switch-hitter." Tim harkens back to the Angela Frandina case and accepts his need to experiment.

611. *Shaggy Dog, City Goat*

TELEPLAY: Eric Overmyer
DIRECTOR: Kyle Secor
BROADCAST DATE: January 16, 1998

Dr. Cox baffles a convention of medical examiners with the case of a man who intends to commit suicide by jumping off the roof of an apartment building and is shot on the way down. Munch and Kellerman are able to determine that the jumper's off-the-wall father (Steve Allen) let go a shotgun blast at his mother (Jayne Meadows), thinking the gun was unloaded. He, of course, didn't know a jumper would pass his window as the pellets flew. Falsone seeks legal custody of his son. Gharty and Ballard hunt down a couple of city goats — the urban variety of hillbilly — suspected of shooting a drug dealer. Gharty shows himself to be as condescending toward white trash as he has been toward blacks. Mike, Lewis, Stivers, Cox, Giardello, the city, and department are all named in a civil suit launched by Georgia Rae. Incensed, Meldrick confronts her, which results in threatened harassment and assault charges against him and his immediate suspension. A deeper fissure is opening between Kellerman and Lewis.

612. *Something Sacred*

TELEPLAY: Anya Epstein & David Simon
DIRECTOR: Uli Edel
BROADCAST DATE: January 30, 1998

This two-hour double episode centered on the murders of two priests. Initial evidence points to a couple of Guatemalan refugees who were supported by the church. They had been living in the rectory with the first victim. Gharty, a former altar boy who still attends mass, is the primary. He is particularly appalled at the killing of priests. As the investigation progresses, it becomes evident the murders were committed in the course of robberies. A corner dealer named Roc-Roc (Avery Waddell) is fingered. Pembleton shows him a chance at life and gets him to give up the actual killer. Stivers is officially transferred into homicide. Stress from the Mahoney situation has clearly pushed an increasingly distraught Kellerman to the brink. He is particularly anxious to find Meldrick, who hasn't been seen since his suspension. Badly drunk, Mike stumbles through the city and beats down a man at gunpoint.

613. *Lies and Other Truths*

TELEPLAY: Anya Epstein & David Simon
STORY: Noel Behn
DIRECTOR: Nick Gomez
BROADCAST DATE: March 6, 1998

A secret society of spy wannabes buried one of their members alive as part of a "training exercise." It comes out that Giardello's shadowy past includes having been a PoW in Hanoi. He helps guide Pembleton and Bayliss through the murky world of intelligence. The subject of a manhunt, Nelson Broyles (John Glover) — owner of a spy paraphernalia shop and leader of the Sons of the Silent Service, a clique of bizarre bumblers who fancy themselves an underground brotherhood keeping alive the Cold War arts of espionage for that day when they are needed — comes to the squad room wearing a dynamite-laden vest. Confident he can resist police interrogation techniques, he surrenders the vest and proceeds to confess in record time. Falsone is denied custody of his son. Road rage between a car and a state road maintenance vehicle gets out of hand, resulting in a crash, killing both drivers and leaving the passenger of the car paralyzed. The state pressures Cox into finding the driver of the car intoxicated so as to absolve Maryland of any possible liability. She refuses to fabricate her toxicology results, and to reduce the pressure she leaks them to the press. She's fired for her integrity. This would be Michelle Forbes's final appearance.

614. *Pit Bull Sessions*

TELEPLAY: Sean Whitesell
STORY: James Yoshimura & Julie Martin
DIRECTOR: Barbara Kopple
BROADCAST DATE: March 13, 1998

With Lewis on suspension and Bayliss taking time to fill his shifts at the Waterfront, Pembleton and Falsone are thrown together. An old man is mauled by pit bulls belonging to his grandson, Harry Tjarks (Paul Giamatti). The dogs were trained and used for fighting. Though convinced Harry didn't premeditatedly kill his grandfather, they are chilled by his lack of remorse. Munch, Gharty, and Ballard join Bayliss at the Waterfront and swap war stories of the stupidest criminals while in the presence of Tony, a creepy busboy who sits at the end of the bar making illustrations in his Bible, on which he writes the names of the detectives. Much to everyone's surprise, Georgia Rae's suit is on its way to a jury trial. Kellerman is certain the presiding judge, Gerald Gibbons, is on the Mahoney payroll, especially when he finds that he specifically requested the case. Sean Whitesell, who played Donald Groves on *Oz* and has a recurring role as Dr. Eli Devilbliss on *Homicide*, wrote this episode.

615. *Mercy*

TELEPLAY: Eric Overmyer
DIRECTOR: Alan Taylor
BROADCAST DATE: March 20, 1998

Pembleton and Bayliss investigate a complaint alleging that Dr. Roxanne Turner (Alfre Woodard) has been euthanizing terminal patients under her care. That she ministered to her patients is not at issue, but whether the treatment she pursued was meant to sustain or terminate their lives is the question. And when does a particular course of action, perceived to be in the patient's best interest, constitute murder? Dr. Turner does not believe in prolonging life at all costs, and sees what she's doing as easing their deaths, not assisting them. Kellerman confronts Judge Gibbons (Rick Warner) concerning his decision to bring Georgia Rae's suit to trial. They speak in the ambiguous phrases of those who don't want to be talking about the subject at hand. Mike surreptitiously tapes the conversation, but it could be interpreted in one of two ways: that Gibbons is on the pad, or that Kellerman is making a threat. Falsone and Stivers handle their first child-killing when a young girl is shot during a pizza-parlor holdup. Gharty and Ballard finally arrest the city goats they've been seeking since an earlier episode. Gharty buys perfume for Billie Lou, the barmaid at the Waterfront.

616. *Abduction*

TELEPLAY: Julie Martin & Anya Epstein
DIRECTOR: Ken Fink
BROADCAST DATE: March 27, 1998

In the moment that a child is out of his mother's sight on a merry-go-round, he is snatched. As the unit responsible for investigating kidnappings, it's homicide's red ball. Falsone is the primary. As usual, the ex-husband is the initial suspect, but is quickly disqualified. The investigation is followed by the producer of an *America's Most Wanted*–type program. False starts included a convicted child molester who lived in the boy's neighborhood and a man who called in to confess. He turned out to have been looking for a way onto TV. Evidence given under hypnosis by the little girl who was riding the merry-go-round beside the victim proves crucial in tracking the vehicle in which he was abducted. The woman and boy are spotted at a diner where police stopped them. The deluded kidnapper was on her way to family in Montreal, where she planned to raise the boy as her own.

617. *Full Court Press*

TELEPLAY: Phillip B. Epstein
STORY: David Simon & Phillip B. Epstein
DIRECTOR: Clark Johnson
BROADCAST DATE: April 3, 1998

Clark Johnson's frequent on-screen absences have been occupied by his off-screen activities, as he directed this episode. An apparently much-loved high school basketball hero is found shot in the locker-room shower. Munch and Gharty find out that he was also a much-feared bully. He pushed one kid too far and was killed. Pembleton and Bayliss have the name and description of a prime suspect in a murder they've been working. They even know the bar he hangs in and his pager number. But they have had no luck in tracking him down. Giardello orders them to bring him in. Dialing the pager, they identify a subject at the bar. When they move in to make the arrest, however, they find they've got, not their killer, but a man transporting enough cocaine to give them the largest bust in Baltimore history. Kellerman — in marked contrast to Ballard — is unenthusiastic about solving the murder of Calvin Barnes, yet another dead soldier from the Mahoney organization. Lewis is seen hovering around the drug corners. Mike takes the tape of his conversation with Judge Gibbons to the FBI. Initially showing no interest, one of the agents advises him off the record that Gibbons has been under investigation for some time and charges are imminent.

618. *Strangled, Not Stirred*

TELEPLAY: Linda McGibney
STORY: Julie Martin & Anya Epstein
DIRECTOR: Jay Tobias
BROADCAST DATE: April 10, 1998

An attractive couple, Nick and Helen Montgomery, meet an attractive young woman at a trendy Charles Street nightspot. The next morning she's found strangled. A second single woman who had been in a bar alone is also killed. The women had been subdued with a stun gun. Ballard gets worked up over the murders for which she fits the victim profile. By matching credit-card receipts from the bars the two women were at, the police pick up on the couple. They give each other up. Killing a woman together excited them, but the husband cheated by killing the second woman on his own. It turns out they had been at this through several cities between Texas and Baltimore. Anonymous tips on the Mahoney killings lead to a spate of arrests. The tips were provided by Lewis. Giardello calls him in and tells him the trial board could lift his suspension, but Barnfather wants him transferred to the District.

619. *Secrets*

TELEPLAY: Yaphet Kotto
DIRECTOR: Edward Bianchi
BROADCAST DATE: April 17, 1998

Two prominent Baltimore financiers commit suicide on the same day, raising suspicions as to whether there might be some connection. It turns out both had received packages of incriminating photos, explaining why each had taken their lives. Josephine Dalton, photographed in a compromising position with her 17-year-old babysitter, asphyxiated herself in her car. Kenneth Alden, caught having sex with his half-sister, shot himself. If they were being blackmailed and the extortion led to their suicides, the deaths were criminal. Both were members of an exclusive country club. Remington Hill (Remak Ramsay) hired the photographer to take the pictures, intending to use them to coerce an end to what he considered shameful activities, which he wouldn't tolerate among fellow club members. This doesn't amount to extortion. However, he was also holding something over the head of the photographer. Feeling guilty over his role in the suicides, the photog murders Hill. Lewis is reinstated and returns to homicide. During the hearing for jury selection on Georgia Rae's civil suit, Judge Gibbons dismisses the case. On the way out of the courthouse, Kellerman accosts him in front of a lobby full of witnesses and threatens that he'd better give up Georgia Rae to the FBI. Two senior Mahoney crew members are found murdered. Bayliss admits his bisexuality to Ballard.

620. *Finnegan's Wake*

TELEPLAY: David Mills
STORY: James Yoshimura & David Simon
DIRECTOR: Steve Buscemi
BROADCAST DATE: April 24, 1998

Bayliss is still plagued by nightmares about Adena Watson. This episode is based on Baltimore's oldest unsolved homicide. Ten-year-old Clara Slone was molested and shot in 1932. William Devlin comes to HQ and tells Bayliss his father was responsible. Det. Tom Finnegan (Charles Durning) was the last cop to work the case and he preserved the files and evidence in his home. Finnegan insists on helping pursue the new investigation. The Slone case bears striking similarities to the Watson case. Bayliss, who had met with Devlin, gives the case to Falsone, but decides to ride along with him and Finnegan. Devlin's father had given his brother his gun and the brother had long since pitched it into the harbor. Police divers recover it and it matches as the murder weapon. So, notwithstanding the elder Devlin's death, the case goes down as closed.

621. *Fallen Heroes (1)*

TELEPLAY: Lois Johnson
STORY: Eric Overmyer
DIRECTOR: Kathryn Bigelow
BROADCAST DATE: May 1, 1998

Judge Gibbons is knifed down in broad daylight. The FBI tells Bayliss about Kellerman's outburst in front of witnesses in the courthouse. Junior Bunk, who found himself out on work release courtesy of Gibbons, despite having taken shots at police officers and killing a bystander, took advantage of his time away from jail to kill the judge. The police arrest a much changed, hardened version of Junior, who refuses to talk. Freed from his cuffs to make his phone call, he reaches into a desk drawer, pulls a gun a cop had carelessly stored, and shoots up the squad room, killing three uniforms and wounding Gharty and Ballard. He's killed in the responding cross fire. Giardello sends the troops out to bring in everyone connected to the Mahoney organization.

A parole officer is gunned down in a hale of bullets. Pony Johnson, a killer arrested in year one of *Homicide*, had been violated back to prison by the parole officer. One of his crew members was living with the PO's secretary, who the PO picked up for work in the morning, making him an easy setup for retribution. Falsone gets him to confess and to put Pony in for the murder.

622. *Fallen Heroes (2)*

TELEPLAY: Joy Lusco
STORY: James Yoshimura
DIRECTOR: Kathryn Bigelow
BROADCAST DATE: May 8, 1998

On a mission, the police hit hard at the East Baltimore dealers. The hunt is on for Georgia Rae. Stivers is overcome by her responsibility for the explosion of violence and tells Giardello that Luther's shooting wasn't clean. Ballard and Gharty are on the mend. As the police raid a home to which Georgia Rae is traced, shots are fired. She is found dead inside. Pembleton faces off on the shooter at the back, but freezes. As the shooter turns on him, Bayliss steps in, taking a bullet, and is gravely wounded. Giardello tells Frank to get to the truth about Luther's shooting. He and Falsone begin by interviewing Lewis, who doesn't give Kellerman up, but doesn't stand up for him either. They bring Kellerman into the box. After being accused of planting a gun on Luther, he inadvertently concedes that Luther's gun was off Meldrick when he shot him. Frank insists to Gee that he won't write up Mike's statement as anything other than what it was. Having his partner near death for saving his life, disgusted by his interrogation of Kellerman, Frank resigns. Giardello gives Mike the option of fighting charges or resigning, in which case the shooting would stay on the books as justified. In either event, he's done as a cop.